OVERLANDER

OVER LAND ER

ONE MAN'S EPIC RACE TO CROSS AUSTRALIA

RUPERT GUINNESS

SIMON & SCHUSTER

London · New York · Sydney · Toronto · New Delhi

A CBS COMPANY

OVERLANDER: ONE MAN'S EPIC RACE TO CROSS AUSTRALIA
First published in Australia in 2018 by
Simon & Schuster (Australia) Pty Limited
Suite 19A, Level 1, Building C, 450 Miller Street, Cammeray, NSW 2062

10 9 8 7 6 5 4 3 2

A CBS Company
Sydney New York London Toronto New Delhi
Visit our website at www.simonandschuster.com.au

A catalogue record for this
book is available from the
National Library of Australia

Cover design: Christabella Designs
Cover image and internal images as credited: Troy Bailey @troybaileyimages,
troybaileydesign@gmail.com
Internal images by Rupert Guinness unless otherwise specified
Typeset by Midland Typesetters, Australia
Printed and bound in Australia by Griffin Press

The paper this book is printed on is certified
against the Forest Stewardship Council®
Standards. Griffin Press holds FSC chain
of custody certification SGS-COC-005088.
FSC promotes environmentally responsible,
socially beneficial and economically viable
management of the world's forests.

IN MEMORY OF MIKE HALL

4 JUNE 1981—31 MARCH 2017

CONTENTS

FOREWORD

BY KRISTOF ALLEGAERT

I have always been in love with cycling – my whole life has been woven by the bicycle. When I was young, cycling thirty kilometres was already a big adventure for me, and then I started dreaming about going for rides of 50, 100, 150 and then 200 kilometres.

Over the years, I have seen half of the world by bike. Cycling is the perfect form of travel – it's fast enough to make progress, yet slow enough to allow you to take in and appreciate the landscape around you. I was into bikepacking before it became more widely known, and I've had the time of my life because of it. Over the years I discovered that my strength was being alone, cycling by myself. There was a start and a finish, but I always knew that in between I was free – just me, my bike, and the elements of nature, weather and the terrain.

But it wasn't until I was almost 40 that I took part in a formal bike marathon. My first was the Transcontinental Race across

Europe in 2013, an ultra-endurance race over distances between 3,200 and 4,000 kilometres that can take between 7 and 10 days to finish. Before then I'd never thought of competing in traditional road races, even though I'm from Kortrijk in Flanders, Belgium, which is the heartland of one-day professional classics like the Tour of Flanders.

When I started the Transcontinental Race, I really didn't know what to expect, but everything worked out the way I had planned and hoped for. And so began a new chapter of my life, of cycling at a whole new level.

After hearing so many amazing stories about cycling in Australia – and especially of crossing the fabled desert of the Nullarbor Plain – a part of me was really excited about racing in the first Indian Pacific Wheel Race – but another part was scared and apprehensive.

How would I feel about this as a race? With minimal sleep and limited food and refreshment available, combined with the harsh sun, what would be the impact on your mind and body, especially if you're coming from a European winter?

It was only three months before what quickly became known as the 'IndiPac' that I committed to being at the start line in Fremantle, Western Australia on 18 March 2017, and racing it. This meant I had to do some big rides at home in Belgium in the cold dark days of winter. Would I be ready? I had also never been to Australia before. I expected that so many who had entered would know the Australian roads far better than me, at least local riders. I had no real advantage. There was also such a strong field of competitors, including from overseas, and I knew that the price of any small error would be high.

It was only after the start when riding alone that I began to relax, knowing the only thing I needed to do was follow my first love: riding my bike from early morning till late in the dark.

Of course, I made mistakes in the race. Everyone does. But when I do, I know the challenge is to fall back on my skills and think smart to find a solution. Races like the IndiPac are full of ups and downs, and challenges which no one can be totally prepared for. That will never change, no matter how much experience a rider has – whether it's me or you. It's not unlike life.

The 2017 IndiPac reminded us all of that, albeit tragically so, but also for so many positive reasons before it ended as it did; as does this behind-the-scenes book, in which Rupert Guinness portrays his first experience of riding in this genre of cycling, and how it not only impacted him, but many others as well.

Welcome to the IndiPac, and also the world of solo, unsupported bikepacking, where cycling is pure adventure.

INTRODUCTION

A COSTLY RIDE

FRIDAY, 31 MARCH 2017

I am feeling great – in my mind. A positive glow is warming me from deep within the layers of fatigue I have built over almost two weeks. Arriving in Adelaide, my spirits are high from the sense of achievement of having cycled 2,830 kilometres, or across a little more than half of Australia, in the inaugural 5,470-kilometre Indian Pacific Wheel Race from the South Mole Lighthouse in Fremantle to the Opera House in Sydney.

There's still so much further to cycle before I can say 'mission accomplished'. But whatever happens from here, I have ridden further than the first 'Overlander' route cycled by Arthur Richardson, a mining engineer from Port Augusta, South Australia, who worked on the Australian goldfields looking for new strikes. Aged 24 and with just a small repair kit and a water bag, he set off on his bike on 24 November 1896 from the gold mining town of Coolgardie to cross the Nullarbor

Plain to Adelaide, a ride which had been deemed by so many as too dangerous. Richardson took 31 days to finish the ride and became the first person to cross the Nullarbor on a bicycle. Later, he famously described the searing desert heat as being '1,000 degrees in the shade'.

Incredibly, in a display of decision-making that might be best described as impulsive, it was during this ride and when suffering worst from his sunburn, saddle sores and exhaustion that Richardson started plotting his audacious plan to become the first to ride 18,507 kilometres around Australia, his plan being to start and finish in Perth. He was pushed by the knowledge that a combined trio – Frank White and his younger brother Alec, and the wealthy pastoralist and amateur cyclist Donald Mackay – were planning to attempt the same feat, but in the opposite direction and with the White brothers starting in Melbourne and Mackay joining them in Brisbane.

Richardson's bid to be the first to circumnavigate Australia by land was audacious in itself. That he pitted himself to beat three others whose plan meant they would help each other added to the audacity of it all. Richardson left Perth on 5 June 1899 – and the White brothers from Melbourne on 5 July – and he beat them, finishing on 4 February 1900. How Richardson did it, riding out into the unknown on lumpy camel pad tracks, across parched desert plains littered with patches of broken rock and scrappy bush, forging pathways that today are bitumen roads, is simply mind boggling.

For me, riding from Fremantle to Adelaide has been a huge challenge in itself. A year ago I would never have imagined attempting it, let alone completing the distance. Not to mention what fulfilling the ultimate goal of reaching Sydney will mean to me, after I've cycled through Victoria and parts of the Australian Capital Territory and New South Wales. I think of Australia as a chameleon with its diversity of terrain – the changing colours and landscapes – and wonder how I might come to learn more about this beast of nature by seeing it first-hand, rather than via documentaries and advertisements and images on postcards and in coffee table books. As with the open ocean in sailing, I know that when cycling alone in the wilderness you should never underestimate Mother Nature. She can be as cruel and angry as she can be beautiful.

So on this fourteenth day of this solo and unsupported ride – held to recognise the feats of the Overlanders like Richardson – I'm definitely feeling the hundreds of kilometres I've ridden every day. I have acute pain in injured parts all over my body. But after a challenging start and several tough days crossing the Nullarbor, I'm now used to dealing with the highs and lows – emotional as well as physical – of each testing day in the IndiPac.

Leaving the Torrens River bike path, I ride slowly up King William Street towards the city centre of Adelaide, negotiating my way through rush-hour traffic and pedestrians. The sight of fresh-faced and neatly dressed city dwellers at a set of traffic lights makes me think of how I must look – and smell. I need a shower, some rest and a little bit of body maintenance, and so does my bike.

All this steers me towards the Treadly Bike Shop, a quaint store that specialises in bespoke single speed, fixed gear, cyclo-cross and commuter bikes. Tucked away in the shadows of Ebenezer Place behind the bustle of Rundle Street, the shop has been monitoring, on the satellite dot tracking system, the progress of every IndiPac rider as they each make their way across Australia at varying speeds and battle a variety of weather conditions. The shop has also offered to be open 24 hours a day to help riders on their arrival into Adelaide.

This offer is too good to refuse. I've had persistent tyre issues, and in the last few nights and early mornings before and just after dawn, problems with my light system that needs someone more qualified than a technological luddite like me to address. Treadly makes for a welcome sight, as does the greeting smile of owner Sam Neeft.

It's just after 9 am. Sam wastes no time to ask, 'How are you? How are you feeling?'

My smile probably says enough, but I reply, 'Mate, I'm so happy, so relieved to be here.'

I am, but my mind is focused on the rest of the IndiPac course and the mechanical attention my titanium Curve 'Belgie Spirit' needs, which is still bearing a thin film of ochre Nullarbor dust. I steer the bike to the back of the shop, where it's put on the rack for service.

My plan is to be as efficient as I can with my time in Adelaide, yet make the best of being here. Several days back I'd decided I'd reward myself for making it this far by taking a day off the race, stay in a nice hotel and enjoy some good wine and food. The pickings out on the road have been slim. But now all I want to do is clean up, eat, rest for an hour or so more and then, with my serviced bike, return to the solitude and isolation of the road that I've grown to love.

As soon as my bike is on the rack, I'm explaining to mechanics Jake Thomas and Andy Rogers my two main needs. The first is to repair the lighting system that recharges off a dynamo hub on my front wheel when I'm pedalling. In recent days, it's failed to do what it should, with only one of the three bulbs producing light. I also need my rear rim and tyre checked for any issues that may have led to me having had three punctures and a slow leak.

I leave them to it and head next door to a café. I order a coffee and a muffin on autopilot, as I've done over and again on my breaks for the past fortnight. Eating, eating and more eating – it's become part of the daily ritual on the IndiPac, like fuelling an old steam train with coal.

At about 9.20 am I return to the bike shop. The news about my lights isn't good, but there are options, which is immediately reassuring. Over the last fortnight on the race, I've learned most problems have solutions – and that dwelling too long on the problem doesn't help.

We are focused, talking about the issues. The guys can't repair my light system; it can only be fixed by the manufacturer. But they can sell me another model. Should I swap the system and have mine repaired once I'm back in Sydney? Or should I continue with what I have, making do with the one working bulb, and supplement it with new, smaller – and cheaper – lights?

I'm leaning towards the former, despite the extra cost. The IndiPac, I have learned, is a costly ride. But I have to choose one way or the other and soon, so I don't lose time.

My attention is broken by the sight of a cyclist entering the shop. It's Kay Haarsma, who accompanied me for some of the final kilometres into Adelaide and the bike shop – one of the now fabled IndiPac 'dot trackers', cyclists who follow race entrants on the dot tracking system, and ride out to meet and cycle with them for short distances. Kay was smiling when she left the bike shop not long after I arrived – she took a photograph of me too. But now her smile is gone, replaced by a look of grave concern.

'Have you heard the news?' she asks.

Sam, Jake, Andy and I look at each other. We clearly haven't.

'Apparently an IndiPac rider has been killed.'

Kay passes us a printed ABC online report of a collision between a cyclist and a car on the Monaro Highway near Canberra.

'It only happened a few hours ago,' Kay adds, as we huddle to read the report.

At 6.22 am, to be precise. The identity of the victim is yet to be confirmed by police and race organisers, but the ABC story gives a harrowing indication.

ON THE PATH OF THE ORIGINAL OVERLANDERS

OCTOBER 2016

'Is the Overlander in you?'

The online advertisement grabs my attention. I absorb the details. The route of the inaugural Indian Pacific Wheel Race, which soon becomes known as the IndiPac, traverses close to 5,500 kilometres from Fremantle in Western Australia to the Sydney Opera House via the Nullarbor Plain, Adelaide, Melbourne, the Victorian Alps, Kosciuszko National Park and Canberra.

Is there ever! I reply to myself.

I've just submitted the final manuscript for my book, *Power of the Pedal – The Story of Australian Cycling* to the publishers at the National Library of Australia, so have some understanding of the Overlanders and their place in Australian history.

The Overlanders were pioneers. In the late 1890s to early 1900s they cycled over much of Australia with some epic rides into and across the interior as well as around the continent's circumference. Their achievements make up a largely unrecognised chapter of Australian cycling history. Their intrepid journeys not only created folklore – as dispatches about their experiences generated much interest in the major cities and towns where they could be published in local newspapers or bulletins – but also helped to forge stronger links between those cities and towns that had been originally founded by migrants, prospectors, and teamsters and bush workers on foot or travelling by horse. Many of the routes they took led to today's roadways.

But the Overlanders highlighted how much faster the trips could be on bike, and promoted the sturdiness of the equipment they used and the brands that supported their rides. Their arrival into a city or town was nearly always met with a massive throng of people cheering them on, from local townspeople and workers to dignitaries and politicians keen to see these extraordinary people first-hand, and also to listen and learn of their adventures. Many were given police escorts to civic receptions.

The Overlanders became stars of their time. They included the likes of George Burston, Percy Armstrong, Arthur Richardson and Joseph Pearson, to William Snell, Frank White, William Virgin, Jack Denning, Pat O'Dea and Jerome Murif, along with A.W.B. Mather, Charles Greenwood, Tom Coleman, Albert MacDonald, Donald Mackay, Alec White, Eddie Reichenbach (aka Ted Ryko) and Francis Birtles, and the last of an era in

Sir Hubert Opperman. Also among them in the 1920s and 1930s, until the Second World War intervened, were women such as Elsa Barbour, Billie Samuel and Joyce Barry.

All came from different backgrounds and had different motivations for their rides, a number of them attracted by the fame and the money they could earn by promoting various bicycle products (from the bikes themselves to gears, wheels and tyres) at a time when the bicycle was becoming a boom mode of transport in Australia. But each was fundamentally bound by a daring spirit that cast aside fears of the inherent risks they would face and enabled them to set off into the unknown, laden only with food and water.

Collectively, the Overlanders' story debunks the myth that Australia has traditionally not been a cycling nation. But Australia's roots in the sport are unique, even if its origins aren't linked to road and track racing as they are in Europe, which is still considered the traditional heartland of the sport.

In Australian history the Overlanders have received far less recognition than they deserve, but the IndiPac could help resuscitate interest in their story, and ensure their rightful place in our national story. Despite never having ridden in a solo, unsupported, ultra-endurance bicycle race like the IndiPac, I know that the inherent hazards faced by the Overlanders, who cycled over brutal off-road terrain, in areas where food and water were scarce and the wildlife a potential danger, were far tougher than any challenges I might face.

I look at the ad for the race again. It's a great opportunity for me to deepen my understanding of the Overlanders: their character, their will, their struggles and their achievements. If I enter, I'll be able to experience a little of what they might have. And if the suffering and difficulties become too hard to cope with, I can always draw on the legacy of their experiences in those torrid circumstances as motivation.

◉

With the seed planted, it doesn't take long for the beginnings of a plan to grow. But apart from proposing my entry to my wife Libby to test the waters, before I push any further with trying to convince her of the plan, I need to get more insight into what would be at stake. Libby has heard me bang on before about going on some grand adventures and for the most part it's been mostly banter spiced with a sense of fantasy. That said, I did sail in the Sydney to Hobart Yacht Race twice, with no open sea sailing experience beforehand. But the IndiPac would be different. I need more information – not just to convince myself that this is something I really want to do and feel I can achieve, but to reassure Libby that I've covered off as many safety and survival concerns as possible before I set off for Western Australia.

First off, I meet up with friend and world-class film maker Anthony Gordon. Among many other features, Anthony produced the documentary on the inaugural Race to the Rock, the 2017 solo and unsupported ride from Adelaide to Uluru, instigated by Jesse Carlsson, who is also the mastermind of the IndiPac. When I meet up with him to chat about the IndiPac, Anthony has just returned from Nepal, where he shot the second season of his series *Everest Air* for the Travel Channel, about a Sherpa high-altitude rescue team.

Anthony's thinking is that my interest in the event is as a journalist. I could hold interviews with riders and other event personalities during the race for the videos that he would shoot and post on social media and later edit for an official IndiPac documentary. He's pretty surprised when I tell him I actually want to race it. As his surprise rapidly shifts to infectious enthusiasm, I become even more hooked on the IndiPac and all it stands for. Anthony likes the fact that, after spending the early and more recent years of my professional life writing about mainstream sport – as well as major cycling events like the Tour de France – I want to take part in an event that even many professional athletes might think is too crazy to consider.

Other factors weigh in to my thinking too. Nine months since taking a voluntary redundancy from the *Sydney Morning Herald* in January 2016, I'm uncertain about a lot of things – my career future for one. I'm also questioning what change I need in my life. I spent many years writing about the performances of elite riders in cycling, which I started covering in Melbourne in 1984. In 1987 I really began to focus on the sport when I moved to Europe and spent nine years living and working in Belgium and France, reporting on cycling at a time when very few English-speaking journalists were forging a career out of it. The largely untapped world of ultra-endurance cycling could offer me just the sort of change I've been looking for.

◉

Given my thirty-plus years as a cycling journalist, Anthony thinks the prospects of getting support from those behind the race, bicycle equipment suppliers, and maybe a charity or cause were I inclined to choose one, could be strong. He reckons the first call I should make is to Jesse Carlsson, who Anthony is already in deep negotiations with about shooting the official IndiPac documentary.

Jesse isn't just the brains behind the IndiPac. Melbourne-based, he has a PhD in theoretical physics, and is a private equity investor and former BMX age-group world champion. He's also a world class ultra-endurance rider. In 2013, he came second in The Divide, a 4,400-kilometre solo, unsupported mountain bike race from Canada to Mexico. In 2015, Jesse also won the 6,800-kilometre Trans Am Bike Race, also solo and unsupported, which races on open roads across America. Along with the Transcontinental Race in Europe, the Trans Am was at the time one of the two major ultra-endurance road events in the world. The IndiPac would be the third such race of this kind.

Jesse is also one of three owners of Melbourne-based Curve Bicycles, which manufactures specialist bicycles such as titanium 'graveler' bikes – hybrids made for adventure riding that allow riders to cycle on the road as well as off it, on trails. Anthony thinks Jesse might entertain the idea of me riding one of the bikes he's designed for a ride like this, and that the Australian arm of Rapha, the UK global cycling apparel company, which is supporting the event, could well be open to outfitting me with their kit, too.

The first conversation I have with Jesse fuels my excitement further. His knowledge of Overlander history is as extensive as his passion for ultra-endurance cycling. When Jesse speaks, he has the exuberance of someone who's just discovered a secret code.

'How will you ride it, to race or to finish?' Jesse asks. He's genuinely keen to gauge my plans, rather than jump to conclusions about my ability.

'Well, my plan is to focus on finishing, but go in with a racing mindset.' My answer doesn't lean one way or the other, I know. But what begins as a conversation about me entering the IndiPac turns into a lengthy discussion about how the IndiPac would recognise the Overlanders' place in history and allow riders to get a taste of what they experienced.

'Even better,' Jesse adds, 'is that we can celebrate the 80th anniversary of Sir Hubert Opperman's record-breaking crossing of Australia from Fremantle to Sydney.' Opperman took 13 days, 10 hours and 11 minutes to complete the 2,875 mile trip in 1937.

Opperman not only etched his name as an Overlander but also as a world star in road cycling – finishing 18th and 12th in the 1928 and 1931 Tours de France, and on the track where he won some of the biggest races in the sport. Not content just to soar in cycling, he entered politics after the Second World War and later became a member of Prime Minister Robert Menzies' federal government in the 1960s, eventually serving as Australia's first High Commissioner to Malta in 1967.

While Jesse talks up Overlander history, he's up front about how hard the IndiPac will be – for everyone, not just newcomers. 'I can't stress enough how tough it will be,' he says. 'For anyone who enters, there's a strong chance they won't finish. People should know that.'

Even the top riders will be in for a challenge like no other, but still Jesse's excited about how the IndiPac will give them the opportunity to square up against each other. 'Never before have we seen the top ultra-endurance riders go head to head,' he says.

Jesse explains that it is usually very hard in this genre of cycle racing to get all the top stars in any one race. That's because most are still recovering from a previous race and only have the energy, time or resources to compete in one or two such events in year. Ultra-endurance, he adds, doesn't offer a lucrative living to the best riders as men's road cycling does. A Tour de France winner, for example, earns millions of dollars. Nevertheless, Jesse has managed to pull in the world's marquee endurance riders and the race promises to be an exciting one.

Even still, Jessie stresses, 'The IndiPac winner won't get a thing. No one will – no number, no T-shirt, no entrant's pack.'

By the time we say goodbye, the seed of interest is deeply planted – and sprouting. And with every discussion with him afterwards, I feel more excitement blooming, despite my increasing awareness of the dangers of traffic, sleep deprivation, exposure in the harsh conditions and wildlife.

◉

But there's more than taking part in an homage to the original Overlanders that draws me to racing the IndiPac. Something inside me wants to be stripped bare – emotionally and physically – by such an epic challenge. I've always loved endurance sports. As a child, no day was better than those spent from dawn till dusk riding my Dragstar bicycle, exploring the area where I grew up in the Eastern Suburbs of Sydney. In later years, I relished marathon surfing sessions; I would only come in to the beach for a quick snack before hitting the ocean again until the last wave of the day, and return home exhausted.

I love the expanse of open space: on land and in the ocean. I've never excelled at sport in confined areas or with regimented patterns of play – from playing fields or courts to swimming pools. Rugby union was the one ball sport I liked, and I did reasonably well in, but it was clear to me very early on that endurance sports were my thing. Rowing, triathlon and road cycling became my pursuits; likewise trekking and, years later, open water sailing, despite lacking skills and suffering from seasickness.

So how did I come to love the pain of endurance sport? Since childhood I've been plagued with insecurity, and always felt the need to prove myself. I suspect the roots date back to my youth, when my lack of ball skills led me to believe I had little sporting ability. I also struggled with my weight, which led to issues about body image and a loss of self-esteem. As a tacker, I absolutely loved hamburgers – especially those with the lot from the local burger shop. But I also loved McDonald's burgers. Their advertising campaign promised a free extra Big Mac to anyone who could list the ingredients in less than thirty seconds when placing their order – and I learned those ingredients very quickly!

My weight and size increased to the point that, at The King's School where I boarded, one of my nicknames was 'Meatball'. As I immersed myself in endurance sports the moniker changed to 'Meathead', and to a more accepting 'Meaty' by Year 12, when I made the First VIII rowing crew. I never took offence. These names probably gave me a sense of inclusion among my peers and allowed me to deny how much I'd stacked on. But while blind to it then, over time my perceived sense of excess weight fuelled my insecurities further.

But I enjoyed school. I was very lucky to have had the education that I did, thanks to my father. When I left in 1979 I happily pursued my greater talents in rowing at the Sydney Rowing Club. But my body weight and self-image issues resurfaced when I joined the competitive lightweight grade. Before every race, rowers must weigh in under a set maximum; and for an individual male at the time that was 72.5 kilograms.

There was little education at that time about healthy weight loss. Some people advised me, however, and over one winter my weight came down. But my obsession with my body weight took a firm grip. The numbers on the scales – my own set as well as the club's – became an obsession, especially during the racing season. The weekly schedule of regatta preparation, competition, recovery – and celebration – saw my week turn into a juggling of priorities.

I liked to socialise after regattas, and started to look for short cuts. This led to an awful cycle of the eating disorder known as bulimia – binge eating, followed by regurgitation. The first time it seemed so easy – at the end of a huge three-course meal on a Monday night out after a weekend regatta. It was painless. And it also stripped me of any sense of guilt for having over-eaten, and thereby compromising my weight for the ensuing week of training and racing. In no time, it became a secret habit.

People in my circle – from family to friends – became concerned by my weight loss and gaunt look. Whenever I was asked if I was okay, I would just reply that I was, despite eventually spending a week in hospital in Sydney to undergo tests, none of which were explained to me, or explained anything that might be wrong. Not once did anyone suggest to me that I could have bulimia. I didn't know the word at the time, let alone its meaning, and the causes and consequences. And while deep down I realised what I was doing was wrong, I didn't recognise it as a condition until many years later; and that it's not just a physical condition, but one that's driven by your state of mind.

Bulimia isn't dealt with simply by admitting to it. The real job of tackling it can take years, a lifetime even. Even today I still struggle with the condition intermittently. The guilt about having allowed it to take so much control heightens the need for secrecy. And in turn that erodes self-confidence, self-esteem and a sense of purpose.

Bulimia has spiralling consequences but the condition can be dealt with in a range of ways. For some, like me, an endurance event such as the IndiPac can provide the focus for getting a handle on it – or trying to. This has worked for me before, when I switched from rowing to triathlon at the end of 1984. When you're swimming, cycling *and* running as part of a single endurance competition, eating well is imperative. But of course the long term answer is to openly acknowledge that it's a part of me and recognise and understand what triggers it.

◉

Racing triathlon became another obsession. Not long after my first event in Melbourne in late 1984 – a 1.5-kilometre swim, 40-kilometre bike and 10-kilometre run – I entered a longer distance Ironman race, the inaugural 1985 Double Brown

Ironman in Auckland, New Zealand. My father was horrified when I quit my job at *The Australian* newspaper to train full-time for the 3.2-kilometre swim, 160.1-kilometre bike and 32.2-kilometre run event (it was then shorter than the traditional Ironman). My 11th place qualified me for the Hawaii Ironman World Championship, in which I placed 48th. But in 1986, after again qualifying for Hawaii, I quit the next paper I'd joined, the *Melbourne Sun News Pictorial*, to once more train full-time.

I was optimistic that I could figure in the top 16, for which prize money was on offer for the first time. And I was driving my father to despair. He thought I was crazy, not only wasting my career, but wasting my life. But I was hooked on the need to not just prove myself as an athlete, but show that I was right in taking a positive risk by leaving yet another job to pursue a dream.

Little wonder that when my 1986 race ended with me abandoning during the bike leg when having difficulty in keeping any fluids down, 'we told you so' seemed to come from all and sundry when I returned home.

I was shattered. I saw only failure. Once more, my self-confidence was shot. And it took me a long time to get over that.

◉

My sense of adventure didn't evaporate, though, and it led me to the world of European cycling. I became editor of the UK edition of the cycling magazine *Winning Bicycle Racing*

Illustrated, published in Belgium. I held this position for a year, and remained as the magazine's chief correspondent for six months afterwards. Then I continued living in Europe for nine years, working as a cycling journalist – four years in Belgium and five in France, for the most part with *VeloNews*.

They were eye-opening years. I covered all the major international bike races and also returned to racing in triathlon. Of course, those nine years weren't without setbacks, but by the time I returned to Australia in early 1996, my sense of independence and self-confidence was restored.

Life back in Australia led to meeting and marrying Libby Bennett in December 1996, and a new appreciation for the country which I'd originally arrived in as a 'Ten Pound Pom' with my parents in 1966 when I was four. Libby and I married a year after we met at a mate's barbecue in Sydney during an end of year trip I made back to Australia from France where I was still living. Six weeks later, on New Year's Eve, while we were on holidays together in Rome, I proposed to her. Libby waited four months before saying 'Yes'. It was a whirlwind year, but one where the flicker of adventure also returned, and so did the desire to challenge myself anew, probably to the despair of those around me. Once I say 'yes' to something, for me there's no going back – there's a sense of responsibility to back up what I commit to, of course, but there's also the fear of losing face. And I also see physical challenges as a pathway to liberation, as temporary as they are.

So for years I found myself looking for opportunities that varied in activity and degrees of difficulty – from running marathons to 24-hour Trail Walker events, to more Ironman triathlons. To say nothing of crewing in the 2000 and 2001 Sydney to Hobart races on the maxi-yacht *Nicorette*. If that race could show me how we can go well beyond our comfort zones and discover greater strength than most of us realise we have, or are ever required to draw upon, the IndiPac could offer me another chance at that. It would also provide me with the perfect opportunity to step out from behind the laptop, to put myself on the line and account for my own performance, rather than someone else's.

The timing was also ideal. When I spotted the IndiPac ad, my life was in a state of flux. My journalistic career was facing uncertainty. I'd also lost my way at work in the two years leading up to my departure from Fairfax Media after the tragic death of my former sports editor at the *Sydney Morning Herald*, Rod Allen. In 2013, Rod had fallen off a cliff at the end of Libby's and my shared 51st birthday party at Cockatoo Island in Sydney Harbour. I believe I was the last person to see Rod alive. At the time, he suddenly ran off into the blackness of night after the party concluded, despite me yelling out to him to wait, after which I showed his wife to the tent where they were to sleep. Rod was found dead the next morning at the bottom of the cliff by one of our friends during an early morning walk.

It had been three years since he died, but it reinforced my belief in living life while we have the chance. We should work to live, not live to work – and we only get one chance. Rod's senseless fate reminded me of how truly tenuous our lives are, a belief that sadly has been reinforced for me too often since.

◉

If I was to race the IndiPac, I needed Libby's blessing. She'd been understandably nervous, but supportive of me racing in the Sydney to Hobart. She'd sailed in open water races herself, and while knowing the dangers, had been reassured by the calibre of the crew I was going to sail with. But the IndiPac is on another scale altogether. That Libby is not a cyclist is not the point. At home, we often discuss the dangers of cycling, no matter where or how far I ride.

Libby has learned much about cycling since we've been together. She followed the 1998 Tour de France with me. When the French number-one-world-ranked Festina team was disqualified for systematic doping, our 'second honeymoon' was systematically put onto the back foot.

To put it bluntly, Libby's fear about the IndiPac was that I would either be killed or suffer from any one or more of the possible accidents or misfortunes that can occur in such solitary long-distance events. What I understood least was the anxiety she would feel not knowing how I was faring or where exactly I would be at any point – despite my progress being recorded on my Spot Gen3, an online tracking device that transmits messages, from life-or-death rescue calls to reassuring alerts about overnight stops.

A heritage architect, Libby is a stickler for detail; although throughout our marriage she has been totally supportive of any challenge I have wanted to pursue, more supportive than I have probably given her credit for. For the IndiPac, we talked in-depth about me being well prepared for any unexpected incidents, and the importance of having the right equipment, technical and otherwise. We discussed strategies for the various permutations of what could happen. But as neither of us had participated in this kind of event before, either as entrant or supporter, deep down we both knew we were talking about the unknown. It was impossible to predict how I might react to any incident.

Still, Libby supported my dream. And after paying the race fee and receiving confirmation of my entry on 1 October 2016, I began planning and preparing. The list of questions that I would never know the answer to until after the race fast grew.

How would it end?

What would the fall-out be?

How would it impact my outlook on life?

Would it lay to rest my past demons, or resurrect lost self-esteem and confidence?

And finally a question I admit I didn't give enough weight to at the time, considering the risks: What impact could such a pursuit have on our marriage?

Who knew if I would find the answers?

But what was definite is that I would never know, otherwise.

PLANNING AND PREPARATION FOR A DREAM

Many experienced ultra-endurance cyclists said I would never know if I was ready for the challenge until after the race began. Only then would I know how I'd handle the numerous challenges, like the physical demands of riding so far, to coping with inherent sudden changes and setbacks. It made sense. The same was said to me by the most experienced of hands of the Sydney to Hobart Yacht Race.

But very quickly my days beforehand become consumed by ticking off a seemingly neverending 'to do' list that included acquiring bike, clothes, sleeping, technical and mechanical items and information on the course route and potential hazards in day and night; and the setting up of a public Facebook page on which I will post live blogs — or vlogs — of my experiences and also use as a platform to also support the 'Helping Rhinos' organisation that is trying to stop poaching of the endangered species.

It's a marathon commitment made harder by my lack of ultra-endurance experience. I have no filter for which advice is valuable or not. I have read the memoirs of a number of original Overlanders such as Arthur Richardson and Jerome Murif, and magazine pieces written on more recent trans-Australia rides and online blogs by participants in any number of ultra-endurance rides. Soon I have so much varied information from so many sources, I can't see through it all, until I realise that what suits one person may not suit another and despite the good intent of all those who advise me, I must follow what I feel will best work for me. Probably the best advice I get is to not have one game plan, but be ready to plan along the way.

The physical training is an easier challenge to get a grip of. Not that I take that challenge lightly. It still takes plenty of planning, time and effort – and support – but like so many who have participated or competed in endurance sport, I'm used to following a hard training regime that requires a balance of long distance and short intensive work and gym sessions once the goal is targeted and I have committed to going for it.

I embark on a five and half month training program under the eyes of two cycling trainers – Frank Conceicao of Albion Cycles in Sydney who I have known for many years but ridden under since 2008, and Mark Fenner of FTP training who works with World Tour road professionals and other endurance riders – and my personal gym trainer, Nicola Vrachnas from Longevity PT at the Regenesis Gymnasium near home in Edgecliff, Sydney.

My cycling program is a mix of structured and improvised sessions, early morning rides in the dark at 3 am and long weekend rides becoming longer by the week concluding with a two-day camping tour to the Wingello Forest south of Sydney and back. In the gym, I do twice-weekly anaerobic and cardiovascular sessions that include treadmill running, exercises and weights, and a once-weekly yoga-stretch class.

My numbers of my final Tanita body composition test two days before flying to Perth on 15 March 2017 confirm I am ready. Since 7 October 2016, when I took my first test after receiving confirmation of my IndiPac entry, my body weight is now down to 79.7 kg from 93.9 kg; my Body Mass Index (BMI) is 25.4, down from 30; my fat percentage 21.3, down from 30, and my fat mass is 17.0 kg against the initial 28.2 kg. It's good that my body fat isn't too low, as the fat stores will be vital for my body to tap into and fuel during the ride.

I'm as ready as I can be. All that's left for me to do now is to take my bike to Frank at Albion Cycles for one last check, pack it and all my gear into a cardboard bike box, go to the airport and then take my flight to Perth in Western Australia.

2

AN AUDIENCE WITH ROYALTY

Peering out the window on the approach to Perth, I grasp the immensity of what is coming. Having flown across the country and seen below the vast expanse of a mostly ochre landscape and patchwork of thin lines that are roadways has reinforced just how huge Australia is. That I will soon be cycling alone down there, in conditions that are among the harshest in the world, is in stark contrast to the business class luxury I have treated myself to on the one-way Qantas flight.

At least I can see what I'll be riding across from above, I tell myself, unlike the original Overlanders who set off on their rides without many clues to go by, bar the word and later odd photo of previous riders who had crossed before them, or anyone who had been by foot or horse.

◉

In the last days leading up to the 6 am race start from the South Mole Lighthouse in Fremantle I feel different to what I usually do before racing in triathlons. With Ironman there's the excitement of finally getting to compete after so many months, weeks and hours spent training. The final event is actually the reward for all the time and energy put into preparing for it.

But nothing can fully prepare you for the uncertainty that comes with doing an ultra-endurance event like the IndiPac for the first time – no matter how much you tap into the advice and experience of other competitors.

It all becomes real on the Thursday night. The IndiPac starters have gathered at the Local Hotel where the highlight is the official sign-in by all 70 entrants. This is followed by interviews with a panel of four of the key contenders, hosted by Jesse Carlsson in his capacity as the instigator of the event. Before us, as we sip on custom brewed Indi-Pac Ale, is ultra-endurance cycling royalty. I'm keen to hear what they say, but also a little anxious that what they say will confirm I've bitten off more than I can chew.

One of the speakers is Englishman Mike Hall, aged thirty-five, a Yorkshireman who lives in Wales with his partner Anna Haslock. Mike, who I haven't yet met and to be honest knew little about beforehand, is a giant of ultra-endurance riding. This isn't just due to his racing successes, which includes winning the 2014 Trans Am Bike Race, the Tour Divide in 2013 and 2016 and for which he holds the record for fastest time, and his victory in the 2012 World Cycle Race, which took him 91 days and 18 hours to complete. Mike is also the founder and director of the Transcontinental Race that began in 2013. And as a supporter of Newborns Vietnam, he led the 2013 and 2015 Vietnam Challenge Rides organised by Cycle a Difference, a charity that raises funds to improve access to and quality of newborn care in the poorest rural areas of that country.

Another favourite on the panel is the Belgian Kristof Allegaert. The forty-two-year-old high school teacher of mechanics hails from Kortrijk in the cycling hub of Flanders in Belgium. Interestingly, road racing in the one-day classics or events like the Tour de France has never been his go. He has focused solely on ultra-endurance racing, which he has dominated. In 2011, Kristof set a record for the Tour de France Randonneur, an unsupported amateur version of the Tour de France, bettering Patrick Plaine's 13 days, 9 hours and 20 minutes set in 1978 for the 4,800-kilometre route with 13 days, 2 hours and 15 minutes.

Kristof has also won the Transcontinental Race three times: in 2013 in 7 days, 13 hours and 45 minutes for the 3,200-kilometre route; in 2014 in 7 days, 23 hours for the 3,600 kilometres; and in 2016 in 8 days, 18 hours and 2 minutes for 3,800 kilometres. He also won the 2015 Red Bull Siberian Extreme in 13 days, 6 hours and 57 minutes for 9,200 kilometres.

The third panellist is Sarah Hammond, from Melbourne. A relatively new face on the international ultra-endurance racing scene, Sarah is fast emerging as a star. She started cycling later in life with road racing, ascent challenges and 24-hour racing. But after testing the waters of mega distance cycling in Audax rides, she quickly recorded notable results in solo unsupported events similar to the IndiPac. In her first such race, the 2016 Trans Am Bike Race, Sarah placed sixth overall. Later that year she won the 2,300-kilometre off-road Race to the Rock from Adelaide to Uluru in Central Australia; it was her third ever mountain bike race and she was also the only official finisher. She won it again in 2017, riding from Albury in Western Australia to Uluru.

Jesse, Mike, Kristof and Sarah aren't the only star contenders. Others include the German–Briton Juliana Buhring, a top-10 finisher in the Transcontinental Race and Trans Am Bike Race; and German-born Steffen Streich who lives in Greece and won the 2015 Trans Afrika Bicycle Race. Steffen came second in the 2016 Trans Am Bike Race; after leading with 110 miles to go, he made a directional mistake on the last day. Four others are the German Kai Edel, who placed fourth in the 2016 Trans Am Bike Race and competed in the 2011 and 2015 Paris-Brest-Paris race in France; Irishman Donncha Cuttriss, who was 13th in the 2011 Race Across America, and sixth, fifth, fourth and fifth in the 2010, 2012, 2013 and 2015 Race Around Ireland respectively, and fifth in the 2015 Trans Am Bike Race; and Belgian Kim Raeymaekers and Dutchman Matthijs Ligt. Their presence leaves no doubt over the strength of this international field that Jesse has attracted.

Despite his racing pedigree that includes his second place finish behind Jesse Carlsson in the 2015 Trans Am Bike Race and finishes in the 2011 Tour Divide and 2014 Transcontinental Race, Kim Raeymaekers came to Australia with an open mind for his hopes, believing that he was undertrained. 'I didn't have any real ambitions for the race,' Kim recalls later. 'I didn't have time to train enough, or the motivation since it was winter in Belgium. I tried to get in shape the best I can within the minimal amount of time. I knew that I needed to get out of the Nullarbor as fast as possible without burning myself to the ground.'

Matthijs Ligt knew most of the Europeans. After seeing the entry list and calibre of riders he understood what it would take to finish well. 'With my growing years of experience in ultra-endurance cycling I had set myself the goal to ride a Top Ten position, preferably Top Five,' he says. 'But this kind of cycling isn't executed in a controlled race environment. The smallest errors can mess up a perfectly prepared race.'

Juliana Buhring did not come with any declared ambition, but her philosophy to racing such events says enough about what anyone can expect from her. 'I rarely go into a race with any real ambition other than to ride as hard and fast as I possibly can and to test myself and my own limitations,' she says. 'I'm not very competitive when it comes to others in the race. In fact, the competition aspect kills a lot of the pleasure of it for me. I generally race against myself and my last big ride, to see if I can better my own time and mileage.'

First to address us before the panel is an Australian ultra-endurance icon who may no longer race but whose presence is so fitting. Rod Evans was twice Australian cyclist of the year, in 1990 and 1994. He has ridden across the Nullarbor five times and in 1988 broke the Around Australia record, completing the 14,000-kilometre trip in just under fifty days. In 1990, Rod broke the late and legendary Sir Hubert Opperman's 24-hour world record set fifty years earlier, covering just under 806 kilometres. Then in 1994 at Perth's Midvale Velodrome, he set four more world records – the 100 and 200 miles records; the 1,000 kilometres record, in a time of 29 hours, 12 minutes and 39 seconds – and a new 12-hour record in the same ride.

Rod was also a friend of Opperman, or 'Oppy' as he was and is affectionately known. Asked what advice Oppy would have given us for the IndiPac, Rod says with a wry smile: 'Cycling is a very easy concept. When the pedal comes to the top of the stroke, you just push it down again. If you do that, you can relax until the other pedal comes to the top of the stroke, and then you just push it down again.'

Rod says we will see some of the roads Oppy rode on, with the Eyre Highway being close to the one he took – especially at Madura, where the old road is on the right. He warns us that one of the challenges we will face is working with the concept of 'how much sleep you can get away with not having'. While today's cyclists can easily find advice and information on what sleep limits are safe, in Oppy's day there was no such precious data. With that in mind, Rod recounts how Oppy once recalled that, during his record ride across Australia, his long-time agent and mentor Bruce Small tricked him into thinking he had got more sleep than he had. Oppy was on the brink of exhaustion and felt he couldn't go any further, despite Small's persistent encouragement. After he pleaded for sleep, Small granted him eight hours.

'Bruce got Oppy off the bike, put him in the car,' says Rod. 'Then he got Oppy's watch and wound it forward 7 hours and 50 minutes, gave Oppy ten minutes' sleep, woke him up and said, "You've had your eight hours, get going."

'Oppy felt incredibly refreshed. "This is fantastic," he said to Bruce. "I feel so good."

'But Bruce knew that Oppy had only had ten minutes' sleep. And what soon concerned him was that Oppy began veering from one side of the road to the other. Bruce was wondering, "Have I really pushed this guy too far?"

'Finally, he decided he couldn't stand it any longer. He came up beside Oppy and asked, "Are you okay?"'

'"I'm fine," Oppy said. "I feel really, really good."

'"But you're weaving all over the road."

'Oppy looked at him. "Mate, it's not me. It's all these other bloody cyclists."'

The room erupts into laughter, but quietens when Rod reminds us of the dangers of riding alone. He also tells us, pointedly, 'Every day you're going to have a massive high and a massive low.' Then, with a smile, he throws out the caveat. 'The great thing about the lows is they are all the stories you will tell when you get home.'

We're all listening; and no less so Jesse, Sarah, Kristof and Mike. Rod's respect of tradition, and the IndiPac's role in recognising it, helps to fuel the sense of imminent adventure. And while we all have varying levels of experience and ambitions, we're bound together by this.

This bond is reinforced at 4 pm the next day when we gather at the South Mole Lighthouse for a group photo. Then we each dip our bike's rear wheel into the waters off the beach in Bathers Bay. The beach is small and nondescript at first sight and adjoins the seawall to the lighthouse, but is significant in Fremantle history, being the embarking site in the late 1800s for Aboriginal prisoners sent to Wadjemup (Rottnest Island), many of them fierce warriors and leaders in conflicts over frontier settlement.

In an age-old tradition, the early Overlanders dipped their rear wheel into whichever sea they started their epic rides from, and the front wheel into the sea upon finishing. For us, this means the Indian and Pacific oceans, the latter off Sydney's Bondi Beach, even though the official finish line is in front of the Opera House in Sydney Harbour.

But right now, dipping my front wheel is the last thing on my mind. There are 5,470 kilometres for me to cycle first.

I HAVE NEVER RIDDEN THAT FAR IN A DAY

Day 1: Fremantle to Merredin

Start: 6 am   Finish: 7.35 pm

Riding time: 12 hours 35 minutes

Distance: 319.7 km   Metres climbed: 1,995 m

Average speed: 25.1 kmh   Temperature: 13–21 C

The noise of rain on a tin roof has a soothing effect when you are wafting comfortably in and out of sleep. Unless you are due to be cycling in the early morning – and especially on the first morning of a solo unsupported race across Australia. The sound, like light taps on a cymbal, is almost hypnotic.

Not that I've really slept well, but knowing I'm not the only one to have had a restless night provides some solace. The glow piercing from under the doors of other rooms when I went to the bathroom down the corridor earlier confirms that others are restless with anticipation as well. As does the sound of riders unfolding and folding their maps, tinkering with equipment or pottering around because they can't sleep. But after I fall into a deep slumber, it seems like no time has passed when 4 am ticks over and I must get up, shower, dress, eat and ready myself to cycle a few kilometres from the Local Hotel in South Fremantle in darkness, and in an early blow to spirit, light rain and an early morning chill.

Frankly, I'm not really in the mood for the start of a 5,470-kilometre race. But I can't turn around now. I'm too far down the track to change my mind. So it's best to not think at all, just follow the others as they soft-pedal in pre-dawn silence to the South Mole Lighthouse where the race will start.

While we had all been there the day before, the green glow of the lighthouse is literally a beacon for us. As too are the many red rear lights of riders already arrived – from entrants to the supporters who intend to ride out with the IndiPac peloton as it negotiates the exit from Fremantle and towards the first stretches of isolated forest and bushland, and then desert.

◉

For Ironman triathlons, I don't chat much before a start, preferring to find peace, relax and limit any building anxiety. It's the same now. At the end of the breakwater near the lighthouse, there's continuing light rain and a blustery wind. Word gets out that there should be a tail wind for the start, which is good – it will push us along. I remain silent, barring a chat with one or two spectators I know, and recording my first vlog, part of a series I will post on Facebook throughout the race.

Then, just as I think I have all bases covered, I realise I haven't. With minutes to spare before the start, I still haven't activated my Spot Gen3. This satellite tracking device won't just show our names alongside colour-coded dots on the race map through its GPS, but will also act as a safety tool. We have the option of three messages. One button, activated by pressing 'okay' at the end of each day, will send a message to anyone whose email address we have registered, letting them know we are safe and where we are going to rest. A second button can send out an alert for assistance, if needed. The third button is for the most drastic of circumstances, such as an emergency evacuation, and to be utilised in life or death situations only.

I feel a flush of panic. The one thing that's going to monitor where I am in a massive continent isn't even working. I feel as though I'm about to miss the start of a 100 metre sprint – that I will suddenly be left behind – but then remind myself that ahead is the best part of 5,500 kilometres and possibly four weeks of cycling. One of the most important bits of gear I have, the Spot Gen3 was one of the first things I bought for the IndiPac, having it sent from Spain. Not mastering its operation has been one of my lapses, and now I've been caught out for not taking the time to trial it. I should have spent more time figuring it out on my training rides. 'Dumb,' I say to myself.

Mid self-remonstration, I notice that nearby is Ryan Flinn – AKA 'Rhino' – a fellow entrant and growing identity in Australia's ultra-endurance cycling world. We had met the previous year, in Paris, on the night after the Tour de France finished. Rhino had left a lasting impression on me. After our traditional Monday-after-the-Tour lunch that I and other Australian journalists and cycling 'friends' have attended since Cadel Evans' historic 2011 win, Rhino joined me and some other 'survivors' at a nearby café. He talked about his plan to ride from Paris to Bordeaux that night. I thought he was mad, or at the very best joking. He wasn't – joking, that is.

Now, almost eight months later, I'm standing right next to him. With barely a couple of minutes before the start I desperately blurt out, 'Rhino, mate. Can you start my Spot?'

'Sure, no problem, Rupe,' he says with his trademark smile and calm that embarrasses me. 'There you go. You're all set.'

With his press of a button, my device is operational. I figure that there is still more than enough time ahead to get my head around the rest of its operation.

As soon as the red lights are flashing on my Spot Gen3, Jesse Carlsson orders the start of the race.

We are off. Seventy riders in a field spread for age as much as for talent. Lochie Kavanagh, at eighteen the youngest rider, has had only several months' experience cycling and only signed up for the IndiPac after completing his Higher School Certificate the previous year. Seventy-four-year-old Paul Adrill began cycling after suffering a stroke at sixty-five and is riding to promote the benefits of an active life. Having previously cycled from Perth to Sydney, he's also using the IndiPac to commemorate the sudden death of his triathlete daughter Cheri Lutz in 2016. In a preview of the IndiPac by *Sydney Morning Herald* journalist Garry Maddox which was published this morning, Paul joked that his wife Express Posted him to Perth and told him he had to find his own way back.

In darkness, we negotiate ourselves toward the east. Sydney is several weeks away at best. I haven't really determined a destination for day one. I figure I'll get a sense of where to stop nearer night-time. A lot will happen between now and then.

A number of riders bolt from the start and make a furious race of it up front. They include Mike Hall, Dutchmen Matthijs Ligt and Jan-Willem Bobbink, Irishman Donncha Cuttris, Australian Sebb Dunne, Belgian Kim Raeymaekers, Germans Juliana Buhring and Kai Edel and the Greek Vasiliki Voutzalii. Sarah Hammond flies by me as we leave the lighthouse breakwater. We share a wave and smile.

'Hey, Rupe!' Sarah yells as she passes me with a wave.

'Have a great race, Sarah,' I shout back.

'You too. See you in Sydney!'

I know immediately that will be the last I see of her until then.

Kristof Allegaert, I only later learn, is the last to ride away. I certainly don't see him pass me.

As dawn emerges, my first kilometres are slow. I get caught in the traffic of locals cycling with us. I also feel tense. I have made real the idea of riding across Australia – or of attempting to. I think about the Overlanders as they left on their rides – many were sent away with fanfare too, foremost being Richardson when he left Perth on 5 June 1899 for his ride around Australia, two and a half years after his historic crossing of the Nullarbor. Even the Governor of Western Australia, Sir Gerard Smith, was there among the fans and sponsors to cheer his farewell.

But not all Overlanders had send-offs like this, such as the Irish-Australian engineer Jerome Murif, who became the first person to cycle across Australia from south to north in 1897, riding from Glenelg, near Adelaide on the Gulf of the Southern Ocean, to Port Darwin on the Arafura Sea. In his memoir *From Ocean to Ocean – Across A Continent on A Bicycle*, Murif, who began his ride at age 34, recalls his departure from the Pier Hotel where he had been staying: 'I shook hands with the landlady ... told her I might not be back for tea and not to keep it waiting, and quietly pedalled away on my glistening Diamond, without a single person being by to see me off or wish me luck.'

But he wasn't disheartened by the low key farewell: 'There was the glorious sense of having resolutely acted as an independent part. A glad feeling of being alive, untrammelled, free. And so we gaily sped along. It was a very dance on wheels.'

◉

Unlike Murif, I'm a bit apprehensive. Looking ahead, there's plenty to be worried about. I don't really have a grasp of how hard I should ride with so much distance ahead, so I rein in my pace as I head towards the hilly outskirts of Fremantle.

The route takes us through the top of the Korung National Park, then north through the Beelu National Park to the town of Mundaring and finally right onto the Great Eastern and Southern Highways and out into the wilderness. It's all new road and terrain for me. I feel foreign, even though it is Australia.

I haven't conducted any reconnaissance of the route on my bike or in a car, apart from some parts outside Adelaide in January while riding in the BUPA Tour during the Santos Tour Down Under in South Australia, and then in the Southern Highlands of New South Wales. Before long, I'm surprised by the steepness of the Perth hills – and by how many locals are cycling out with us in a show of support. I assume the rule of entrants not being allowed to ride in anyone's slipstream won't count until the field is less congested. There are slipstreams everywhere right now, but who can question such valuable goodwill and support at the start of an event that began as a dream?

The early part of the ride provides a great opportunity to chat with supporting riders. Part of me wants to settle into a pace I'm comfortable to ride at alone, but I'm swept up by the enthusiasm of the cyclists riding with us for these early kilometres, knowing that in a few hours I will have more than enough time to ride alone – perhaps too much. Many riders ask me about my reasons for entering, my hopes and fears.

Enjoy the company, while you have it, I tell myself. *There are thousands of kilometres of solitude to come.*

Rain has been building and the wet weather sets in. I'm soon drenched but still comfortably warm thanks to the rain jacket I have on – supplied by Rapha cycling apparel who are supporting me with clothing for the race – and the effort needed to climb. I am actually grateful for that. It could be far worse. I could be wet and cold, chilled even. It has happened before when wearing kit that may be cheap but ineffective. To get a cold now, let alone any time, could be so detrimental. My first worry is whether I've packed all my gear correctly into the Apidura packs – one under the handlebars, top tube and the saddle and one behind and either side of the head stem. I decide to stop and check.

If it is wet, there's nothing I can do about it now, I tell myself. *I can only take it out to dry later.*

I remain focused on finding a rhythm. As riders pass me, and me them for the rest of the day, I realise it might take days for a reliable pattern to emerge. Even as I'm thinking about it, my rhythm and speed increases to something akin to an 180-kilometre bike leg of an Ironman triathlon – just under the threshold of riding hard, but not too hard to exhaust myself.

It surprises me. A pace like this is manageable over a five-hour Ironman leg, but here I'm looking at three to four weeks in the saddle. I'm feeling good physically, so I continue, but my inexperience is playing with my mind. In any case, the leaders are much faster than I am. Others have passed me as well. As a newbie to this kind of event, the only real way to gauge my pace is by trial and – no doubt – error.

◉

With about 130 kilometres ridden, on the approach to York, the oldest inland town of Western Australia, there is finally the semblance of solitude. Five kilometres out from the town and with rain still falling, I come across the first IndiPac 'road angel'. These race supporters, we have been told, come to the route offering IndiPac riders food and drinks, which is allowed if available to every rider. Rather than ride off-route five hundred metres into York, I seize the chance to embrace this angel's offerings. I refill my three 750-millilitre drink bottles, drink a few bottles of water and electrolyte, eat a banana and take another.

Soon after getting back on the road, I hear the sound and then sight of Sam Jeffries and James Raison, South Australian riders I had chatted with earlier in the day, on the approach. I thought they were way ahead of me.

'Hey, Rupe. How's it going?' yells Sam as he passes.

'All good, mate.'

'Have a good one,' says James as he rides by soon after.

'You too. Keep it going.'

They're soon out of sight. They must have stopped for lunch in York, surrendering their initial lead on me. But I soon see the benefit of their decision. They have fuelled and rested properly and are now feeling strong. While I got a brief rest, enjoying the road angel's offerings, I'm not in the same state of recovery. I also wonder what York is like. *Too late*, I think. *Keep moving.*

Not that I'm concerned about being passed by Sam or James. I know plenty of other riders will catch and pass by me in the days and weeks ahead, and vice versa. But still, as I continue alone on to Central Wheatbelt towns Black Rock and then Merredin, I start thinking about the best times to rest and why, and the need to be smart about those decisions.

◉

With about five and half hours of steady cycling in the legs, I still feel good. The training I've done is standing me in good stead. I feel even better when I see the sun trying to push through the grey skies. But then begins one of many IndiPac phenomena. Just as I think I've found and held my rhythm, it deserts me . . .

and then returns. I've never felt this in an Ironman. I learn later that this fluctuation is common in ultra-endurance cycling, but it still tests both the spirit and body, especially when it first strikes.

Then, once I've refound my rhythm, I'm thrown one of the first of many glitches of the IndiPac when my iPhone flips off the mount secured on the head stem of my handlebars. It happens just after I pass Nathan Jones, an American who has entered as part of his ride around the world. I stop and, seeing the phone is not smashed, clip it back on, thinking that I mustn't have attached it properly earlier. I also use the break in momentum to have a pee by the side of the road. *All is good*, I think to myself. Despite the hiccup, I'm settling into things. I'm okay.

Soon after, I hear something falling from my bike again. I can't tell what it is but I stop and ride several hundred metres back over the route to check, keeping an eye out. But I see nothing, so resume cycling east and quickly slip back into a rhythm.

About 15 kilometres later, I look down at my handlebars again and – incredibly – see a vacant space where my map and written route notes had been strapped onto the pack. They're gone. The noise I heard before is explained.

Their loss sends me into my first spin. Sure, I know where I am. And where I am going. But for some reason, losing the detailed paperwork that I had spent many hours late at night at home in Sydney working on has now left me feeling stranded.

While I'd been concerned I hadn't studied the race route properly, that map and those notes were a security blanket for my hopes of following the race route correctly. The route itself has been carefully planned by the organisers. It's easy to follow to Ceduna and the end of the Nullarbor, but then there are a number of directional changes that could easily send a rider off route and, according to the race rules, force them to return to the point of error, which means riding extra kilometres and losing time. That, or risk being slapped with a time penalty. I've downloaded the route onto my iPhone via the Ride with GPS and MAProgress apps, and also onto my Garmin Etrex 30, which is a separate handheld GPS device I have as backup. But the hard copy of the map and my handwritten notes gave me the added assurance I needed to not get lost. Given my lack of experience with digital maps, I feel at a major loss. But I'm not about to turn back again.

I can buy another one, I reassure myself. Going forward is what's important, not back, especially this early in the race. I also want to accumulate a solid tally of kilometres to kick-start my IndiPac on a positive note. So I try to shake it off and push on.

Throughout the afternoon I see numerous riders several times. Some I pass. Others pass me, such as Claire Stevens, a Melbourne surgeon who I met three nights before at the rider sign-in at Fremantle.

'How good is this?' Claire yells as she blasts by, turning to look at me with her trademark smile beaming.

I smile and wave in return.

◉

Late afternoon I reach Bruce Rock, 50 kilometres south of Merredin. Previously known as Dalton, the hamlet's population was thirty-six in the 2016 census. It doesn't seem like much has changed. The streets are empty, there's no activity. The end-of-day light casts a gloomy shadow over the town, but thankfully the general store is open for business.

Entering, I see Claire for the first time since she flew by me. She's trying to decide what to eat. I watch what she gets, but should just decide what I want. I grab a salad roll, a packaged muffin, a can of Coke and a couple of Kit Kat chocolate bars.

I'm surprised to see Harley Johnstone, AKA 'Durian Rider'. He is a vegan and one of the pre-race personalities with a huge following of his YouTube channel. He's been flagged as one of the riders to watch. I thought he'd be further up the road, but I give this little thought and am content to focus on what I am doing well – or not.

Then, out of the blue comes Rod Evans, who had addressed us at the sign-in at Fremantle. He gets out of his car parked outside the shop.

Although the fatigue of riding 270 kilometres is setting in, my current plan is to not waste time in Bruce Rock and ride as far as I can. But I'm thrilled to bits to see Rod. He was an inspiring speaker in Fremantle and we had a good chat.

Rod sees me, but first speaks briefly to the Durian Rider and then Claire. But after a while he looks at me and says he has something for me. Rod knows IndiPac race rules don't allow riders to get outside assistance, so I'm curious when he returns from his car holding a small white envelope. When he hands it to me I see the words 'Open when things get tough' written on it.

'It's just if you are on the brink of stopping,' Rod explains with his trademark Colgate smile. 'Open it and read it before you decide. If you don't stop, don't open it – throw it away.'

I'm humbled to receive such a simple but considered gesture from an icon of Australian endurance racing.

Could it be considered outside assistance? I suppose it could be if the message influences any decision I make, should I reach a crisis point and think I can't continue. But if anyone under-stands the spirit of the IndiPac, it's Rod. I slip the envelope neatly into my small pack on the top bar near the head stem, within easy reach.

By the time I finish thanking Rod, Claire has ridden off. Because he's nowhere in sight, I assume the Durian Rider has resumed riding as well. So as the late afternoon shadows darken, I farewell Rod and continue my ride. My aim is to make Merredin, halfway between Perth and Coolgardie.

The looming darkness makes me pick up my pace. I'm ready to ride in the night – I spent many evening hours training for the IndiPac – but I'd prefer to reach Merredin in daylight, especially when I notice my rear red light dimming, limiting how well traffic behind can see me. My front lights are being recharged by the dynamo hub in my front wheel, but I haven't recharged my back-up rear light adequately, so I hope this one lasts till I get there.

Soon I also start to feel hunger flat – when the body has run out of fuel and suddenly feels weak. Clearly I haven't eaten enough throughout the day to sustain the calorie intake I need.

I shake my head. I've committed the rookie error of being swept up by the excitement of the race start and making good early progress with the tail winds. I know better, and should have eaten more on the way. My personal trainer, Nicola Vrachnas, had also continually reminded me to eat a lot and always carry extra food with me. While food options may be limited in the outback, it wouldn't matter what I ate while riding because I would burn everything up, though of course high quality protein, carbs and fats would be optimal when or if I could get my hands on them. I understood before the race that I would have to eat all the time, even when I wasn't hungry; but here I am, day one, having made the error of not doing so.

Hunger flat, or 'the bonk' as it is also often called, is a frightening sensation when you realise what it is. One second you feel fine, strong even; but then it's as if all the energy and strength is being sucked rapidly out of you. By then, it's too late and unless it's dealt with immediately, it can leave a rider wobbling in weakness inside minutes, even seconds. With my energy fading as fast as my rear light, I'm worried when I struggle in the final kilometres before Merredin. Not only am

I feeling weak, but my rapidly fading rear light is dangerously restricting my visibility.

◉

Relief only comes with the lights of Merredin finally in view. It's 7.35 pm. No sooner do I arrive in town, I check into the Olympic Motel, a simple but clean place that is the first I see. A day that began rain stricken is now swept by a dry chill. Over twelve hours of cycling I've made five stops: two for a pee, two for a drink and one to eat at Bruce Rock. And I have ridden 319 kilometres. I have never ridden that far on a bicycle in a day in my life.

I'm immediately tempted to strip down and stand under a hot shower in my room, but instead I follow the advice of many ultra-endurance racers and first make sure all my electrics are plugged in to be recharged, all my drink bottles are refilled and whatever food is left is laid out on a table near my helmet, wallet and other small must-have items, ready for putting back into my pockets and packs the next morning.

Only then do I enjoy the most beautiful of showers. I also wash my cycling kit and hang up my shorts, undershirt, jersey and any other dirty clothes to dry. All that's left to do is eat and sleep. Nicola, my trainer, advised that for dinner I eat protein-rich food to give my muscles some chance at dealing with the fatigue. But I soon realise that eating options in Merredin are limited. At the service station next door to the motel, I have to settle for a meat pie, a sausage roll, a bag of Smiths chips and two cans of lemonade.

As for where I am in the race and who's leading, I've barely given either question a thought, so focused am I on buying food and getting to bed. Not that I escape getting the lowdown. The servo guy, a happy and larger than life figure, tells me I am 'well behind' and that a big group is up the road en route to Southern Cross, 110 kilometres away. I know they're way ahead, but *that* far? His update includes the concern of local police that some riders are hard to see at night. But there's little I can do now about what's in front of me, or behind. My priority is to eat, rest, stretch – if I have the energy – and sleep a handful of hours in readiness to do it all again tomorrow.

With my food in my arms, I dash through the cold and darkness back to the awaiting warmth of my motel room. The air is much cooler now. And it doesn't help that my cycling shoes are damp inside from built-up sweat.

Once in bed, eating and staring blankly at the television, I'm suddenly swept by an uncontrollable chill that goes deep into my bones. A case of the shakes overcomes me. My body is protesting. With the light and the television still on, I curl up into a foetal position, trying to contain the warmth in the bed. But I'm still shaking. Like a leaf. I tighten my grip around my shoulders and tuck my knees in closer in a bid to get warmer. I hope I haven't suddenly been struck by a fever.

Finally, the shaking weakens and after 20 minutes, I feel better. As my body temperature returns, so does my morale, until the urge to sleep kicks in. It's too late to call home to Libby. I feel sorry for not actually trying to call, but I simply don't have the energy to engage in a conversation. She knows where I am and that I'm safe, as I've pressed the button my Spot Gen3 device that sends a pre-written email telling her I'm OK and where I'm staying for the night.

I turn the lights and television off and surrender to the night.

4

HOW DID WE GET OURSELVES INTO THIS?

Day 2: Merredin to Karra Retreat Centre
Start: 6.03 am Finish: 1.46 pm
Riding time: 7 hours 46 minutes
Distance: 180.3 km Metres climbed: 875 m
Average speed: 22 kmh Temperature: 10–19 C

It's 3 am. I'm wide awake, fuelled by the adrenaline of getting stuck into day two. The IndiPac is all still so fresh and new. However, my plans for a quick 'get-up-shower-dress-feed-and-go' are thwarted. I am soon fluffing round, seemingly doing a lot, but in reality achieving little. At 5 am I'm still at the motel, sitting on my bed talking live on Facebook, when I should have been out the door. There is time to Facebook later. I phone Libby, who by now is about to leave home for work in Sydney, where it is 9 am. It's a short chat. She'd seen my dot on the tracker parked at the motel and figured I was staying there the night.

But I want to reassure her that I'm up and about, in positive spirits and about to hit the road again.

It's not until 6 am, after breakfast at the servo next door and in full daylight that I straddle my bike. Repacking my kit isn't as fast or as easy as I thought. But I tell myself this is something I'll get better at.

My plan today is to ride to Coolgardie. Norseman, 462 kilometres away from Merredin and the last port of call before crossing the Nullarbor Plain, is too far to reach. But if the conditions are right and I feel strong enough, I don't dismiss the possibility of cycling beyond Coolgardie. Kristof Allegaert arrived there at 2.15 am, to end a first day of 615 kilometres, almost twice as many as me. Simply amazing. It serves as a reality check about the calibre of riders who will be leading – if not winning – this race.

I was too tired last night to think of the advance the front runners have already made. Not that I have delusions of catching them. I must keep to my own plans, ride within my capabilities.

◉

While trying to find some rhythm on the Eastern Highway, my focus turns to the task of dealing with a cross headwind.

The Coolgardie Pipeline is to my right; later it is to my left. This surprises me because it seems I have only been riding straight.

Without my noticing it, the road must have crossed sides. Running from the Mundaring Weir on the outskirts of Perth, the pipeline is the centrepiece of the Goldfields Water Supply Scheme that was commissioned in 1896 and completed in 1903 to channel water to the eastern goldfields of Western Australia, in particular to the towns of Coolgardie and Kalgoorlie. It still has a vital role today, supplying water to more than 100,000 people across households, mines and farms.

Early Overlanders would have been very familiar with the pipeline route, and ridden across the same rugged terrain that lies around it today – not the smooth bitumen road that I'm on of course, struggling as I am with a cross headwind. The pipeline itself would have been a handy landmark for riders to follow, knowing that its destination included towns and outposts. But if the feats of Allegaert and others near the front of the IndiPac seem incredible, those of the pioneering Overlanders, who laboured through hot desert sands sparse of shade and laden with sharp rocks and thistles, were phenomenal.

◉

As the blue sky and dry weather of this morning lift my mood, I think of what I learned on the first day of the IndiPac. One of the changes I've already made is to attach a light to my helmet in readiness for riding late in the day or in case the battery pack to recharge my lights runs out. I want to keep them all fully charged, harder than imagined with the accumulated fatigue of cycling swaying attention to detail. But I want to be fully prepared if extra light is needed. I now realise the importance of time management and the gains of doing the little things after a day's ride in preparation for the next day as soon as possible, rather than surrendering to the temptation of leaving them for later when they can slip the mind.

This is all positive reflection, thanks to a decent rest overnight. As the kilometres and a couple of hours pass, I feel strong – even passing some riders who had ridden into Merredin after me but left town earlier than I did.

My plan is still to ride an average of 300 kilometres per day – allowing for a daily regime of twelve to fifteen hours in the saddle, a few rest stops, and four or five hours' sleep. With such a plan, I hope to be as fresh as possible at the back end of the IndiPac when the route crosses the Victorian Alps and the mountains of Kosciuszko National Park and then again after leaving Canberra and passing through the Southern Highlands before the approach to Sydney.

It's not long into the morning when the first of many road trains of the day passes by me. For months I have heard about road trains and their danger, of their speed and size and the inherent risks of not only being struck but even sucked under their wheels by the slipstream. Before the IndiPac began, I was anxious about the first time a road train would pass me – I had no firsthand experience.

If anything, I was relieved when the first one passed me by on day one – a two-trailer – and was surprised by how calm I felt, although I knew I couldn't drop my guard. And rightly so, as in the days ahead the train sizes increased to three and even four trailer-loads, and with that their sound and the strength of the vacuum, especially when they had only a narrow lane as they negotiated a train barrelling in the other direction. On every occasion I was passed I felt very small, powerless, no matter their size. The sight of road kill – from animals battered to being flattened – was a sobering reminder of what could happen.

I employed a simple but precautionary safety measure in daylight: as soon as I saw or heard a road train approaching from behind – the rumble of speeding wheels on rough desert roads was a trademark alert – I would raise my right arm to signal to the driver that I knew they were approaching, and then after it passed, I would rise my left and wave to signal 'thanks'. At night, or in the darkness of a pre-dawn morning, they are easier to see because their headlights, and even rear lights, shine as strongly as a lighthouse and are visible from kilometres or minutes away. I could never be a hundred per cent certain whether the truckies behind the wheel could see me and knew they had passed me safely, but I had a responsibility to myself – and them – to do my best to be visible. Thankfully though, so far, truck drivers appear to respect our place on the road by giving a wide berth as they pass, even though I learn later from other riders of several near misses.

But there's no denying the strength of a road train's slipstream as it passes – it's powerful, especially the vortex of reverberating air when oncoming trucks pass each other. In every instance, there's very little room for error. The thought of being sucked into and under their wheels is simply terrifying, and I try to put it out of my mind as they pass. My instinct is to freeze and stiffen, but I force myself to relax instead and hold a firm but comfortable position on the saddle and handlebars and breathe calmly and slowly from deep within my core. This allows me to remain alert and ready to steer left off the road and out of the path of danger if needed.

Another lesson learned from day one is to stop earlier to eat and drink more regularly, especially if it's raining. Riding on when you're feeling strong can pay dividends, but it can also be costly if it leads to forgetting to refuel, or to restock for later when there may not be anywhere to buy anything. It's an easy mistake to make in wet conditions when dehydration is just as common as in dry weather, despite the perception that the risk of dehydration is less when riding in the rain. It's a mistake that can be easily made when swimming: just because you're wet doesn't mean you're not sweating and don't need to rehydrate.

So while my plan is to overnight at Coolgardie, my first intended stop for the day, after 110 kilometres, is at Southern Cross, but only for something to eat and drink and to rest a little.

◉

Another town on the Golden Pipeline Heritage Trail, Southern Cross is in wheat and cereal crops heartland and has only a small population of 681. It was founded in 1888 by gold prospectors and named after the Southern Cross constellation. Once you get there, you can tell it functions as a service town to the surrounding communities, busy as it is thanks to its supermarket, petrol station, post office and pubs, and a railway station.

On the approach to Southern Cross, I experience an interesting psychological shift. Since Bruce Rock, I've become used to being alone, with only my thoughts to motivate me. But on the horizon I see the blurred vision of a rider in dark blue. As I close in I notice the trademark pink and white hoops of a Rapha jersey. One of my two jerseys is similar.

I suspect the rider has seen me. I don't know if they're male or female, but I'm quickly catching them up – and then all of a sudden I'm not. Whoever they are, they must be digging in to keep ahead of me. It feels strange, but I succumb to the competition and pick up my pace to reel in the rider ahead of me, which I eventually do.

I finally draw up alongside Mark Ferguson, AKA 'Cycling Maven', from Melbourne with the popular YouTube channel of the same name. I'd chatted with him at the race sign-in.

'Rupe!' he yells with a beaming grin.

'Maven! How are you, mate? Great to see you!'

'I knew that was you coming. I've been watching your dot

close in on me all day, brother. So I put in a big effort for the last five kilometres.'

'I thought so, mate,' I say. 'I was going deep there too.'

The Maven had reached Merredin the previous night after me at 10 pm, but left at 4 am, which explains why I haven't seen him. Now we're around five kilometres outside of Southern Cross we settle back into a manageable pace that suits both of us. I'm behind him yet well outside the minimal distance allowed to avoid an illegal slipstream effect. For a few minutes we return to our own thoughts. Mine steer me to what the Maven had said about observing my progress, which is via his own Garmin Etrex 30. It reminds me that I need to get my head around mine as soon as possible.

Then we reunite, riding abreast, also as IndiPac race rules allow, and chat about our respective first day and a half.

'How did we get ourselves into this?' I ask, jokingly.

The Cycling Maven laughs. 'This is insane.'

After a while we settle back into our own rhythms. This time I'm ahead, and soon the Maven is out of sight when I glance behind. I'm chasing the horizon again. I enjoy another moment of strength, knowing full well that there are inevitable lows to come. My plan is still to stop at Southern Cross, the last main town before Coolgardie, despite the probability of there being smaller places on the way.

The sight of the Southern Cross road sign is welcome but I wonder if I have ridden harder than I needed since leaving the

Maven. He will likely stop at Southern Cross, too. If he does, will I stick to the time I had set myself to stop and continue ahead? Or will we continue our banter from where we had left off, and find ourselves resuming the IndiPac side-by-side again? It is a race, of course, but I am enjoying our chats.

◉

Southern Cross is all but closed on this Sunday afternoon. As I ride downhill and into town along the wide and traffic-free main street, I wonder how the week must pass for those who live in towns like this. There must be busy periods during the week, but the silence and inactivity today is pretty depressing at best. I didn't expect a celebratory welcome from the locals, but I thought I might see some farmers and their families shopping or socialising.

I turn off the highway and stop at the Yilgarn Coffee Lounge, a small place, but the only thing that seems to be open – later I discover there's a service station at the other end of town. An elderly woman is standing in front of the café. There is no one else around. I figure she must run it.

'Good morning. Are you open?' I ask her.

'You're late. The others rode through hours ago,' she replies.

'I may be late, but I'm not last and I know others are coming.'

I'm a little put out by her seemingly curt welcome but she walks back inside. I follow her in and take a seat, thinking about what to eat and drink. Unwittingly, I'm committing the novice ultra-endurance rider's mistake of faffing around, wasting time. Finally, I order two toasted sandwiches, a cup of tea and a cookie to eat while my sandwiches are prepared.

I check my phone to see how the Cycling Maven is going on the dot tracker, as well as other riders such as Doug Migden, a friendly and chatty sixty-year-old American doctor and experienced ultra-endurance rider from Seattle who I met in Fremantle, and had also passed on the road.

I wonder if they'll stop here too. How will I engage with them, considering this is a race? I'm really starting to wrestle with that particular issue.

Am I actually racing this? I ask myself. *Or am I riding it to try to finish?* Then I wonder if there's really a difference for someone like me, unlike those leading. I'm already scores of kilometres behind them. I'm feeling tired already, and it's only day two!

I can't come up with the answer. I stop trying to, and look back at my iPhone and the dot tracker. All I see is what those following the IndiPac from home can see: dots and their names on a map of Australia edging closer to me with every passing second.

The first to enter town is the Cycling Maven. I see his dot stop. Is he wondering where to go in the solitude of this Sunday? Then his dot turns and edges towards where I am waiting for my sandwiches and tea. In less than a minute I hear the sound of a bicycle, then see his silhouette against the sunshine outside. He comes through the door, grinning. I'm smiling too: good times.

'Mate,' I warn him, jokingly, 'when you order, don't bother saying what you're doing and expect praise for it. I was just told I was late when I arrived.'

We laugh. I sense we may be here for a bit longer, especially when two more faces appear through the blinding sunshine, those of Michael 'Crutchy' Crutch who hails from the Southern Highlands of New South Wales and, I learn, is a friend of my cycling coach Mark Fenner, and Canberran Michael James. Crutchy and Michael had met the night before at Bruce Rock. I hadn't seen Crutchy but had spotted Michael and his trademark red hair at the start of the day at the servo in Merredin.

As the four of us discuss our options for the day, my Spot Gen3 device, attached to my bike outside, starts to beep. We can all hear it. It's been going off regularly and I have no idea why. I talk about my frustration, and the Maven tells me it should be attached to the exterior of one of my packs. I have it tucked in my pack under the top bar of my bike frame, but that's been cutting it off from the cleanest detection of the GPS and been hindering the recording of my progress. I feel pretty embarrassed. Again, I'm paying the price for not having road tested my equipment properly before the race.

Forgetting that vital day time is slipping by, we talk on. My ears prick up when Michael says that he and Crutchy might stop before Coolgardie for an early finish and aim for an early start. I'm open to the idea. There are cross headwinds building outside and trying to reach Coolgardie, let alone Norseman, this late in the day could be a stretch. In the toughening conditions, the potential long term benefit of saving some energy with an early rest could pay dividends, especially if we're back on the road very early in the morning when there isn't any wind forecast. But where else is there to stay before Coolgardie, other than to bivvy at a stop area or by the side of the road? Before I even ask the question out loud, Michael James adds with a wry smile and a wink of someone who has wisely done their homework: 'I know of a little place to stop at.' I don't know what the Maven is thinking but it sounds interesting to me.

After a last purchase of some lollies – there is an abundance of options, many of them brands that offer a fond throwback to memories of my youth – and another home-made cookie for the road, I leave Southern Cross with the Cycling Maven, before Crutchy and Michael. I've already spent a fair amount of time in the café and they still have to eat and pay. But the idea of an early stop is still floating in my mind. I could slow down and wait for them if I warmed further to the idea, as I'd need to know where they're going to stay. Or if they pass me, I could simply watch where they stop.

◉

There's far more traffic on the road today, especially trucks. I'm grateful for having had my nerve already tested by them earlier in the day. Sunday, I'm told, is often the day truckies finish their runs and return home. But more surprising than the truck traffic is the amount of rubbish on the roadside – it amazes me that there's so much, so far from bigger townships or cities.

The Cycling Maven and I pedal on, but making sure we're not racing together, and regularly pass each other, each chasing the horizon as we experience our own spells of strength and weakness. A pattern is forming. I catch Doug Migden, who apparently did not stop at Southern Cross and notes the yellow reflector straps on my left and right ankles.

'I respect a guy who respects safety,' Doug yells as I pass.

I grin and give him a thumbs up and forge ahead, helmet down, into the testing headwind. *When will there be some relief? I ask myself. Surely the winds will turn.*

Soon I find myself some distance clear of the Maven and another Melbourne rider, the bearded Nick Skarajew, who I passed after Southern Cross.

Maybe I am racing, after all, I tell myself. But as soon as I articulate it, my day turns into one of physical and mental punishment, and as a consequence the Cycling Maven and Nick pass me.

My will to continue on to Coolgardie is waning fast. So much for the idea of racing. The idea of an early finish looks better with every pedal stroke, and the decision is all but firm when Crutchy and then Michael sweep by me. While not knowing exactly where they're planning to stop, I do know it's on the left of the Great Eastern Highway. In this part of the country, there can't be many places.

Thirty-two kilometres on from Southern Cross I pass the Yellowdine Roadhouse and see the Cycling Maven and Nick are taking a break, and other riders are too, Claire Stevens among them. Having come to terms with my plan to stop, I cycle on and we all exchange cries of encouragement.

My idea is that I will text the Cycling Maven and Nick when I stop, in case they have a change of heart and opt to stop early too, rather than trying to reach Coolgardie.

◉

My relief is instant when I see the blurred image of two riders near a sign that reads 'Koora Retreat Centre' – and a tray of 'Trail Angel' drinks that awaits thirsty IndiPac riders. I slow and join them for the 500-metre ride off-road into the vibrant green of Boorabin National Park. When we pull up at an intriguingly rustic establishment, I have no regrets about changing my original plan for the day. This is what the IndiPac is about: planning as you go, seizing opportunities as they arise, and hoping they pay off.

But it *is* a big call. Coolgardie is still 120 kilometres away. At this time of day it's achievable, even though the cross headwinds are building. But my mind has come to terms with an early finish, and with that an early dinner, an early sleep – and a very early rise.

As we ride slowly up a dirt track, grateful it's in daylight, we're welcomed by the bearded smile of a tall man in blue working overalls. The Reverend Peter Harrison owns the retreat centre with Reverend Dr Anna Killigrew. Both are Anglican priests and chaplains licensed by Perth's archbishop. Anna isn't here, and despite it only being 3.30 in the afternoon, Peter has already begun cooking with a view to Michael's called-in request to serve dinner at 5 pm to fit in with our plan to get to sleep early and leave sometime between 1 and 3 am.

Peter proudly shows us around the centre. It's so pleasant to see where we are staying before nightfall and we savour the simple but charming character of the centre that usually caters for large spiritual or religious gatherings or companies wanting an isolated business retreat. Then, after installing our electronics for recharge, preparing our food and bikes for our departure, and showering, we're back in the kitchen listening to Peter's stories of his many adventures in this wilderness.

Checks of the dot tracker in the meantime show that the Cycling Maven and Nick have opted to continue on to Coolgardie. At first, I wonder if I've let myself down. Had I dug in, I might have been with them now, closing in on my initial target destination. But after day one, having ridden longer than I ever have in my life in a single day, a step back now could pay off later. I have to back my call, and keep an eye on the long term objective – not waste energy with 'what ifs'.

To Peter's credit, huge serves of spaghetti bolognese and drinks of water are on the table on the dot of 5 pm. There's even the offer of a cold beer, if we want one. 'A number of stubbies have been left from a previous group. They're still in the cool room,' Peter says.

I immediately, reply, 'Yes, please.' Peter continues to entertain with stories of past visitors. He's also curious about the IndiPac. But with each mouthful of spaghetti and each swig of beer, fatigue quickly starts to take over. As the sun starts to set an early evening chill arrives. I'm suddenly enchanted by the prospect of bed.

The plan is to rise at 2 am and reach Norseman before nightfall. There we'll rest before heading the following day into the notorious Nullarbor Plain. I have read, heard and watched so much about this terrain, and am wary of it. But as I slip into bed, I'm in a good place mentally, and I know already that's something I can't take for granted.

The IndiPac, I soon learn, has claimed its first withdrawals. The first is Harley Johnstone, the Durian Rider. To be fair, he did begin the IndiPac with an injury from a recent cycling crash.

The other is more surprising. Jesse Carlsson, the mastermind behind the race, has been forced to stop on day two due to ongoing abdominal issues that he'd been battling for eighteen months. Announcing his withdrawal, Jesse revealed his participation had been in doubt right up until the day before the race started. In an Instagram post that was reposted on the IndiPac

Facebook page, he said, 'Given the time and effort I'd put into the race, and the rare opportunity to race an incredibly talented roster, I had to try. I was hoping my body would settle in [. . . but] I'm unable to keep battling through this time. Sorry for the let-down, folks. I had high hopes for this one.'

What a race, I thought to myself. *Pedigree and experience counts, but neither guarantees success.*

Best for me that I enjoy the comfort while I have it. There'll be a lot less of it in the days to come, if not the weeks. As I turn the lights out and shut my eyes, I think of the race leader, Kristof Allegaert, the last entrant to pedal away from the lighthouse in Fremantle. According to the dot tracker, he's already hundreds of kilometres ahead of me. By the end of two days in the saddle, Kristof has reached Caiguna, with 1,151 kilometres ridden. For him, it's been another signature day with more than 500 kilometres under his belt.

And close behind him is Mike Hall. Mike briefly took the lead at Widgiemooltha after 691 kilometres, but approaching Norseman, Kristof slipped back into first place. Kristof later revealed in his IndiPac diary that they both left a service station where they'd stopped at the same time. It was an awkward moment. But they quickly lost each other.

5

IT'S GONE

Day 3: Karra Retreat Centre to Norseman
Start: 3.05 am   Finish: 8 pm
Riding time: 13 hours 02 minutes
Distance: 303 km   Metres climbed: 1,324 m
Average speed: 22.1 kmh   Temperature: 5–24 C

Only one thing is harder than getting out of the warmth of my
bed when I wake at 2 am, and that's getting onto my bike and
riding off into the cold and inky blackness of the wilderness at
3 am. But this is the plan committed to by Michael, Crutchy and
me the day before. I'm tempted to sleep in comfort until dawn
and then resume. But I can't do it, not this early in the race. Not
on day three. If I succumb now, I'll succumb over and over.

As I step out from my small but cosy room into the biting
cold, a few metres away in the dining area I see the towering
figure of our host Reverend Peter Harrison already preparing our breakfast of coffee, cereal, toast, more toast, more coffee

and fruit. No sooner have I eaten, I'm in the kitchen making honey sandwiches for the road.

The hour from wake-up to departure seems to fly by. All that's quicker after we negotiate the gravel pathway back to the highway is the speed at which Michael and Crutchy ride off. Not that it worries me, but as their red rear lights disappear into the blackness ahead I realise I'm utterly alone.

It is a remarkable feeling. I feel isolated and exposed, but not afraid. All I can see are the metres before me illuminated by my front light and head lamp. There is no sign of habitation. The solitude and silence, exacerbated by the lack of any wind, are calming. Within minutes I'm settled and really enjoying the experience. As dark as Centennial Park in Sydney was at 3 am while training for the IndiPac, it had never been like this. All I can hear is the whir of my wheels as I ride at a comfortable rhythm, the beat of my heart and the sound of my breathing. The more I think about it, the more exhilarated I become. But I make a concerted effort not to ride too hard and waste the energy I'll need in the day ahead.

As the kilometres click over, the effort creates a comfortable warmth. Soon I am sweating. The calm is broken only by the odd truck or car passing. Still, I start to feel fatigued with the sensation of constantly riding uphill. With the emergence of dawn, the pitch blackness around me has begun to break. The skies above turn deep royal blue, then a lighter shade with each minute.

Finally, the orange glow of the sun slowly rises above the horizon. It's one of the most breathtaking experiences I have ever had: being alone, without a soul in sight, and witnessing such a simple yet glorious occurrence, one repeated every morning for hundreds of thousands of years, with only the tweets of waking birds breaking the silence. As I reach the crest of a hill I stop. I have to take it all in.

◉

It's 6 am. I have ridden 65 kilometres since leaving Karra, and am still 55 kilometres out from Coolgardie. Besides enjoying the quiet and using the stop to stretch a little, eat, drink, and check over my bike and packs, I post a live video on Facebook to share the moment with anyone following. The phenomenon of the dot watcher is not yet completely clear to me, or the growth in dot watcher numbers. But in my video I explain my plan, which is to stop at Coolgardie, then try to make Norseman by the end of the day, another 180 kilometres away, for an estimated total of 300 kilometres.

It will be hard, but I'm feeling positive, in high spirits and in good health and only a few new niggles. On day one, I had spasms across the back of my shoulders, but they disappeared. On day two, my left knee was sore, but now it's feeling much better. Today's complaint is my right ankle, an ailment I noticed for most of the previous 10 kilometres before stopping. That stretch of road had been stripped for new bitumen, exposing a gravel road corrugated by the wheels of work trucks. It made for a bone jarring ride, sending sharp, painful shudders through the sole of my foot to my now swelling ankle.

Short rest stops like this one are invaluable for managing niggles like this with self-massage. Still, I can't afford to waste time, and the passing of a car snaps me out of the comfort of the momentary rest. It's time to continue on to Coolgardie in the gloriousness of this new day.

◉

About an hour later, making steady pace towards Coolgardie, I see hands waving from both sides of a car that's emerging out of the haze of the horizon. It's Anthony Gordon and Troy Grice, who I have not seen since day one. Anthony interviewed then me from the car while I was riding and then drove off to join the front of the race. Race leader Kristof Allegaert has ridden more than 1200 kilometres and is now well into crossing the iconic 90 Mile Straight of the Nullarbor – at 146.6 kilometres, it's the longest straight stretch of road in the Southern Hemisphere – so I'm surprised to see Anthony and Troy. But their energy and encouraging gestures are great to see.

They make a U-turn after passing me and drive up alongside me with beaming smiles. After exchanging 'G'day's and 'How are you?'s, Anthony fills me in with where the Cycling Maven and the others with him are. He and Nick Skarajew aren't that far ahead.

'They've just left Coolgardie. They got there last night,' says Anthony.

The news is encouraging. I realise I haven't t lost that much ground by stopping early the previous day, and dare to think that maybe, with the good feed and night's sleep and the kilometres I have already ridden this morning, my call is paying dividends.

With the leaders forging ahead, Anthony and Troy have driven out of Coolgardie to trace back over the route and catch riders further behind like me on film. They plan to then re-join the leaders, who are set to take more distance on the rest of the field.

Anthony updates me on the race up front. Kristof, he says, is stomping. So is Mike Hall, who is also on 90 Mile Straight, averaging 26 kilometres per hour and setting the scene for a terrific tussle off the back of three to four hours of sleep over the last two nights. Also racing strongly is Sarah Hammond, the lead female, in sixth place overall and approaching the 1000-kilometre mark with 930 kilometres ridden in the first two days. It's mind boggling, really.

Kristof's and Mike's progress is remarkable, but Sarah's is understandably sparking plenty of interest. Could she win? We banter about it. Sarah's strong showing, and those of other women in the IndiPac, a number of who have passed me, demonstrates that peak ultra-endurance cycle racing isn't determined by gender.

Anthony interviews me for an official race update, which lifts my morale considerably. I talk about self-assessment and explain the struggles I've faced and how I've discovered the IndiPac isn't just about pedalling, but about management – time management, rest management, operational management, the whole gamut – and how mistakes will happen, but how you react is crucial to how well you recover. Unwittingly, as I talk to camera, my bike speed increases. Subconsciously, I'm riding harder.

Anthony finishes the interview and he and Troy drive off into the distance, and I fall into a slump. I am alone again, under a glorious blue sky and a sun that is warming by the minute. But I can't believe I allowed myself to be swept up by the boost in mood caused by their company to ride as hard as I did for camera.

The price? I labour into Coolgardie.

The town was founded in 1892 when gold was found there and by 1898 it was the third-largest town in Western Australia, after Perth and Fremantle. Coolgardie was among a growing number of goldfields, and a hub of activity at a time when the bicycle was becoming increasingly popular among gold diggers wanting to get to the next find as quick as possible, and messengers working for services, such as Overlander Percy Armstrong who moved to Coolgardie in 1894 after becoming the first person to cycle from Croydon in the Northern Territory to Melbourne, Victoria, in 1893.

By 9 am a lot has already happened today. Most people I know are only just arriving at work. Coolgardie is still stirring as I stop at the Caltex petrol station and convenience store. It's a welcome sight. I'm ready to eat again.

The importance of refuelling in a race like the IndiPac can't be forgotten. It's imperative to keep eating. And each time you stop, it's vital to buy food for later, especially in the wilderness where shops can be scarce, if not non-existent. You must store fuel by eating some food straight away, and stuffing more into your jersey pockets or packs, or by strapping it onto the bike somehow. Whichever way you do it, you've got to keep consuming food and drink. It's the mantra.

Loaded up – both inside and in my packs – and after a spirit-lifting call to Libby, I leave Coolgardie after forty-five minutes at the servo, knowing that the next roadhouse is in an abandoned gold mining town named Widgiemooltha, 80 kilometres away. Norseman is 100 kilometres further on.

I smear a thick, fresh coat of sunscreen over my face, ears, arms and legs, remount and pedal out slowly from the cooling shade and back into the hot sunshine. Day three has really only just begun. I'm feeling good again, but am ready for more dips and rises. The IndiPac was always going to be tough, I knew that when I entered. But I know it better now, even after two and a bit days.

This is living, I tell myself. *This is what I wanted from the IndiPac.*

It's as good a Monday as anyone could get, certainly better than sitting in an office. Lifted by the thought, I slowly pedal down Bayley Street, which leads through the heart of town, passing the Goldfields Exhibition on my left and an array of other heritage buildings. A few hundred metres out of town I turn right onto the Coolgardie Esperance Highway towards Norseman. My exit from Coolgardie also prompts me to think about Arthur Richardson. In 1896 he rode off from here for his then epic ride across the Nullarbor to Adelaide, which took him 31 days.

Back then, Coolgardie would have been a hotbed of activity that serviced a surrounding patchwork of goldfields in an otherwise remote and desolate desert. The town seems remote for me, requiring a ride of two-days-plus from Fremantle to reach now, so at the turn of the 19th Century it would be been even more so. I imagine the scene of camels, horses and buggies, and even motor vehicles leaving their mark. I imagine Richardson creating a stir as he embarked on his daring ride to Norseman and then across the Nullarbor Plain to Adelaide, and the masses as they surrounded him in curiosity as he mounted his bike and set off to the east on a dirt track that would soon turn to a trail of camel pads, unlike the bitumen road I am riding on.

As huge as the challenge of riding on to Norseman and then across the fabled desert is for me, at least I know what awaits – the secure knowledge of food, water and safe shelter. Richardson only faced uncertainty, like so many Overlanders of his era. His only certainty was that the unknown awaited him.

◉

The heat seems to rise with every kilometre. And the road too. As does the pain in both my knees, my right ankle and my butt.

I'm not far out from Coolgardie when I notice movement in a shrub to my right. Something golden brown emerges. At first I think it's a rabbit, but as it runs across the road and looks at me from about 30 metres ahead, I realise it's a dingo. It's probably more scared of me than I am of it, and it darts off to the other side of the road and out of sight. Still, I check behind me after I pass where it has left the road, wanting to make sure it's not chasing me from behind. But all I see when I turn is open road – a barren, exposed road at that.

It strikes me how little wildlife there has been so far. I'd expected to see more – dingoes, kangaroos, emus, snakes, spiders – and had feared they could be one of the biggest threats.

As I slip into a zone of thought that is deepening by the day, time seemingly slips by. But as Widgiemooltha nears my speed starts to slow radically, mainly due to sudden sharp pain in my ankle and knees. I stop by the roadside at least three times over the last 15 kilometres before reaching the roadhouse to stretch and loosen my aching joints. On the final gradual rise my speed slows to 15 kilometres per hour. I try to not think of the 100 kilometres beyond the town to Norseman.

I think only of reaching this stop. I imagine the relief of the shade inside the roadhouse, and of the chance to sit down and massage my aching joints and gather my thoughts. *It's only day three . . . How can I feel this bad, this early?* I ask myself while fighting on.

I'm worried. It's my first real struggle so far, the perfect storm of accumulated fatigue, pain, heat, wind and the knowledge of the distance yet to travel today. What a difference from the exhilaration of this morning.

As I reach the crest of what I think is a rise, I see the Widgimooltha Roadhouse. I'm desperate for food and drink. I also need to take some time to reflect on what I'm doing. The sight of an IndiPac bike outside the roadhouse tells me I won't be alone. Whether that rider has just arrived or is about to leave, I don't know. And whether the rider will be good company or not as I wrestle with my emotions, is also something I don't know. Will I need time alone? Will some company take my mind off my struggle and ease the pain?

The answer comes quickly and positively as the bell on the door of the roadhouse chimes as I walk in, and a young, dark-haired cyclist in a hi-vis orange jersey looks up and gives me a nod and a smile as he scoffs down a huge plate of hot chips.

◉

Sam O'Dea, a twenty-five-year-old from Bendigo in Victoria, has only just farewelled the Cycling Maven and Nick Skarajew as I arrive. I have been closing in on them, faster than I thought.

Sam's jersey is from Vegan Athletic Apparel. A technician for Mercedes-Benz in Bendigo, Sam is a vegan, hence his chips-only meal. Mine consists of two cans of lemonade, a hamburger with the lot and a plate of chips. I sit down and release a huge sigh. Sam recognises the sentiment and smiles back while simultaneously putting more chips into his mouth. It helps to know he shares my world of pain. I sense he has been there not too long ago but is coming out of it.

It's easy to be honest about how exhausted I feel. I don't hold back. I don't even have the strength to.

'Mate, I am absolutely busted,' I tell Sam. 'I had to stop three times in those last 15 kilometres.'

'I know what you mean,' he says, reassuringly. 'The others [the Cycling Maven and Nick Skarejew] only just left. I needed more time.'

I'm still worried about what exists between here and Norseman – 100 kilometres. 'I'm not sure I'm up for it,' I tell Sam.

But I know Sam is up for it, and when I see his determination my belief in myself sparks. When my meal arrives I focus on devouring it rather than the negatives of how I am feeling, and with every mouthful a semblance of strength returns. *Of course I'm going to ride on to Norseman*, I tell myself.

A part of me hopes Sam will want to get going alone before I finish eating, and not want to be slowed by a fifty-five-year-old. I give some strong hints to let him know it's okay if that's how he feels. But he is too kind, and waits for me to finish eating. He'll ride at my pace. Once we're further down the road, I remind him, he needn't wait if the urge to ride off strikes him.

We cycle side-by-side as the rules allow. Kilometres separate the riders ahead of and behind us. We ride and chat, ride and chat. It's as if we have known each other for years. In his cycling kit, Sam has a not too dissimilar look to Richie Porte, the Tasmanian professional road cyclist who races for the American BMC team and is a Tour de France contender. I know Richie well, so I wonder if that's why I feel so at ease chatting with Sam. But of course the truth is that Sam is an easygoing, decent young guy, who enjoys company.

Remarkably, as the afternoon light deepens, the soreness in my right ankle, both knees and my butt abates. By the time we get 50 kilometres outside Norseman, the sun is starting to set and the surrounding green bushland hardens to a silhouette. I'm riding at quite a good tempo – reasonably hard, but with a nice cadence. Now I'm feeling on top of the day, my physical sufferings draining away.

But suddenly, as I ride over the crest of a rise and pick up speed on the downward slope – with Sam a few hundred metres ahead of me – I find myself careering off the bitumen shoulder through shin-high shrubs and over the clay roadside that's still

ON YER BIKE: The cycling adventure begins for me on
a tricycle at age three in Hyde Park, London, 1965.

BIG WET I:
As per Overlander tradition, dipping my rear wheel into the Indian Ocean on the eve of the 2017 IndiPac.

REMOTE:
Day three of the 2017 IndiPac en route to Coolgardie.
Photo by Troy Bailey

Open when things get tough

ENDLESS: One pedal stroke away from the longest, straightest stretch of road in Australia.
Photo by Hugh Moore

BARREN: Our smiles hide the pain during a quick rest stop on the Nullarbor Plain.
Left to right: Me, 'Tracking Jack' (Jack Heyward) and 'Humungous Hugh' (Hugh Moore).
Photo by Hugh Moore

WATCH OUT: Camels, wombats and kangaroos await travellers on the Nullarbor.

NATURE'S MOVIE: Sunrise at the Nullarbor Roadhouse is mesmerising.

HOT, HOT, HOT:
When it hits 46 degrees,
it's time to load up
with extra water.

SO FAR:
Reaching halfway of the
2017 IndiPac near Tanunda,
South Australia, reminds
me how far I've come, yet
how far I still have to go.

EPIC: Kristof Allegaert in cruise control during his extraordinary race in the 2017 IndiPac. *Photo by Troy Bailey*

POWER: Sarah Hammond's consistency during the 2017 IndiPac left many asking if she might win. *Photo by Troy Bailey*

LEGEND: Mike Hall on the road to Cabramurra in one of the last images of him before his death in the 2017 IndiPac. *Photo by Troy Bailey*

WHAT A RIDE: Preparing for the 2017 IndiPac tribute ride in memory of Mike Hall in Surry Hills, Sydney. *Photo by Alexia Ford*

IN MEMORY: 2017 IndiPac riders at the Opera House steps paying tribute to Mike Hall. *Back, left to right:* Kai Edel, Jan-Willem Bobbink, Jesse Carlsson, myself, Steve Watson, Frank Proud; *Front, left to right:* Donncha Cuttriss, Sarah Hammond, Kristof Allegaert, Matthijs Ligt, Eelco Wijmans, Juliana Buhring. *Photo by Curve Bicycles*

damp after recent rain. Despite managing to ride over several divots that would spell disaster if I lose control, I find my way back on the road and stop to gather my senses.

It's a huge wake-up call. *Don't get complacent,* I tell myself after explaining the near-miss to Sam, who has stopped.

I regather my thoughts and calm myself. We continue riding, this time side-by-side, and resume chatting as the kilometres tick away beneath our wheels.

◉

Excited about the prospect of reaching Norseman before dark, I decide to check the time of day and look down to where my iPhone has been positioned on the Quad Lock device.

'Oh, no!' I yell out, stopping.

Sam turns to ask, 'What is it?'

'It's gone. My iPhone has fallen off . . . again,' I tell Sam. 'It fell off a few times before but after the last time I doublechecked I had it on properly.' Now I lament not having connected my phone to a lanyard and strapped it to the handlebars.

'Where did you lose it?' Sam asks.

I remember taking it with me from our lunch stop, and then re-attaching it soon after. One strong possibility is that it's by the side of the road on the stretch where I nearly came a cropper 10 kilometres earlier. But 10 kilometres is a long way when you have to go back and re-ride it again slowly. Sam kindly suggests he could try to check its location on the Find My Phone app. I tell him that my app is not turned on. I can see he wants to help, but there's nothing he can do really. This is a solo unsupported race. I know I have no choice but to look for it on my own.

'You ride on. I'll do a U-turn, ride back to where I nearly crashed and try to find it,' I tell Sam. Who knows? If it did come off when I sped off course, it could be visible due to reflection from the sun. It's unlikely; but I turn, and ride the 10 kilometres back in the hope it's possible.

My morale takes a hit from losing so much time so early in the race, and I can't help but think of Sam making good progress to Norseman, progress that I would otherwise be making too. But really there's no other option. I need the phone. I have to try and put the frustration out of my mind, and am surprised when I reach the stretch where I nearly crashed. My point of exit off the road is so clear I can see the marks from my tyres in the clay.

And there's no sign of my phone, despite numerous passages up and down the road to look for it. I even dismount and walk over the area, and beyond where I rode off route, thinking that it could have been flung further into the bush. But with the sun rapidly setting, any chance of spotting it is diminishing by the minute. After about 40 minutes, I decide to cut my losses and ride on to Norseman, although the chances of getting there in daylight are now slim at best. As for my phone, I try to console myself with the thought that perhaps one of the riders behind me will see it. Not that I rate that a very strong chance.

Committed to my plan, I quickly get back into the groove and find my rhythm. I start to ride hard, driven by getting to Norseman as soon as possible. I was once looking at a sunset arrival and now it's likely to be well into night-time. I also need to assess the ramifications of having lost the phone – the foremost being no longer able to directly call Libby, or anyone else for that matter, emergency or not, and not being able to take photos or record the live videos I'd promised to do – at least for now. The other issue is that I can't access the IndiPac route maps that I had downloaded. I have them on my Garmin Etrex 30 but they were so much larger and easier to read on my phone – my eyesight isn't what it used to be.

As frustrating an end to the day as it is, I can't fully address any of those problems until I reach Norseman. The town's historic goldmining points of interest would have been fascinating to me earlier, but now they matter little to me – what's more important is that it's the nearest place for food and rest before tackling the infamous Nullarbor Plain.

I focus on pedalling as fast as I can, looking forward to being able to relax. As the sun goes down, I appreciate the view of the glistening waters of Lake Cowan to my left, and then in both directions as the highway crosses the southern tip of the lake before the final kilometres into Norseman. It's been some time since I have seen so much open water. And given the days ahead, it will be a while until I do again.

◉

As dark falls, relieved and fatigued, I ride into the centre of town to look for a telecommunications shop. Not that I expect any business to be open at 8 pm, but I want to canvass options for getting a new SIM card the next morning for the old mobile I've brought with me as back-up. Soft-wheeling through the quiet streets, everything is indeed closed. Even the local pub is about to shut up – and there's no sign of any kind of store that might sell SIM cards for the morning. My priority shifts to finding somewhere to sleep and something to eat and drink.

I head back to the neon lights of the Norseman Eyre Motel near the edge of town. After checking in, I ask the reception-ist if I can use a hotel phone to call Libby. I want to let her know I'm okay and update her on the situation. She will have seen that my dot has arrived in Norseman, but I also know she will have been concerned about seeing it back-track over the race route. This early into the IndiPac I don't want Libby to worry and I feel an urgency to reassure her. The motel receptionist obliges by very kindly offering me her private mobile to use, rather than a hotel line which I would have to pay for.

It was good I did call and explain. Libby was still wondering what I was doing going back on the route.

'I can't speak for long, Lib, but don't worry, I'll work on a solution as soon as possible.'

I feel I've rushed the call, especially as Libby has other questions to ask; but I don't want the receptionist to think I'm taking her help for granted. But at least Libby knows I'm safe and that I'm working on a solution.

Now, though, frustratingly, I'm told the kitchen is closed. The receptionist directs me to the BP servo across the road for an alternative dining option – another loading of takeaway food. She also tells me the servo sells smart phones, which lifts my spirits and dispels my fears about being incommunicado for any length of time. But first things first. I go to my room and follow my end-of-day ritual of recharging and refilling and organising things that I will need the next day within easy reach. Only then do I have a hot shower, change my clothes and head across the road to buy some hot food for dinner, and some extra supplies for later that night or the next day. I also buy a smart phone that comes with a pre-paid SIM.

I even leave with a new road map. Hearing me explain to the attendant how I had lost the downloaded route maps on my phone, a woman who had come in to pay for petrol asked if I needed a road map. When I said yes, she rushed back out to her car, grabbed hers and handed it to me saying, 'Please take mine.' I thanked her profusely for her generosity – having a hard copy map in my hands again provides terrific reassurance; it's like a security blanket to me. I privately pledge to make sure this replacement one makes it as far on the IndiPac as I do.

I still need to get access to the downloaded race route, and get around to learning how to best read it on my Garmin Etrex 30, which is still in my top tube pack. Having this map appeases my fears of taking a wrong turn – even if that is unlikely in the days to come. The road across the Nullarbor Plain is virtually straight.

With food, drink, map and new phone in hand, I return to the motel feeling much happier. But my buoyant mood turns to shock as I enter the motel reception. At a table in the dining room some IndiPac riders are waiting for their dinner. They had arrived before me and must have ordered their meals before the kitchen closed. I join them – Ryan 'Rhino' Flinn, the Cycling Maven, Sam O'Dea and Nick Skarajew. I ask for some cutlery and eat my takeaway moussaka while they tuck into their 'a la carte' meals. The one luxury I share – besides the comfort of a table and a soft-seated chair – is a cold beer.

But it's a gathering of like-minded spirits, to say the least. We toast day three of the IndiPac, share stories of our respective struggles and tap into the brighter side of our various misfortunes. The worst tale is Rhino's. He had a lightning start and had ridden 450 kilometres on day one, but had to nurse himself into Norseman in the middle of the day due to pain in one of his knees caused by a bad adjustment of his saddle height after putting a new cleat on one of his shoes. He was busted when he arrived at Norseman.

I feel for Rhino as he ponders his options. But as he enjoys a glass of red wine, his positive spirit, which many would see through his vlogs, begins to shine brightly, as do those of Sam, Nick, the Cycling Maven and myself. We all agree we're having the adventure of a lifetime, and the highs will be as memorable as the lows. While we're all physically dead tired, the chat is animated, so much so that the story of my lost phone prompts the Rhino to attempt (in vain) to start up my new phone – and we almost forget we still have thousands of kilometres still ahead of us.

Then Nick asks, 'What time is everyone getting up and going?' Back to reality.

Opinions vary. Although riding together as a group or in team time-trial formation isn't allowed, it's within the rules for us to leave at the same time, and we agree to 4 am.

◉

Walking back to my room, there's a chill in the air. When I wake in several hours' time to begin day four – the day I begin my run across the notorious Nullarbor – it may well be chillier.

In bed I eat a bar of chocolate, drink a cup of tea and try to start the new phone, but to no avail. The time wasted is time lost to recovery, I admonish myself. The future of communications with Libby isn't going to be solved tonight and the best I can do is take advantage of the chance to sleep and be as fresh and strong as possible for the early start.

As to where Kristof Allegaert, Mike Hall, Sarah Hammond and other race leaders are, the thought barely crosses my mind. I learn later that Kristof is still leading after reaching Border

Village in South Australia, with 1,500 kilometres ridden; and that some riders up front have been struggling, including Juliana Buhring who has had an allergic reaction to some painkillers for a knee injury. Word is, she plans on re-starting the race from Fremantle once she gets treatment.

6

THE NOISE ONLY GETS LOUDER

Day 4: Norseman to Balladonia

Start: 4.22 am   Finish: 2.30 pm

Riding time: 9 hours 01 minute

Distance: 188 km   Metres climbed: 273 m

Average speed: 19.7 kmh   Temperature: 17–23 C

Many have ridden the Nullarbor Plain before, but for me this iconic stretch of land that stretches 1000 kilometres, from Norseman along the Great Australian Bight and to Ceduna, is a huge box to tick off on my bucket list. I've never crossed the Nullarbor by car, bus or train, let alone by bike. To do so now will be a huge personal feat in itself.

At 3.30 am I walk across to the servo diner for breakfast and to buy extra food and water. I've already drunk a couple of cups of tea and eaten a chocolate bar and a muffin in my motel room while re-packing my gear, wiping down my bike and lubricating the chain. I'm getting much quicker and more efficient at these daily tasks, knowing where and what order to put my gear back in for easy access should I need anything during the day.

I need to fuel up for the big day ahead so I buy another muffin and a coffee and consume them while studying my new paper map. Today's is a simple route: straight onto the Eyre Highway, named after the explorer Edward John Eyre, the first European to cross the Nullarbor in 1841, then to the roadhouse community of Balladonia, an Aboriginal word meaning 'big rock by itself'. Not that I notice any such rock there, so immersed am I in fatigue when I arrive. Balladonia was first settled in 1879, and from 1897 to 1929 it was a station on the Perth–Adelaide telegraph line, but it's probably much better known for being near where debris from the Skylab space station landed upon re-entry in July 1979. Today, remnants of the Skylab are on display in the Balladonia Roadhouse, which received a phone call from then United States President Jimmy Carter, apologising for the fallen debris after the local Dundas Shire chief executive presented NASA with a littering fine. The spectacular cliffs of the Great Australian Bight are accessible by four-wheel drive from Balladonia, and of course, more importantly to me, the town is the last stop before the Southern Hemisphere's longest straight stretch of road, all 146.9 kilometres of it.

◉

There's no shortage of motivation to tap into this day. As 4 am nears, there's no sign of Sam, Rhino, Nick or the Cycling Maven, but no matter. This is an individual race. I'm ready to get going; to ride as many kilometres as I can before the arrival of sunrise – and the heat, which has been kind due to the wet start, but in the exposed desert it can't be underestimated, especially with such little shade.

I finish my coffee and stock up on more supplies: bananas, muffins, chocolate, yoghurt-covered muesli bars, and a packet each of salted cashews and jelly beans which I mix in one sealed plastic bag. I grab an extra 2-litre bottle of water and secure it with an ocky strap under the aerodynamic tri-bars attached to my handlebars in addition to the three re-filled 'bidons', or drink bottles, that I already have in position on my bike, and a can of Coke, which I drink while I continue packing away my supplies. It's a full load.

As I activate my Spot Gen3 device, alerting all who are following me online that I'm up and ready and soon to resume riding, I hear the click-click-click of a spinning rear derailleur. I look up and see Sam emerge from the dark. He is ready, bar needing to make a quick purchase or two, so I have no issue waiting for him. We roll away from the servo just after 4 am and head into the pre-dawn dark and silence on our way to the Nullarbor Plain, its name aptly derived, as I discover when the sun comes up, from two Latin words – 'nulla' (nothing) and 'arbor' (trees).

As suspected, the chill in the air is biting, but in no time the steady pace has my blood flowing. While I've looked at the route on my map, I'm still unsure about the specific details of the course ahead. I figure I only need to head east and follow the Eyre Highway. The kilometres tick by under my pedals and I forget about where Rhino, Nick and the Cycling Maven are. I settle into a good tempo, soon buoyed by the sight of another glorious sunrise, which leaves me rueing the day that I don't have a functioning phone to capture the image with.

The gradual transformation of night into day is sublime: the glowing red of the rising sun appears as a simmering slice on the horizon, then grows into a big round ball, its light defining the arid landscape. A few trees and a maze of low saltbush and bluebush scrub are in black silhouette, while crisp, cloudless blue skies are unveiled. The moment is so captivating that my hurts – from the chafing in my shorts, niggling pain and building fatigue to self-doubt – simply disappear. It is sheer bliss.

When I next pass Sam I can't help but tell him how lucky I feel. If nature and isolation are drugs, I am high on them. 'How beautiful is this?' I tell Sam, smiling. 'Whatever happens in this IndiPac, witnessing this one sunrise would be reward enough.'

With the sun fully up, the heat of the day and accrued kilometres start to take their toll. I find myself falling into a trance following the white line along the edge of the road. There's some strong momentum from the weight of my packs, which I estimate to be between 10 and 12 kilograms, and a sudden gust of wind from my right sends me careering off to the left of the road, straight into a clay embankment. The impact sends me head first over the handlebars. Fortunately, I escape injury, despite landing on my left shoulder, which had undergone an operation in 2014 after a series of five dislocations.

But more worrying is the pain in my right ankle, which suddenly changes from constant numbness to a sharp stabbing pain. And it begins to swell up.

◉

Sam and I arrive at Balladonia separately at around 2.30 pm, with me coming in behind him. With 970 kilometres behind us, we plan to leave at midnight after a feed, shower and rest, and make a bold bid for Madura, 338 kilometres away.

About an hour later, Sam and I are showered and in dry clothes, and the Cycling Maven, Nick and Rhino arrive one by one. My room has extra beds so I offer them a share in it, as I have Sam. It all helps to minimise costs.

The Maven and Nick take up my offer. Their plan is similar to mine – to resume riding overnight. They quickly head off to shower and change. Rhino is uncommitted, contemplating a quicker turn around. But he's still happy to share a couple of Cooper's Pale Ales with me.

I have no qualms about enjoying a beer on the IndiPac – and on this occasion I drink three. This is a race, yes; but I'm not at the pointy end where the leaders are approaching Adelaide, a little under 2,000 kilometres away. For a rider like me, who planned to make the best of their rest time while not wasting time either, a beer or two will help relax me and ensure I get to sleep quickly.

It is all good banter this afternoon. I chat with Rhino, and then with Sam, the Cycling Maven and Nick after they've showered, and also with the bearded Ben Cadby, AKA 'The Mango Rider'. Ben hails from Hobart in Tasmania and the IndiPac is part of his planned ride around Australia. While opting to stop for a longer break like we have, he ends up setting up his bivvy outside the roadhouse.

As the beers take effect, I can sense Rhino is going to ride on: he has that grin. He mentions a collision of two big weather systems that are rolling in from the north and the west. What that means exactly is beyond me – my meteorological credentials are limited – but basically they promise wind and rain. Rhino's thinking is that it will be best to get going and stay ahead of the poor weather, rather than prolonging the time spent at Balladonia and risking getting caught in the conditions to come. My reaction? I just order a third Cooper's, telling myself I don't mind the wet and will just deal with it.

Rhino's decided: he starts preparing his bike. I sit on a bench outside the roadhouse and borrow the Maven's phone to make some calls – the first to Libby – with the backdrop of the late afternoon sun and blue skies behind me. Rhino throws his leg over his bike, clips his feet into the pedals, mounts and pedals slowly out of the car park. He turns left onto the Eyre Highway to begin his night time run to beat the impending storm. I give him a wave then return to the shop to buy more food and drink, even though I've already bought extra supplies. Better to have too much than find out too late that you need more, or learn that the store is closed at midnight when I plan to leave. But I don't waste too much time scanning the shelves.

Back at the room, Sam is already fast asleep, though he's woken by the noise of me, the Cycling Maven and Nick coming in at the same time. It's about 6 pm, maybe earlier. A major downside to sharing a room is that there's no privacy. With each person having something different to do or attend to, or different ailments or concerns to moan and groan about, there's no quiet for anyone.

For me, the biggest worry at the moment is my right ankle. It's swollen to the size of a cricket ball and is turning red. I send a message to my trainer Nicola, who asks me to send a photo of it to her. She soon replies, recommending some deep self-massage and that I strap it with a compression bandage. I use one of my arm warmers, tightening it over the area, proving the usefulness of travelling with multi-purpose items.

Amid the chat, laughter and moans in the room, the Cycling Maven decides to phone his partner Hannah in Melbourne. From my bed, I overhear him.

'What? They found the phone? How? Who? That's amazing!'

It can't be, I think. *Are they talking about my phone*? I don't want to leap to conclusions, but am excited enough to get out of bed and move closer to the Maven as he's chatting to Hannah from his bed. Nick and Sam are wide awake too. So much for sleep.

The details are sketchy but apparently the partner of another IndiPac rider read about my lost phone on Twitter – and she alerted him to look out for it on the road. Hannah doesn't know who the rider is, or his location on the route, but gives me an adrenaline rush that makes sleeping harder once the Maven finishes his call. I can't help but think of the odds.

Suddenly, we're all talking again, even though each of us tries to remind the others that we need some sleep. Time is ticking by fast in the dark before our planned midnight departure. Why we have agreed on the same departure time is simple: if someone decides to leave at a certain time, they'll be woken up by the noise, so everyone else may as well leave then, too.

◉

Finally, just as sleep takes over, I'm woken by the sound of droplets of rain on the tin roof. The noise grows louder.

I pretend it's not raining, that this is not one of the weather fronts that Rhino was talking about before he rode away. It's a short-lived belief. Any pretence is dismissed when Nick asks, 'Is that rain?'

I picture Rhino cycling in the darkness but still dry, looking behind and seeing the clouds building.

We wait beyond midnight, vainly hoping that the rain may pass. We wait. And wait. But the noise only gets louder. The front is upon us.

7

A CHALLENGE JUST TO FINISH

Day 5: Balladonia to Caiguna

Start: **10.07 am**   Finish: **8 pm**

Riding time: **8 hours 47 minutes**

Distance: **181.1 km**   Metres climbed: **273 km**

Average speed: **19.7 kmh**   Temperature: **12–23 C**

'Is anyone awake?'

We all are. No one has had any deep sleep at all.

The window of dry weather that Rhino mentioned has firmly shut. If anything, when I finally get up, shower and re-pack my bike in the dark, the wet weather looks like it has set in. It's about 4 am. I figure I may as well wait until full light, so I put the extra time to good use by having a hearty breakfast and preparing for a long day of riding in the wet.

The extra time in bed gives me more time to rest and massage my swollen ankle, and to think about how I could better position my drink bottles, or at least one of them. Whenever I pedal out of the saddle, my right knee bumps the right hand drink bottle. My response has been to direct my knee outward on the upstroke, but this constant shift in direction has triggered the pain in my ankle. I don't have the same problem with my left knee because it's not striking the bottle on that side as hard. I figure I'll re-position the right hand bottle onto my tri-bars, and keep the handlebar pack to store various sports and chocolate bars, which take up less space and offer no obstruction to my knee and leg movement.

The delayed start also allows me to chat with Andrew Webster, a journalist mate from the *Sydney Morning Herald*. He wants to write an IndiPac report in his weekly column. The Cycling Maven has loaned me one of his two phones, this time for the rest of the IndiPac, knowing that my broader mission – besides finishing the race – includes posting videos on my Facebook page. After eating a plateful of eggs, sausages, toast and all the other food I'm now accustomed to shoving down my throat, I wait with a fresh coffee to take Webster's call. He said I'd be the subject of the Q&A segment in his Friday column four days away. I suspect he might have a bit of fun at my expense – which I'm fine with, especially considering the value of a laugh at this stage of the race.

When he calls as scheduled, however, I'm taken aback – not by him, but myself. Without warning, the sound of a good mate's voice triggers a switch in me and my voice quivers with emotion.

I can tell he's concerned but I reassure him with a nervous laugh that I'm all right. I tell him this sort of thing is bound to happen out here.

His questions are to the point, as always. He begins by asking, 'What's doing?'

I explain over a coffee at the roadhouse dining room that I am 970 kilometres into a 5,470 kilometre ride. I explain about my lost phone of the day before and he's a bit shocked to learn that I'm still using a paper map. I remind him that they still work, but fill him in on the news that someone had found my phone, but that's all I know at this stage.

Webster's keen to know how my legs are holding up.

'I'm going to find out shortly, mate. Yesterday they were sore. And my right ankle has blown up.'

Then he wants to know about my arse. Everyone always wants to know about your arse, I've learned. It's one of the key questions I'm asked – by people I meet at roadhouses, anyone I talk to on the phone, and in comments on social media. 'Mate, I've tried to change my position but my bum is . . . sore,' I tell Webster. 'The worrying thing is that it's going to get worse. I'm feeling parts starting to go already. My fingers are numb. My feet are numb. When you're on the road it's pedal stroke by pedal stroke.'

I also remind Webster of one of the reasons why I'm doing the IndiPac. I tell him the story of the Overlanders in the late 1800s and early 1900s, their intrepid willingness to confront the very real prospect of not surviving, which is what Jerome Murif wrote several days into his 1897 south to north ride from Glenelg in South Australia to Port Darwin. Speaking of his suffering thirst one day before finding a well to drink from, Murif wrote, 'It would not be particularly difficult for one who does not know the country to perish hereabouts. Just the wrong turning, or meet with a disabling accident, or lose the indistinct track, and in one single hot day the business may be done. Solitary graves are plentiful.'

I also take the opportunity to tell Webster that I'm riding the IndiPac in support of 'Helping Rhinos', the UK organisation that works to stop the poaching of and extinction of rhinos in Africa by creating awareness and raising funds with a range of partners from around the world. But then I get back to my own personal reasons for racing, that I really want the challenge of being part of something unique, and of being stripped bare. I want to see how far I can go – the emotions can come and go, but in the end I'm going to find out exactly what I'm capable of. Then Webster asks if I'm listening to music as a way of finding extra motivation – I'm not. I'm just listening to the rhythm of the bike and the sound of the wind.

◉

Leaving Balladonia, my aim now is to reach Caiguna, 181 kilometres away – a far sight shorter than Madura, which was the original plan before the rain delay. Race leader Kristof Allegaert reached Caiguna on day two. The town itself was established in 1962 to assist the traffic crossing the Nullarbor for that year's Commonwealth Games in Perth, and it also happens to be the starting point for official Central Western Time (CWT) – a time zone I hadn't even considered during my IndiPac preparation. I wrongly thought the only time zones that would matter would be Perth (minus three hours to Sydney) and Adelaide (minus thirty minutes to Sydney). Central Western Time requires you to advance your watch by forty-five minutes upon arrival at Caiguna. It's a simple enough thing, but it's easy to overlook and be confounded by when making calculations for future departures and arrivals.

When I set off from Balladonia, Sam is the only rider with me. We pedal off quietly but happily, despite the weather. I feel better for being back on the road, sometimes side-by-side with Sam, other times with good distance between us but our red tail lights in sight.

There's no glorious sunrise today. The continuing rain means we're greeted only by lightening grey skies. But I feel reassured by the Cycling Maven's phone, which is firmly tucked inside one of my jersey pockets where it can't unknowingly fall out. The Maven's conditions were that I don't try and position it on the Quad Lock device on my handlebars and I'm very happy to oblige. Having the capacity for direct contact again with Libby, my family and friends really bolsters me, as well as the knowledge that Maven downloaded the race route onto it as well. And now that I have internet access again (pending wireless avail-ability) I can resume my live recordings. I race into the damp ahead with a positive spirit.

◉

Heavens knows how the Overlanders did what they did. Often their best and sometimes only form of communication was by passing messages to travellers they came across, knowing it could take days or even weeks to reach the intended recipient, or by sending a telegram from the smaller outposts that they passed through. But then many of the Overlanders were loners who often didn't feel the need to communicate. While today's racers can look after themselves in the wilderness, they also know where they're heading, or at least where the nearest township is. The original Overlanders knew little of what lay ahead, yet could comfortably set up camp and settle as if the stony scrub were their home.

It makes me wonder how their live Facebook posts would go down today. I reckon Francis Birtles would have embraced it. In 1906 he became the first person to cycle from west to east across Australia, and whose consequent trips by bike and car included his London to Melbourne drive in his 'Sundowner' Bean over 1927 and 1928. Birtles wrote often about his trips in magazine articles, authored two books and illustrated them with his own photographs – *Lonely Lands* (1909) and

Battle Front of Outback (1935) – and also produced the film *Across Australia* in 1912 with footage of emus, crocodile hunting, sugar cane growing, shark fishing and pearling on Thursday Island. And there was also Eddie Reichenbach (AKA Ted Ryko), an avid photographer who set a new record for cycling from Adelaide to Darwin in 1914. After his record ride he set up a photography studio in Darwin from where he sold postcards of his adventures on the bike throughout the Northern Territory and the scenes that he saw. The thought of both or either Overlander posting on social media raises a smile from me.

Not that a day on the IndiPac is guaranteed to pass without problems for the modern-day Overlander. Challenges are always lurking. My most immediate on this day sounds simple, even quite possibly stupid. But in the wilderness, little things – good and bad – tend to take a greater shape. For me, the first problem is not knowing exactly where the signpost indicating the 90 Mile Straight – or 146.9 kilometres – actually is. Sam assures me it's 'soon' after the Balladonia roadhouse. Stupidly, I think 'soon' is just after we turn left onto the highway, and the further I go without it in sight, the more frustrated I become.

Thankfully, I feel good physically, and that buoys me as I pedal on. As do the prevailing silence and the sight of the vast landscape as daylight gradually increases. It's mesmerising, in fact. Even on a drab and wet morning, the Nullarbor Plain has a unique beauty – a remote, vast and largely barren landscape tempered by weather conditions most never associate with it. If anything, the wet weather has emphasised the colours of the Nullarbor, with the soil a deep and rich ochre, and the patchwork of low scrub much greener than I'd ever imagined in a desert. It all contrasts with the black of the bitumen beneath my wheels, rather than the trademark grey I've been riding on to this point.

Finally, after 34 kilometres – or an hour and forty-five minutes of cycling – I reach the sign that signals the beginning of the 90 Mile Straight. I have read about this famous stretch of road for months; seen photos of travellers – many on bikes, others in cars – with smiles of accomplishment for having got as far as the sign or for being on the cusp of crossing the stretch of desert that follows it. I always wondered how I'd feel once I reached it, with the prospect of the hard ride ahead.

Despite the rain and cross headwind, the forecast is for a direct headwind. The skies also appear to be clearing up. I'm officially 1,004 kilometres into the IndiPac when I arrive at the famous signpost, something to celebrate – even if the race leader, Kristof Allegaert, reached this mark three days earlier and rode over most of the straight in the dark, with Mike Hall and Sarah Hammond on his trail.

I arrive not long after Hugh Moore, AKA 'Humungous Hugh'. I had passed him the day before when he was suffering badly from an Achilles injury. He stayed overnight in the Balladonia roadhouse motel as well. But earlier this morning he swept by me and Sam. When I roll in to a stop, Humungous Hugh and

I take photos of each other by the yellow and black signpost. Hugh, a retired bank accountant from Geelong in Victoria, chats to a family – two parents in their mid-30s and two children aged about ten – who are travelling around Australia in their camper van. Sam arrives, then the Cycling Maven and Nick. Now we all take photos of each other. Who knows how far we will go in the IndiPac? But we all know that to stop at this landmark and not capture the moment would be a loss.

Not that we waste any time. It's another 204 kilometres to the Cocklebiddy roadhouse, and after that, 147 kilometres to Caiguna. This will mean fourteen hours in the saddle for me. I still can't believe the original plan was to reach Madura, a mere 92 kilometres after Cocklebiddy.

As I stand by the signpost I suddenly feel very emotional. I realise that it's day five, a juncture that many said beforehand would possibly be a turning point for me, physically and mentally. It starts without warning, with a sudden tightening of stomach and then a welling of tears in the eyes – I feel it all build and am powerless to stop it. Eventually I contain the moment, but not without my eyes glistening and voice trembling. This significant point in the road – after which there are no services for water or food supply for 146 kilometres – has got the better of me.

Truth be known, my emotions have been changing like light switches: click, click, click, click: good, bad, good, bad. At the start of the IndiPac I vowed to post in my Facebook vlogs exactly as I felt. I wanted followers to see for themselves my response to the accumulated physical and mental fatigue, no matter how erratic. And here they are – my emotions are chopping and changing, from humour to tears, from assured positivity to wavering doubt. I have nothing to hide, or be ashamed of. I just want to share the experience with people – for good and bad. One moment I might feel on top of the world; the next, I'm sobbing – and for no apparent reason, unless there's something buried deep beneath layers of denial that the stresses of the IndiPac has managed to peel open. Maybe all the wide open space is the trigger, without the immediate pressures of the inner city life I am so accustomed to. Maybe the truth is that in my heightened state of fatigue my vulnerabilities are allowed free rein.

Out here, riding in the wilderness, I often find myself thinking of family one moment, and work and friends the next. I can't explain why. Is it something to do with the raw environment of the IndiPac being a solo and unsupported race perhaps, how alone I really am out here? Or perhaps it really is just the perfect storm of fatigue, injury and pain, and emotion hitting at once. Certainly, riding into a headwind for a spell seems to take an eternity, even if you've only covered 300 metres. 'How am I going to get through 5,500 kilometres?' you ask yourself. But you can't think like that. You can't think of the full sum of what lies ahead, only the parts, kilometre by kilometre.

I have settled on my strategy to get through the days ahead: when I see a sign that says a town is 150 kilometres away, I break it down into 10 kilometre stretches. Then I chop away at those parts. People refer to this as 'eating the elephant' – a phrase that means taking on massive challenges bit by bit. If necessary, I treat myself at one of those points and take a break, either to have a stretch or a pee, or just allow myself some mental respite.

The race leaders are already well past Ceduna, some 976 kilometres away. Suddenly, when I think of that achievement and the divide between me and them, the emotional taps open again. I'm gobsmacked by how fast the front runners are racing and that they're just so far ahead. I don't feel strong. These seasoned riders have travelled almost twice as far as me, often on just an hour's sleep a day. It's bewildering.

Then I realise that the main hazard from here won't be the next 146 kilometres, but the issue of the first major right hand turn of the route – into and out of Port Augusta. From there, I'll need to negotiate the race route on to Adelaide using my downloaded maps, unless I can get my head around the machinations of my Garmin Etrex 30, which I still haven't done.

Standing there at the signpost, I distract myself with other thoughts. I think of the little miracle – of Steve Watson, AKA 'Cloudrider', the racer who found my phone coming into Norseman. I'm overjoyed, and can't wait to hear more about it. I owe Steve a big one; but who knows when I'll be able to pay him back, let alone meet up with him?

◉

This far into the race, I now understand intimately how many elements can impact a rider's mindset and physical wellbeing. For all I read and researched about the nutritional challenges of the IndiPac, I'm still stunned by both the amount and type of food other racers and myself are eating. It's unbelievable how much you need to consume in a race like this. Preparing for the race, I stripped down from 97 kilograms to 79 kilograms by training on the bike, in the gym and by diet, and this morning, while cleaning my teeth, is the first time I've noticed any real weight loss. In the mirror I saw the person I used to be as a twenty-four-year-old lightweight rower trying to weigh in somewhere between 72.5 and 69.8 kilograms.

For all the food I've been eating – from double orders of hamburgers with the lot and large servings of French fries to chocolate muffins washed down with buckets of chocolate milk – I have never felt full or bloated. Even when resting I feel the calories burning up. How the original Overlanders, riding on packed bikes that could have weighed up to 35 kilograms against the 25 or so of my bike, survived on the dried meat, flour and tea they took with them is astonishing. My metabolism has kicked in like a mule and accommodating a high fat and calorie intake with ease. I reckon I'm consuming up to 12,000 calories a day, but I hear others are using between 15,000 and 20,000. It's such a contrast with my thinking and behaviour when I was wrestling with bulimia. Huge food and calorie consumption is the common denominator, but the bulimia was a condition driven by disordered psychology, whereas right now my vast caloric intake is being driven by a body pleading for more. No matter how much I eat, it can't seem to get enough.

The whole experience is blowing me away. How my body is responding, discovering what it's capable of; not to mention the support and feedback from family, friends and dot trackers monitoring every rider's progress – with some even meeting us en route – to Facebook followers. I haven't always kept up with the many, many messages of encouragement because of the need to keep riding and limit my spare time. But when I do briefly check in, they mean such a great deal; from those wanting to support or inspire me, or to urge me to keep things in perspective, to those who have also been humouring me.

◉

Nine and a half hours later, I am still on the fabled stretch. It's been raining all day and the wind is still up. It howls, and not just when I stop for a breather. When I ride, it filters through my spokes and the ghoulish scream makes me feel vulnerable and alone – which I am.

I stop at Caiguna at about 8.30 pm. I'm surrounded by a desolate flatness. The billowing clouds range from white to grey to black. The day was going well but suddenly my strength of body and mind have again hit a low. My plan was to make it to Cocklebiddy, 65 kilometres from Caiguna. But as I've learned on the IndiPac, plans change often and reaching Cocklebiddy now seems unlikely. There's no need to decide immediately, however, as I opted to revise my plan once I got to Caiguna. Whatever option I pursue from there, I will still need to have a good feed and recharge my lights. I can't afford the risk of not being seen by vehicles approaching from behind because of a dimming rear red light, like on day one to Merredin.

With the wet weather prevailing, I've used my lighting systems much more than I would have thought. It's easy to see oncoming traffic and hear it approaching from behind, but if cars, caravans and trucks are all using their lights on such a dim day, then I need to as well, not only for my own safety but also out of respect for others on the road. I haven't yet had any trouble with drivers on the Nullarbor; road train drivers in particular are aware that there are riders out here, scattered over long distances and days apart.

Suddenly I'm back on a high, knowing that as the end of another day gets closer, the luxury of a hot shower, dry clothes, a feed and sleep awaits. I'm learning to appreciate each moment of joy like this, rather than lamenting hardship. So rather than rue the wetness, wind and isolation in such a barren environment, I embrace the uniqueness around me and listen to the sound of the wind in my ears, or of it passing through the turning wheels. I love it especially when I'm riding into a cross wind and it creates a rhythmic hum. I don't like to listen to music as I ride – one reason is of course for safety's sake, but another is so that I can hear the sound of my heart beating, which also helps me to stay focused, in control of my pace, and motivated.

A downside to this is that my focus tends to zero in on the white line shouldering the road. On such a barren and straight stretch as the 90 Mile Straight, I discover that my momentum can tip me into a trance, which occasionally means I lose a real sense of where I am on the road. This only helps me to act on the acknowledgement of fatigue – if I'm tired I'd rather finish a day's riding earlier, rest and be refreshed, and resume riding earlier, even if it means riding early morning in the dark – as I did from the Karra Retreat.

For me, it's about gauging the difference between calculated and silly risks. For a rider of my ability, new to ultra-endurance cycling, riding before dawn after a rest falls into the former of the two options. Riding into the dark at the end of the day when the sun is setting – or has set already – when I and most on the road are usually tired definitely leans to the latter.

◉

Not a day on an endurance race like this passes without the minutiae of physical challenges and hurts – the head, legs, arms, hands, feet or knees. Thinking of battered body parts, my right ankle has held up well today, so that's another big plus. But the big picture is to do my best to reach the finish in Sydney. That's still a long way off, however, and thinking too much about it can be damaging. By the hour, I'm now learning the value of breaking each day down into mini goals. Rather than being in race mode, I now realise the ride could take me four weeks to finish, not three as I thought earlier.

I remind myself that while there are other solo unsupported ultra-endurance races – such as the Trans Am Bike Race and Tour Divide in the United States, the Transcontinental Race in Europe and Race to the Rock in Australia – there's still no benchmark for a good or bad performance in the IndiPac as this is its debut. The important thing is simply to do my best, rather than carry the additional pressures of my own or others' expectations. As I near the 1,200-kilometre point, I realise it will be enough of a challenge just to finish.

I'm not doubting myself or my abilities, simply adjusting to what's required of this demanding event. If anything, being a part of a new race is a real buzz. No one will ever do the first IndiPac again.

◉

Hours pass. As my fatigue mounts, my pace slows into the headwind. As the grey sky turns to black, the lights of the Caiguna roadhouse are a welcome sight. I finally roll to a stop at 8 pm. I've decided to stay here.

And I'm not alone. The Mango Rider, Ben Cadby, arrives within minutes. Humungous Hugh, who astounds me with his form and resilience by constantly passing me on the road, is already there eating dinner. The Cycling Maven, Nick and Sam are not far behind.

It doesn't dawn on me to ask if there is a room available. I'm so hungry, I order a meal straight away, once again a hamburger with a separate serving of French fries, a can of Coke and bottle of mineral water to wash it all down with. When I ask about a room, I'm told that the last one has already been booked. But its taker, the Mango Rider, very kindly offers it to me – he's decided to ride on into the night instead.

Is Ben just being the generous bearded soul that I know him to be? Or has he truly had a change of heart, motivated by the late arrival of the strapping American, Anders Petersen, who has already decided that he will ride on after arriving at Caiguna to find there were no rooms available? Anders and the Mango Rider will gain plenty of kilometres with their call, edging ever closer to the end of the Nullarbor Plain, no matter what speed they ride at.

I graciously accept the Mango Rider's offer, pay for the room, and return to the dining counter to order another hamburger with fries. And no sooner, the Cycling Maven, Sam and Nick arrive, hungry and happy that there is space for them to sleep for a few hours after a shower and feed. The Maven and Sam are in my small room, which now looks like a Chinese laundry with wet cycling gear draped over cupboard doors, the chair and on every hook and rail in the bathroom. The Maven grabs one of the two single beds to sleep in, while Sam makes do on the floor, despite suffering severe back pain, the result of a broken back that he sustained several years before. Nick accepts Humungous Hugh's offer to sleep in his room.

As always, after a shower and a feed, there's time for thought gathering and reflection on how the day unravelled and what is to come. We learn too that Caiguna is where IndiPac racer Juliana Buhring had an allergic reaction to painkillers for a knee injury and decided to return to Perth for further treatment with 1,151 kilometres ridden, hitching a ride with a road train driver. I'm astonished by her strength of mind when I hear later that she's going to re-start the IndiPac once she's recovered. But then, those who know Ju Ju, as she is affectionately known, wouldn't be surprised.

I use the time at Caiguna to check Facebook. More messages have been posted beneath the vlog I posted earlier in the day. Some are uplifting, aimed at motivating me; others are laced with humour and if you didn't know the person you could easily take things the wrong way. All kinds of messages will sustain me as I ride on, though. I'm quickly learning that while IndiPac riders are vital to the event, so are its dotwatching supporters.

8

BUSTED LIKE I HAVE NEVER BEEN

Day 6: Caiguna to Mundrabilla
Start: 3.30 am   Finish: 10.45 pm
Riding time: 13 hours 40 minutes
Distance: 272.9 km   Metres climbed: 485 m
Average speed: 19.7 kmh   Temperature: 14–25C

It was either a deep sleep or a short sleep. Whichever, when I wake at 2.30 am, it feels like I've barely slept at all.

The day starts with the customary stuffing around in the dark. This is the smallest room I have stayed in so far in the IndiPac – it's maybe five metres by three – and sharing it with the Maven and Sam means there isn't a lot of room, even with our bikes and packs outside.

Sam isn't moving much and I ask how his back is. He's clearly in a lot of pain – more so than earlier when we turned the light out. Figuring that he's weighing up his options, the Cycling

Maven and I continue to get organised. By now the process of repacking bags and food has become pure instinct.

Sam is still lying down. The plan is to leave at 3.30 am. I'm on schedule, as is the Cycling Maven. I assume Nick Skarajew and Humungous Hugh are up and getting ready as well, but I give it little thought. I'll still leave at the time we set in any case, and I expect the Cycling Maven will as well.

I make good progress in getting ready, but it's clear from Sam's silence that he may not be leaving with us. When he confirms his back is still hurting, we suggest that he try to get more sleep in one of our vacated beds, see if his back pain eases and only then make a decision about whether he should continue riding or not. I feel for Sam. He's been great company on the road and his youthful enthusiasm for the race, and for cycling in general, has been really uplifting. It would be a shame not to see him continue, but damaging his back further by continuing on seems senseless.

I'm ready just before 3 am. I'm heartened by Sam's decision to sleep some more and make his call on the IndiPac in daylight. Should he decide to withdraw, which is a clear possibility, at least he'll be at a roadhouse and better placed to find a safe way to travel back home to Melbourne, rather than risk being stranded on the Nullarbor Plain and having to hitchhike.

After activating my Spot Gen3 device, there's still time to drop into the roadhouse for a breakfast. I say 'a breakfast' because I'll probably have a second one when I get to Cocklebiddy, 65 kilometres down the road. I eat a toasted ham and cheese sandwich, a chocolate muffin, a piece of fruitcake, and drink a fruit juice and a long black coffee. I load up on more food to eat while riding over the next few hours as sunrise unfolds.

Little is said among the four of us making this early start – me, the Cycling Maven, Nick Skarajew and Humungous Hugh. We'll just get on our bikes and roll out individually when we're ready, expecting that we'll all cross paths – possibly several times – during what will be another long and hard day. When I ride out, the Caiguna roadhouse lights dim behind me and I'm almost immediately enveloped in inky blackness. I focus on what is ahead with only the dim glow of my front light leading the way.

◉

The hours before dawn can be dangerous. Local animals awaken and are often lured to a messy fate on the highway, as the sight and smell of road kill in the daylight constantly reminds. The threat of kangaroos, emus or dingoes running out and into my path is a present one, as is that of wombats later in the route when there is more bushland and hills. To minimise the danger I turn on my helmet lamp, to supplement my front and back lights. I've learned already that I need to use more lights – not just to see with and be seen by, but to ensure I have back-ups. The helmet light allows me to scan 180 degrees – to my left and to my right and then further ahead – for any approaching animals, and also to try to get a better perspective of the landscape around me.

The helmet light might be ugly but it helps make me visible to drivers of oncoming trucks and cars. And in a race where every day is full of procedural do's and don'ts, the risk of taking a helmet light off when you don't need it is that you can forget to put it back on when you do need it later on. For now, at least, I believe it is far better and simpler to just leave it attached so I can use it when I need to.

When dawn rises today, however, there is no shortage of light. When I stop at 6.38 am to record a live video about 25 kilometres out from Cocklebiddy, I'm in my best ever spirits thanks to the beauty and calm around me. Sure, sunrise is a daily sight out here, but seeing the emergence of dawn – from the first semblance of light and a sliver of sunshine, to the transition to a full blown new day – is just as exhilarating every single time. It's not just the warmth of sunshine that lifts me – although of course that's welcomed – but a sense of joy and peace, a spirituality of a kind, that accompanies the magnificent display of pure nature untouched by the pollution of city life. And I am right there, standing right amongst it, enjoying it unfold – and for free!

Today, the lightening sky is crowned with a huge rainbow from early showers, and made one of the most beautiful sunrises I've ever seen. Then, as if on cue, the sun emerges from the horizon, a giant orange ball. The silence is broken only by the chirping of tiny desert birds awakening in the surrounding shrubs – and then the crow of the Cycling Maven 25 metres down the road, welcoming his audience of 'Cracking human beings' on his own live video. I can't help but laugh.

◉

Despite my concern for kangaroos leaping out at dawn, I haven't seen any – except for the poor buggers struck by vehicles and now rotting by the roadside with a stench that burns the nostrils. The further I ride on, the more I'm beginning to smell road kill victims before I see them, which at least helps me to avoid them.

Still, day six has started as well as it could have. I'm generally feeling good. My legs are tired as they should be after five days of pedalling further than I ever have before, my knees ache from the constant pressure on them, and my right ankle is still a little sore from the extra pressure that I had inadvertently put on it, favouring it over the left ankle while pedalling – but not as much as it was a couple of days ago when I was really worried that it might go to pot completely. Other than all that, my spirits are high and I'm keen to get to Cocklebiddy, and hopefully early enough to make sure I'm nearer the front of the line for breakfast than the rear. I reckon there'll be quite a few hungry souls on the road this morning.

The highs of IndiPac are like a trap, with potential lows lurking around every corner, literally as much as metaphorically. But after such a positive start to the day, and with the rain having abated to a glorious dawn, the Cycling Maven and I share some great banter as we catch and pass each other and spend joyous spells cycling alongside one another. We're looking forward to Cocklebiddy, to the respite it will offer, in particular for the Maven, and that second breakfast – although, to be honest, I'm not feeling all that hungry considering what I ate at Caiguna and have continued to eat since.

But the discussion of a second big breakfast reflects our good mood. Heaven knows, there's not a lot else at Cocklebiddy to look forward to. And the 'Welcome to Cocklebiddy' sign leaning against the wooden post near the entrance to nondescript roadhouse says as much in a say-effacing way. It reads: Population 8, Budgies 25, Quails 7, Dogs 1, Kangaroos 1,234,567.

The former Aboriginal mission on the southern edge of Western Australia's sheep grazing belt was a water source during World War Two until saline water was found under the layer of fresh water, and all that remains of the mission itself are its stone foundations. The small roadhouse is called the Wedgetail Inn, and the surrounding area is better known for its underground caves – foremost being the 6-kilometre long Cocklebiddy cave which is 90 per cent underwater. Also in the vicinity is the Nuytsland Nature Reserve, about 50 kilometres south, which includes the Eyre Bird Observatory, on the site of the historic Eyre Telegraph Station, which operated from 1897 to 1929.

But none of this is on my mind as I near Cocklebiddy. Even thoughts of breakfast are cast aside when I feel a softening of the pressure in my rear tyre several kilometres out. It's a slow leak – my first. With rain clouds building again, I wrestle with the idea of stopping immediately to replace the inner tube, or trying to make it to Cocklebiddy where I can change it under cover, which will mean riding out of the saddle with my weight on the front wheel. I take the latter option and only just make it. Like a dying breath, the rear tyre suddenly releases its remaining air in the driveway of the roadhouse, and I feel the wheel rim underneath me as I ride slowly across the parking area. But soon I'm under cover and dry – a major positive, even with the minus.

Before changing the inner tube, I succumb to the warmth inside the roadhouse. Normally I'd attend to any mechanical problem before thinking of resting, the thinking being that the immediacy of the problem means I'll carry out the repair properly, or at least not forget anything in the process as I might do by waiting until later. Out of mind, out of sight is a risk that can pay a hefty price. But right now I'm swayed by the sight of the Cycling Maven inside already ordering a big breakfast of eggs, bacon, sausages and baked beans. Thinking I'm not hungry, I order a cup of tea.

Our presence is noticed by a number of truck drivers. Their heads turn as if we're cowboys from out of town arriving unannounced into the local saloon. We break the ice with a respectful 'G'day' and explain we're racing our bikes across Australia. We tell a driver sitting near us that we appreciate the patience that the truckies have shown us on the highway so far. Later I hear reports of some fractiousness between a cyclist and a truckie, but my experience has only been positive to this point. We ask the truckie for any advice and request that he relay our thanks on CB radio to others. But I have no idea if he will.

As the Cycling Maven and I chat, I notice he's barely touched his mountain of food. He says he isn't hungry now, and invites me to pick at his meal – which I do, reluctantly at first. But then one pick becomes two, then three, and before I know it I'm finishing most of the plate he ordered. My body is clearly in need of more food, despite everything I've eaten on the road since. In the Maven's case, his mind had told him that he was hungry but his body said something else. Everyone reacts differently and at different times on marathon endurance events like this.

Before long, I realise I've yet to change my rear inner tube, and had best get a move on. The only distraction is that I know I'm being watched. I glance to my right and there are two truckies curious about what I'm doing. By now I'm used to getting whimsical glances, so just smile and say hello. Suddenly I realise there's someone dressed in shorts and a T-shirt standing right next to me. He's a cyclist who has just stayed overnight at

Cocklebiddy. He's riding across Australia too – but in the opposite direction. We chat, but I begin to lose focus on changing the tube, which is not as quick as I'm used to. My Focus Izalco road bike has a quick release system to take the front and rear wheels out, but in order to have greater structural strength under the front and rear forks, my IndiPac bike, the titanium Curve 'Belgie Spirit', requires an allen key to unlock the axle and then take the wheel out from the forks to replace the tyre.

I try to look busy, hoping the cyclist will sense my frustration and leave me alone. I feel guilty because he seems friendly enough, and certainly enthusiastic. But before I have to take the next step and say, 'Sorry, I had better get on to this and get going,' the Cycling Maven makes a timely exit from the roadhouse. With his trademark smile, he walks straight up to the cyclist and engages him in conversation.

Before long I've replaced my rear tube and throw the punctured tube into a rubbish bin.

◉

The road from Cocklebiddy to Madura, 91 kilometres east, becomes hillier, especially where the highway rises to the Hampton Tablelands. The area around Madura, first settled in 1876 as a pastoral homestead, provides a refreshing change of scenery too, with bush and trees. For many years, Madura was known for producing polo and cavalry horses – later known as 'Walers' – for the British Imperial Indian Army. These horses were used in a number of British campaigns on India's rebellious Northwest Frontier after being transported overland to Eucla before being loaded onto ships. Madura is also where Australian Army engineers stayed while upgrading the road during World War Two. It was the only place in the Eucla artesian basin that had free flowing bore water, perfect for grazing stock to drink, even if it needed desalination for human consumption.

Before getting to Madura I must first climb to the top of the Hampton Tablelands where the Madura Lookout provides a spectacular view of the Madura Pass and the Roe Plains. Between 15 and 45 million years ago, the sea levels in this area changed constantly due the effects of the Ice Age. This is geological history that I learn later but don't need to know it right now to appreciate the beautiful landscape laid out before me. When I look behind me from the top of the Tableland, I get my first sense of having ridden some real distance since leaving Fremantle. The expanse of land below is vast. It's hard to comprehend that once the route over this climb was a rubble-strewn, unpaved pass that would challenge today's four-wheeled vehicle drivers.

Descending into Madura is like arriving at an oasis. It's by far the most beautiful site for a roadhouse so far. I knew I'd been climbing for some kilometres, but am surprised by the sheer steepness and length of the drop to the turn-off that comes up suddenly on my right and could easily be missed if riding at night.

It's lunchtime now and with another four hours of riding under my belt, I'm hungry. I'm also hot. The descent into Madura has cooled me, but my core body temperature has risen considerably on the climb to the lookout. Only when I enter the air-conditioned roadhouse do I realise how hot I really am. It's a small bar area but the people are friendly, and I order as I always do: a hamburger with chips. I also order a cold Coke, something I rarely drink in my other life, but have increasingly done so throughout the IndiPac. The Cycling Maven arrives soon after me, places the same order, but with an extra serving of vegetables. My burger and Cola hit the spot, and with the day having gone so well and 150 kilometres ridden so far, I once more feel on top of everything – to the point that I'm happy enough to accept the Cycling Maven's suggestion that we have a few shots on the billiards table. This is despite common sense saying that we should sit down, rather than spend time on our feet, bending over precariously in various shooting positions. Still, a few minutes of skylarking with the cue and several errant shots provide some mental relief.

Leaving Madura, I feel great. There are about 120 kilometres to go for the day, but I'm counting down the kilometres, knowing I have already ridden further in the day than I have needed to. Before long though, the winds pick up again and once more

I am riding into them. The Cycling Maven isn't far behind me. Nick, who arrived in Madura after me, is now ahead up the road, having set off before me, as did Humungous Hugh. Inevitably, my buoyant mood wears off, much like a once fresh battery running flat.

Fighting the wind wastes energy, so I focus on trying to find a rhythm I can maintain, to be at one with the bike and be positive about the challenge ahead. Then, about 40 kilometres from Madura with the sight of a range of hills to my left, I feel that all too familiar softening of my rear tyre again. My heart sinks. 'Oh, no,' I bemoan out loud. 'Not again. Surely not.'

There's no chance of making it to Mundrabilla, 80 kilometres away, before dark. Normally the fact that Mundrabilla is where Australia's largest meteorite was discovered would interest me, but not now. The last thing I want is to be stuck by the road, isolated in the pitch black of night and fumbling as I try to replace a rear tube under only the light of my head lamp and bike – especially in the rain, which now seems likely to return, judging by the building mass of black clouds.

It seems strange that rain is playing such a role in my first crossing of such a fabled desert. While it may limit the heat, it does create other problems which I hadn't thought of before. The foremost is that the rain turns the usually dry desert dust, earth and sand into a sticky clay that, as soon as I stop off the bitumen – or veer off due to a road train or caravan passing too close or when I drift off due to fatigue – gets stuck in the cleat of my bike shoes, in my pedals and wheel rim and, if I fall, in the rear derailleur, chain and brakes.

I should have been better versed in the weather forecast, I tell myself. It may be uncommon, but it's certainly not unexpected for rain to fall in the middle of Australia. I think back to the story of the pioneering Overlander Percy Armstrong, whose last nights of his 1893 ride from Croydon in the Northern Territory to Melbourne in Victoria – the first north to south ride by anyone – was slowed by rain, and thick muddy roads cut up by teamsters. On his last night, four spokes were torn out of one of his wheels when he cycled into a culvert. Instead of riding on, he had to stop and repair the damage at night by the glimmer of firelight.

I shudder. I don't want to be running repairs in the dark. So with sunset approaching, I have to think fast. I wonder if there is something wrong with the back tyre or rim; maybe something is piercing the inner tube. *Did I check the tyre properly back in Cocklebiddy when I replaced the tube? Maybe the chatting outside the roadhouse while I replaced the tube distracted me? What did I miss?* All these questions fly through my mind. Suddenly, I realise my error in throwing away the punctured tube at Cocklebiddy. I should have kept it and repaired it. At this rate, I could easily use up four tubes – and there's nowhere out here to buy new ones. And with the rules of the race firmly in my mind – it's a solo and unsupported race – no one can give me one of theirs, either.

I force myself to cast the regret aside, as well as the frustration of my predicament, knowing that this late in the day and with so many kilometres still to cycle, time is of the essence. The priority is to get on with changing the tube and check the inside of the tyre again – and make the best use of the remaining daylight to do it.

◉

As soon as I stop, I phone Libby. While I'm borrowing the Cycling Maven's spare phone and am conscious of limiting my use, it's a no-brainer to dial home and reassure her that I'm okay. But I also need to be quick, to limit my riding time in the dark.

'Hi Lib,' I say when she answers, trying to sound calm, but I know there's a terseness in my tone. 'I can't talk for long, but just want to let you know I'm all right. I've had my second flat for the day and still have to 80 kilometres to ride, so I'd better keep going.' I can finish the call on a positive note, though, and update her on the fact that the Maven has lent me his phone and I can stay in regular contact. She can see where I am on the dot tracker, too, of course.

We say our goodbyes and I hang up. It was an abrupt call, laced with my own frustration. I feel bad – Libby deserves better – but I figure it's better than no call at all. Libby was barely able to get a word in, but she understands that the urgency isn't due to any major problem, rather my need to make as much progress in the daylight I can.

I'm not opposed to riding in the darkness, as I'm comfortable doing so in the very early morning hours of day; but towards the end of a day I'm tired and prefer to stop earlier than later. I'm also short-sighted, and when fatigued it's an issue that can worsen.

I'm wrestling with the dual needs of staying calm and working with a sense of urgency but I force myself to be methodical. Before long, it's done and I'm ready to resume riding. Knowing I've had two rear flats nags me for a while, but the sooner I get back into a cycling rhythm, the sooner I will reach Mundrabilla and I push on.

◉

Darkness soon takes over, and with that comes the need to get into my night-time mindset: for the first time on the IndiPac I really feel isolated, but I can't let emotion get the better of me. *Embrace it*, I tell myself. It's not panic, but just a realisation of where I am – in the middle of a desert and kilometres away from anyone, let alone anywhere. If I let that thought get to me, well . . . it could get the better of me. So I just accept it. I think of all the messages of support from friends and family – and they begin to strengthen me. Rain begins to fall, a headwind begins to build, and then the blackness overrides it all, but reassuringly

I'm in a positive frame of mind – I'm riding with as much optimism as I have had all week.

Inevitably, the high from riding in the loneliness of night wears off – especially when I realise I have ridden less distance than I think by misreading the kilometre signs.

One rare great moment on this stretch is my sighting of a tall broad-chested kangaroo by the left side of the road. It has to be more than two metres in height. I'm grateful I'm riding so slowly – between 12 and 14 kilometres per hour, into the headwind and rain. It's staring right at me, and I hope it isn't going to jump unexpectedly into my way and cause a crash. Its stance suggests that it won't, that it was just eating when I appeared. But still, as I edge nearer and the kangaroo is in the sights of my head lamp, I still pray that it doesn't suddenly change its mind and lunge out. I have a fleeting image of me sprawled out, injured on the Nullarbor in the dark, kilometres from anywhere and no one to help.

I'm still hesitant as I ride towards it, ready for a sudden change. The animal is absolutely beautiful. Its posture is majestic – proud, but calm. In the golden light cast from my head lamp, its brown fur contrasts with the blackness behind him. We continue to exchange eye contact. Then it looks slowly to its right, pauses for a moment and gracefully hops away into the bush. My headlamp remains fixed on it as it disappears out of sight, leaving me in total silence. Now I feel really alone, but also exhilarated by the experience of sharing this brief minute of solitude with the kangaroo. It lifts me and I'm soon back pedalling at a nice clip. *This is what it's all about*, I remind myself. *This is living.*

The kilometres seem to pass quickly. Mundrabilla can't be that far away, I figure. I'm not even looking at my Garmin computer all that regularly, being more focused on the road ahead. Then suddenly, as the wind strengthens, my burst of enthusiasm begins to wear thin. Thoughts of how truly isolated I am out here on the Nullarbor and in the thick of night return. *Here we go again ... Another bad spell,* I lament, and then prepare for a now trademark wave of suffering.

Fatigue is resurrected too. I try to reach for positive thoughts, urging myself to fight off the negatives; but with nothing to see except the road in front, the sense of riding further and further into isolation returns, and is broken only by the odd road train or car passing.

◉

I'm astounded by how dark it is out on the Nullarbor. It's nothing like riding in Centennial Park in Sydney at 2 am in the morning, as I did in training – even if that's considered dark, being largely blocked from the ambient light of the CBD. This is blackness, real blackness, out here. And it really strikes me when I stop for a pee and turn my lights off out of curiosity. I may as well have covered my eyes with my hand. The eeriness of the total lack of light is compounded by the silence and the knowledge of just how desolate it is out here.

My awe is broken by the sound of something rustling in the shrubs to my left, a sound that's coming my way. I quickly turn my lights back on, jump on my bike and somehow find a sprint – well, as close to a sprint as I can find. I don't know what was making the noise and I don't want to find out. And then my weary mind gets the better of me. I begin to wonder if whatever it was is following me. Maybe it's a dingo, and perhaps there are others with it, following my trail, waiting for me to tire to the point that I stop in exhaustion and become easy prey . . .

I take a deep breath, focus on pedalling and after a while my fears dissipate. Clearly my mind's playing games with me. But now something else is worrying me – I'm thinking about how much pain I'm feeling – with the rain falling, every pedal stroke seems slower. My back is aching, and so is my backside, my right foot and ankle; and my knees as though they are about to explode, like the legs of a chair under too much weight. The wind, the rain and the pain. It seems all is against me. It crosses my mind to stop and sleep by the road.

As I ride on, I notice a series of dark clumps on the side of the road, which is steaming from the heat of the day and the rain. My first thought is that they're piles of cattle dung, which is strange, because I haven't seen any cattle at all for days.

Now the darkness begins to add directly to my woes – no longer because of any fear of what might be out there, but more because I can't see far enough ahead to get a sense of what the terrain is like, of where I am, or how much further I have to go to reach Mundrabilla. This is the worst I have felt since leaving Fremantle.

Then the road rises and I have to work harder to keep riding.

A Kombi van passes me, then stops. The couple in it offer me a drink, but I politely decline, explaining that race rules don't allow any outside assistance. I'm not sure they understand, I may be mumbling. But they smile, wish me well and drive away.

I haven't passed anything that might indicate I'm closing in on the roadhouse, other than signposts with an 'M' and a number of kilometres. But then I start to read those wrongly: one sign indicates fewer kilometres to go, the next seems to indicate more. It really begins to do my head in.

After what seems like an eternity, I see the slightest of flickers in the distance ahead. It must be Mundrabilla.

I dig in like I never have before in this race. But the light seems to get no bigger or closer. It even disappears, then returns, and disappears again. Is it a parked truck, or a camper van? Surely not. Finally, the light gets brighter. I realise it's been going in and out of view because the road is winding up and the hillier terrain nearer Mundrabilla has been occasionally blocking it.

As I reach the crest of the apparent rise, there is more than a flicker of light. It's constant. It's larger. And then there is more than one light. Finally, the Mundrabilla Roadhouse is there on my left.

I soft pedal off the highway, the sound of my wheels over the loose gravel my only companion. I have absolutely nothing left. Reception is closed, but I see some activity over where the rooms are. There are bikes outside. Clothes are hanging off them. I know the Cycling Maven, Nick Skarajew and Humungous Hugh are here somewhere. I'm hoping there's a bed in one of the rooms, or even just a little floor space to sleep on.

Then, like a genie out of a bottle, the Cycling Maven steps out from one of the rooms. His trademark smile is beaming. I roll over to him.

'Mate,' he says. 'We saw you on those last kilometres. We knew how you were feeling – we were just willing you on.'

It's 10 pm. I am busted like I have never been busted in my life – this day has broken me physically and emotionally; it's been my hardest ride ever. Not the longest in terms of kilometres ridden, but definitely the most brutal. I collapse down onto a stool outside the room. The Maven tells me he has bought food – there's a sandwich, a chocolate chip cookie, a slice of cake and a can of Coke waiting inside for me. I can't thank him enough.

And of course I'm looking forward to a hot shower and a good night's sleep.

Later, when I check the dot tracker, I'm amazed to see how far ahead Kristof Allegaert and his nearest challengers,

Mike Hall and Sarah Hammond, are. Kristof has backed up a 400-kilometre ride the day before with a 350-kilometre haul from Port Augusta to Wirrabara, where he arrived just before 5 pm and left shortly after to ride three more hours.

But I'm just happy to be in a bed in a motel room, sharing the banter, even the moans and groans of a punishing day, with three other IndiPac survivors. As Rod Evans said in Fremantle, it will be the tough days and moments that we will remember forever. And I will remember this day . . .

My train of thought and the peace of mind I have found is broken when Humungous Hugh enlightens me about the clumps of cattle dung on the road. They are in fact curled up snakes – death adders – that have come out of the rain stricken desert to warm themselves on the heat of the bitumen.

'That'd be right,' I say, laughing.

I turn the lights out. This IndiPac is sheer madness.

9

LIKE FROGS CROSSING
A LILY POND

Day 7: Mundrabilla to Border Village
Start: 12.36 pm   Finish: 3.51 pm
Riding time: 3 hours 15 minutes
Distance: 77.8 km   Metres climbed: 153 m
Average speed: 23.9 kmh   Temperature: 18–22 C

The sound of heavy rain doesn't disappoint me as it may have a few days earlier. It wakes me – well, it wakes all four of us in the room at Mundrabilla Roadhouse – in time for our scheduled 4 am departure. The Cycling Maven, Humungous Hugh, Nick Skarajew and I exchange our concerns about riding in the downpour. After yesterday's ordeal, I'm happy to wait it out.

Among us, Nick seems the keenest to get under way despite the foul weather. His tail is up. He wants to chase Rhino – Ryan Flinn – and, before arriving at their home city of Melbourne, bridge some of the lead Rhino has gained since leaving us at

Balladonia. I repeat my mantra that I'm set on reaching Sydney. I want to be strong for the last 1000 kilometres through the mountains and, after Canberra, the Southern Highlands and Royal National Park to Sydney.

Hugh repeats his own mantra: 'Play the long game'. The Cycling Maven is tossing up whether to go with Nick, or to stay. Nick opts to make a break for it, despite the continuing rain. After changing into his kit and checking his bike, he is gone, joining Ben Cadby – the Mango Rider – who was staying in a nearby room. Once Nick is dressed and organised, and his packs are loaded onto his bike, he is gone. The room is quiet and the Maven, Hugh and I wait out the rain till dawn.

◉

One of the downsides of sharing rooms is that you are hostage to anyone else's intent to head off. Preparing to ride creates noise and eliminates any chance of anyone getting the sleep they're hoping for. In any case, this morning my aches and pains make it hard for me to continue sleeping. But lying in the warmth of my bed listening to the rain fall is soothing. If I'd been alone, I doubt I'd have gotten up and ridden in this weather.

'Who would have thought that we'd find rain our biggest enemy in the bloody Nullarbor,' I say to no one in particular.

We three aren't the only ones hesitating, either. When I do get up, I take a peep at the dot tracker. It's been a tough and wet first week this far back in the field, and sure, the leaders are doing an amazing job, racing as fast as they are with so little sleep. Reports filter back of them sleeping in public toilets, which does impress me as much as it shocks me – I can think of other places I'd rather rough it in than a toilet block. But the constant wet and wind from the front coming in from the north-west has taken its toll on others, as well as me.

Only the night before, I learned about the extent of the problems of another rider I had met earlier on the road. 'Tracking Jack', AKA Jack Heyward, was also having a tough time of the race. Like me, he had really suffered riding those last kilometres to Mundrabilla, and even lay down by the side of the road, using the handlebars of his bike as a pillow – clearly not knowing about the snakes. More worrying, he has a saddle sore that is worsening with each pedal stroke. This morning he shows us a photo of his open wound. It's weeping, which can be really dangerous in cycling. The sheer pain aside, the risk of infection is very high, and if it does set in and it isn't treated in time, it can be fatal.

Thinking of Tracking Jack's situation reminds me of the need to check my own condition in the same area. I have a 'hot spot', which makes it almost painful to sit on the saddle. And while it hasn't developed into a saddle sore, it is starting to get bigger. All I can do is ensure the sore – in fact my entire groin area – stays as clean as possible, and that I keep applying the chamois cream every day.

And like other riders, I've got a check-list of other concerns. My right ankle is still sore, but manageable, and both knees are in a constant state of change that ranges from numbness to pain. My feet are becoming increasingly sore, especially the ball of my right foot which frequently has the sensation of burning, or no feeling whatsoever after a rash of pins and needles.

But none of my ailments will stop me from riding today, at least once the rain abates – which it finally does. The little extra rest has given me some additional time to treat my aches and pains. After eating the first of two breakfasts – a cheese sandwich, a chocolate bar and a can of Coke – at 6 am – I have a second breakfast of eggs and sausages after 8 am when the roadhouse kitchen re-opens. The time spent over breakfast allows us to catch up on the race, especially on race leaders Kristof Allegaert, Mike Hall and Sarah Hammond who really are setting a cracking pace.

It's fantastic to see the images on the IndiPac website of Kristof arriving in downtown Adelaide at peak hour this morning. He was welcomed by hundreds of people – from Adelaide Mayor Martin Haese to blue and white collar workers. Kristof, interviewed by Jesse Carlsson, who is following the leaders, was visibly moved by the welcome party. Kristof later recalls in his IndiPac diary how the mayor even wanted to make him a citizen of his city. Kristof was also taken aback by how many people came out of their houses to watch him cycle past as he headed through the suburbs.

Fittingly, the spontaneous public welcome in Adelaide for Kristof was akin to what the Overlanders experienced in the late 1890s and early 1900s whenever they arrived at a major city. This was like history being remade, I felt; a throw back in time.

Mike Hall and Sarah Hammond have also been greeted in Adelaide with true Overlander respect – Mike a little later in the day and Sarah at 10 pm. Sarah was overwhelmed by the support but joked that the sight of dot trackers seemingly coming from out of nowhere onto the bike path to greet her was like being in a zombie film. Her remark triggered a huge laugh in the crowd there to see her in the CBD, and then she ignited a cheer when she revealed she was way ahead of her daily schedule for kilometres ridden.

'Can you catch the boys up the road?' asked Jesse, while interviewing her.

'I don't know,' she said, laughing.

◉

I laugh too when I see the Rhino's latest Facebook update. Like many others, I'm interested to learn how he's travelling. Is he 'flying like an eagle', as he told his Facebook followers after he bought a toy eagle? He named it 'Eagzzz' but it soon became known as 'Rheagle', a combination of rhino and eagle. Rhino had attached Rheagle to his handlebars before I bade him farewell at Balladonia where he ditched some of his load for lightness and speed, including his bivvy bag, water bladder and two water bottles. Later he loses his fabled toy.

Typically, today Rhino has a humorous but interesting message to pass on to anyone with a dodgy knee like the one he suffers from. That is: don't put goanna oil on your knee – or any afflicted area – before you put on your cycling shorts lacquered inside with chamois cream to protect the crutch from infection. Otherwise, as Rhino says, the layer of goanna oil turns the chamois cream into something akin to the menthol rub Deep Heat in a way you would not wish upon your worst enemy.

◉

For all the gains of the extended spell at Mundrabilla, the downside is that my body starts to stiffen up. It takes some time for me to get my rhythm back after the Cycling Maven, Humungous Hugh and I finally get going at about 12.30 pm. There is no secret to the solution: keep pedalling and the rhythm will return. When it does, however, I'm still feeling somewhat flat. My legs feel heavy, despite the welcome assistance of a little tail wind. The previous day has taken a lot more out of me than I've expected.

I quickly resolve that I'll treat today as a rest day of sorts. After the late departure from Mundrabilla, I aim for an early finish and stop at the Border Village roadhouse, 77.8 kilometres away, where race leader Kristof Allegaert arrived at midnight on day three. My plan is to have a big day of riding tomorrow.

After 65 kilometres I arrive at the Eucla Roadhouse, which requires riding up a two-kilometre climb – the first of the IndiPac since leaving the Perth Hills behind me on day one. Eucla is the easternmost point of Western Australia and the ride is enjoyable, though I would never say I am a climber, but getting to ride in a different gear, uphill and with a handy tail wind after cycling on so much flat terrain and into cross and headwinds is a welcome novelty. The difference a change makes!

I don't really notice that the temperature has risen to 33 degrees, which in desert parlance isn't that high. I'm alone, but ahead of me are the Cycling Maven and Humungous Hugh. I have no idea what has become of Tracking Jack, and I wonder how he has got on with his saddle sore. Nearing the climb, what was a blue speck is clearly the Cycling Maven who has stopped halfway up. I can hear him recording a live Facebook post. Clearly the hill has given him a new backdrop after endless days of reporting from flat desert plains.

Passing the Maven and now at the top, I see Humungous Hugh who has stopped to take some photos. I ride on, but turn off to the Eucla Roadhouse. I want a cup of tea. I assume the other two will probably do the same, even though we've only been riding for about two and a half hours. But after stopping in front of the Llewin Way Whale, an imitation grey whale in the car park, and talking to a woman who has asked what we are doing, I realise they have ridden on to Border Village, just over the Western Australian–South Australia border.

I learn later that, because of the relatively steep climb out of the Roe Plains, Eucla is the only town in Western Australia that has a direct view of the Great Australian Bight. Sadly this doesn't dawn on me at the time. I'm tired from the accumulated days in the saddle, happy about having got this far and overjoyed at being so close to where I plan to rest up before a longer haul in the saddle the next day. With a little over 13 kilometres to go, it was easy to miss the signs that would have steered me to the fabulous sight.

But Eucla itself has an interesting history. When the telegraph line opened in 1877, the town was one of the most important telegraph stations on the line, and was a vital conversion point when South Australia and Victoria began to use American Morse code – otherwise known as the Victorian alphabet – while Western Australia used the international Morse code we are familiar with today. The old Eucla telegraph station is now regarded as one of the loneliest sights on the Nullarbor Plain. All that remains are broken down stone walls which are often swamped by the shifting desert sands and the dunes they create.

I decide I might as well enjoy the rest of today's cycling and ride the last kilometres to Border Village at an easy pace. I still can't help but appreciate the beauty of the Nullarbor Plain – its barren expanse, the utter silence in the mornings after daybreak, the glorious sunsets. These are going to be my last kilometres of cycling in Western Australia and I want to take it all in. Which I do, embracing the majestic desert landscape all around me, including my first sighting of emus pacing just outside Eucla.

I think of how I will spend my hours in Border Village. Rest is crucial, but I should use the daylight – especially now the sun has pushed the rain clouds away – to give my dirty and smelly clothes a good wash and my bike a thorough going over too. At the end of the first week, it's also a chance to grant myself a bit of respite and think about week two.

Crossing the border into South Australia is a poignant moment for me, which I celebrate by taking a selfie in front of the road sign that welcomes me to South Australia. I turn around, look back at the horizon and farewell Western Australia. Then I roll slowly towards Border Village. The stop-off point is multi-purpose and operates on a 24-hours-a-day, seven-days-a-week schedule. It's a Western Australian agricultural checking point where anyone who is entering the state from South Australia must declare any fruit, vegetables, plants, seeds, soils, honey and animals in their possession. And it's also a service centre for petrol, diesel, accommodation and dining. There's also a desali-nation plant, and it's also the gateway to the spectacular cliffs of the Great Australian Bight.

As I roll in, I notice the giant Kangaroo statue. The 'Big Roo', AKA 'Rooey II', is in the quirky Australian tradition of celebrating 'big' things – a tacky but light-hearted attempt at attracting tourists. 'Rooey II' was triggered by the 1987 defence in Fremantle of *Australia II*'s 1983 victory in the America's Cup. It was thought that the Cup would lure interest from the east coast of Australia, which would also lead to increased road traffic across the Nullarbor Plain.

◉

My priority now is to stop. I ride by Rooey II, past reception to the bungalow-style apartments where the Cycling Maven and Humungous Hugh have parked their bikes. I'm hoping there is a spare bed, but it's clear that many other apartments are free. It's only 3.50 pm, but I plan on making the most of my early finish and getting up at midnight for what will be a big day of cycling to the Nullarbor Roadhouse. Seeing there is a third bed in the shared cottage, I settle down.

Time passes by very fast. I get through my usual routine, as well as washing my kit and hanging it out in the sun before the late afternoon desert chill takes over. Once it's all done, there's time to enjoy a Cooper's beer in the roadhouse where the Cycling Maven and Humungous Hugh are already doing the same. Several televisions are screening live sports events. A travelling couple are enjoying a bottle of wine outside in the shade of the terrace. With each sip of Cooper's, I begin to forget about the IndiPac. *I could be anywhere in Australia right now*, I tell myself. I enjoy a second beer with my dinner, then buy a third.

My mind wanders back to the trials of the original Over-landers. *No way could they have enjoyed this*, I think, looking at the cold stubby in my hand and recalling images of their camps with wilderness all around and only a tent and a billy on the boil their only comfort.

And then the American rider Anders Petersen and Tracking Jack arrive at the bar. The fact that we're all at the same roadhouse at the same time is as much the circumstance of distance as ability. As the Cycling Maven quips, us crossing the Nullarbor Plain with 200-or-so kilometres between roadhouses and the security and relative comforts that they provide is a bit like frogs trying to cross a pond by hopping onto lily pads.

I'm quite surprised to see Tracking Jack, but it's still not clear from what he says if he'll continue or not. He talks of his wound, the pain and the risk of infection. Common sense says he shouldn't continue, but who am I to suggest that? That he is asking the question himself shows he understands the risks.

Besides, giving advice or intervening in someone's decision about whether to continue or not could breach the race rules. In any case it's clear that Tracking Jack realised the severity of his situation and phoned the nearest hospital at Ceduna, 408 kilometres away. The nurses instructed him on how to treat his wound after he showed them the image of it taken on his phone. He shows us the image again and I still wince. To say I'm impressed by his foresight to call the nurses in Ceduna and treat it as per their advice is an understatement.

'I can't believe you did that yourself,' I tell him, before taking another swig of my beer. I'm impressed not only by his courage to go through with the self-treatment but also by how well the nurses instructed him. Jack also pointed out to the nurses that several other IndiPac riders may be needing the same treatment.

'Ain't that the truth,' I weigh in.

A saddle sore isn't yet my problem – although I do have an extremely sore arse and I'm still concerned that one point in particular could develop into one. It's now a sharp and hot pain, and touching it makes it hurt more. But I know it's not infected, so I remind myself to continue washing the area well and regularly. Still, it's good to know that Tracking Jack has passed on the message that others are suffering, so the nurses can be ready in two to three days' time if needed.

Before long, the accumulated fatigue of the last two days hits me – no doubt aided by the three beers I have now drunk. The sudden shift prompts me to re-stock on food and drinks, including those I'll consume for one last snack after my dinner before I go to sleep.

Before turning in I bring in my washing and re-pack it, and then make sure everything else is in order for an early departure – my lights, Garmin, food and drinks. At lights out, there's still a bit of chit chat.

'All set to go at midnight?' the Cycling Maven asks.

'Yup,' replies Humungous Hugh.

'No chance of rain stopping us this time,' I say, jovially.

But deep down I know that as soon as I tumble into sleep, I'll be awake again, as if nothing has happened.

And I know that will suck.

10

A DAY OF
SHEER HELL

Day 8: Border Village to Nullarbor Roadhouse
Start: 12.35 am   Finish: 8.15 pm
Riding time: 10 hours 45 minutes
Distance: 187.9 km   Metres climbed: 301 m
Average speed: 14.9 kmh   Temperature: 17–24 C

We barely speak as we wake up in our bungalow. None of us – me, Humungous Hugh or the Cycling Maven – counts the customary moans and groans. It's not the midnight start we planned, but at 12.35 am it's close enough. We're going to make good kilometres before dawn.

Instinct takes over as we get ready to leave. We are more like zombies than alert, ready-to-ride cyclists, but there's still enough motivation to get on the road as soon as possible. I go through the motions. I know today will be hard, but getting as far as possible before the sun rises is a real lure.

Leaving the bungalow, the sound of loose gravel under our wheels as we roll out from the car park is sharp and clear in the silence of a desert night. The sight of other bikes outside doors tells me more riders have arrived since we turned in. I wonder who they are. I haven't checked in on the race tracker to check. In fact, it's been some time since I have.

At the roadhouse I buy some more supplies and have a quick breakfast. It's hardly breakfast time, but needs must be met! Back in the bungalow, I'd already started eating what food I had on hand, so now is the chance to stock up one more time before I head out from Border Village and into the darkness that awaits me on the Nullarbor.

I'm not exactly sure who'll be leaving at the same time. I figure the Cycling Maven and Humungous Hugh are as good as ready to go, but we tend to roll out individually, though usually still within sight of each other's lights. I soon learn the American, Anders Petersen, is with us too. In time, we'll all pass each other or ride along side-by-side, but strictly in compliance with the rule that we race as individuals. In any case, we'll all be heading for the same destination at day's end and we'll certainly see each other during the day, whatever pace we ride.

◉

The darkness after leaving Border Village is as intense as it was on the night I rode to Mundrabilla. But it is a pleasant dark – calm, serene and dry. The first kilometres roll out under my legs freshened by my extended rest break. After the heat of yesterday, the Nullarbor Plain is still warm. I keep my Rapha gilet on for the first kilometres, but only until I get a sweat up from the tempo. As the course starts to roll, as predicted we catch and pass each other, and at times share spells alongside each other in pairs, chatting intermittently.

Suddenly, the Cycling Maven, who is up ahead by himself, stops. When we reach him he says he has to take a dump. It would be easy to ride on, for all of us to do so. But after my nightmarish run into Mundrabilla, after which Cycling Maven kindly bought me food and offered me a spare bed, I'm happy to wait for him, as are the others.

It's a beautiful minute or two spent as the Cycling Maven heads off behind a bush. I first sit on the highway, then lie down spread-eagled, fully stretched out with my arms wide, staring into the bright star-lit skies above. It's one of the most sublime moments in my life.

It's good knowing the others are taking some time out, too.

Remembering what I thought was cattle dung on the road to Mundrabilla, I call out to Humungous, 'Hey, mate, keep an eye out for snakes.' I can't help but glance around to check myself.

Humungous cheekily chips, 'There, behind you Rupe.'

I can see we're all now lying down on the bitumen, and call out to the others to keep an eye out for trucks. 'We don't want to be falling asleep here on the highway.' I mean it in a lighthearted way, but the onset of fatigue and the sudden need for sleep can strike at any time and without warning. It's a serious threat out here.

It's still amazing, though, this view of the stars and of being stretched out on a desert highway with not a road train, car or camper in sight. I feel so small against the combined vastness of the desert around me, the star-lit sky and the infinity of space above me. It's so calm, so quiet and so relaxing, I could easily stay here all night.

But it's a fleeting thought and it's not long before the Cycling Maven is back and we're off again, onwards to the Nullarbor Roadhouse.

◉

Humungous Hugh is keen to set a good tempo, but after a couple of attempts to follow him, his pace is too much for me at this time of the morning. The Cycling Maven, on the other hand, appears to be struggling. Well, judging by the sight of his front light fading behind me in the darkness. But just as he is almost out of sight, he surges forward again. He's going at his own pace, in his own time, which is what the IndiPac is really about.

Soon we all find ourselves moving ahead, then dropping back. It's still reassuring that we can all see each other's lights – rear or front. If any of us runs into trouble, at least one of the others would wait until our light reappeared. We never actually discussed this as a plan. But I sense it's what would happen.

I use the quiet time to chat with Anders. He is a former American high school footballer who took to triathlon and marathon running and has now embraced ultra-endurance cycling. He may not have a cycling background, but as we chat I discover he's a genuinely affable person, and also has the calmness of temperament and strength of mind that will help him grind out a finish in any ultra-endurance event he enters. 'It would be nice to catch up in Sydney for a beer,' I tell him. There's still a long way to go in the IndiPac, but you never know when it will be the last time you see someone. I just want to get the invitation out there while I think about it.

I drop back to check where the Cycling Maven is and see his front light re-emerge from the dark. Humungous Hugh is forging ahead, but not out of sight. Anders continues tapping along, but then he suddenly wobbles. I suspect it is tiredness. Then I see the same from Hugh. And I'm told by the Cycling Maven that I'm wavering on the road a bit, too. I'm also yawning, and so is Hugh, which only makes me yawn more. Yes, I'm fighting an enormous bout of fatigue. My eyelids feel heavy, like they have weights attached to them; and all I want to do is let them close and sleep.

'Hey guys,' the Cycling Maven calls out from behind. 'Just saying . . . I can see we're are all riding a little skewiff. Maybe we should stop for a rest?'

There's no disagreement. We're all on alert for a turn-off to the nearest parking bay, and some much needed shut-eye. Yup . . . fatigue and the need for sleep can strike at any time.

We soon take a right off the highway and soft pedal a couple of hundred metres inland. Hidden behind the bush in the parking area is a picnic table. A camper van has already stopped, its passengers no doubt fast asleep. I wonder if the sound of our wheels on the gravel road will wake them. Will someone step out, wondering who the hell is out there? We turn off our lights and remind each other in whispers to be quiet as we prepare to settle down for some shut-eye – my first by the road in the IndiPac.

My biggest fear is snakes, especially after hearing about the death adders. But no sooner have I blown up my mattress and pillow, and lain down under the space blanket, I'm in a deep sleep. I'm only woken by the chill and early light of dawn about ninety minutes later. It is quite some chill. I'm shaking with it, and accept that my slumber is over. But I haven't had even a minute to worry about snakes, or much else. And I feel so much better for getting some sleep, as do the others.

It's been an interesting experience, my first bivvy. I know a number of the more experienced – and harder, or more resilient – IndiPac riders are sleeping out, if not every night.

I'm glad I've done it at least once. The original Overlanders would have slept wherever they could: under bushes and
trees, in abandoned stockmen's and teamsters' huts, on the
verandahs of churches and pubs, the platforms of railways
stations. Not to mention of course any offered accommodation
from farmers they met on the way, which would have included
welcome home cooking and perhaps a hot bath, and a chance
to shave and wash clothes.

We re-pack our kits and prepare to re-join the race route,
which is at this point about a kilometre inland from the coastal
cliffs of the Great Australian Bight. The chances are that I will
never come back here – 'Certainly not on a bicycle,' I tell myself.
So I decide to turn off the highway with the others and ride to a
lookout when the opportunity arrives.

When we reach the lookout a foggy haze is hanging over the
steep cliffs. But the Bight is still spectacular. There's no doubting
that I'm right on the edge of a vast continent. I try to imagine
what it was like 85 million years ago, when Australia and
Antarctica were still joined and then began to slowly separate,
a process that was finally completed about 30 million years ago.
The steep and jagged cliff face to the wild open ocean below
certainly looks like a giant bite has been taken out of the land.

It may be time lost, but with 95 kilometres already ridden
since leaving Border Village before dawn, seeing the majesty of
the Bight for the first time is well worth it. Besides the memory
I will keep for my whole life, seeing the Bight has lifted my

morale, which is much needed, knowing that I face 80 or so kilometres before getting to the Nullarbor Roadhouse, and that there's likely to be a strengthening wind on the way as well.

⊙

The fog and early chill soon dissipates as the sun rises to full strength. And the wind continues to pick up speed, soon turning into a torturous headwind. The boost of strength that I felt earlier after resting by the roadside has disappeared, especially when I feel the sensation of my rear tyre flattening again. It can't be. But it is. I have another rear puncture.

I'm about 50 kilometres from the Nullarbor Roadhouse when I stop by the side of the road. I'm as crestfallen as I have been in this race. It's my third puncture. I just can't believe it. But I have to deal with it.

No sooner do I stop than I realise how strong the heat really is. Without the wind cooling me as I ride, it smothers me. Even worse, as I start taking my rear wheel out, and then the tube from the tyre, I notice for the first time the ferocity of the Nullarbor's march flies. They seize the opportunity to bite me, which is not just painful, but plays havoc with my concentration on the repair job at hand. I'm not just brushing them away, but slapping them off me. And the more I do, the more aggressive they return to bite me again, even through my lycra shorts.

Somehow in the chaos unravelling around me, I manage to continue with the job. With the tube repaired, I check the tyre. There has to be something inside it for me to have had a third flat. But I can't see anything. Meanwhile, the march flies continue their assault. *This is insane*, I think to myself. *I've never seen flies attack like this.* It's excruciating. All I want to do is get back on the road and, most importantly now, out of the heat. I intend to put the repaired tube away and use one of my two new spares, thinking that will allow the fixed one to fully seal.

But when I reach for a new spare, I see it is a 25 mm, not a 28 mm like the ones I've been using. I get the other new tube out and see the same thing. I'm completely blown away, and start to lose a grip on the situation. For the life of me I don't know why I have 25 mm spares when I need 28 mms.

I feel so bloody stupid. Right now I don't know what I'm going to do. I'm having difficulty thinking straight, let alone dealing with the heat and the incessant attacks from the flies. Not to mention the accumulated fatigue. And now there are also black crows circling ominously above me.

Suddenly I'm recalling what Jerome Murif felt one day in 1897 during his Glenelg to Port Darwin ride. As he wrote in his memoir, *Ocean to Ocean*: 'Millions of flies, myriads of venomous mosquitoes.' Maybe the 'venomous' mosquitoes haven't ravaged me yet, nor yet the deep-rooted thirst; but the flies certainly have and his sense of desperation resonates strongly with me.

At 50 kilometres from the Nullarbor Roadhouse I feel completely stranded. I don't want to be stuck out here at night repairing tyres. This has really compromised everything. If I don't focus on getting to the roadhouse without another puncture, I will be royally screwed.

I decide to use the repaired tube and hope I can make the distance incident-free. The only other option I can come up with is to hitch a lift to the Nullarbor Roadhouse, sort my rear tyre issues there in the comfort of an air-conditioned room and then, as per IndiPac rules, return to this same spot the next day and resume racing from here. But I dismiss it, realising it's best to make do with what I have.

Eventually I refit the repaired 28 mm tube, pump it up again and get going. It has been the stupidest of mistakes.

◉

The march flies continue to bite, even through my socks. *Murif would be laughing if he saw them at me now*, I think. But I soon realise that the faster I ride the less they bite me. And after getting some momentum back, the 50 kilometres ahead of me begins to seem manageable. I should be at the Nullarbor Roadhouse in no time. But the wind continues to build, and the heat seems to rise. Every niggle in my body converges in a united chorus line of pain. When I look ahead, all I see is a shimmering horizon. I have no idea where anyone else is – the

Cycling Maven, Humungous Hugh and the others – except by now I know that they are well ahead of me. I feel alone, really alone.

I don't think about checking the dot tracker. All I can think about is reaching the roadhouse as soon as possible – and not getting another flat tyre. The one certainty is that when I do reach the Nullarbor Roadhouse, I will be staying there to rest. So much for taking a short break and continuing on from there.

This has turned into a day of sheer hell, and it's not over yet. The kilometres click over painfully slowly, but I count them down with every road sign indicating there are 5 kilometres less to go. I'm so tired that I misread the markers on occasion. I even wonder if it's all part of a plot. The mind can wilt very quickly under such trying conditions.

When the roadhouse finally appears in the haze of the horizon, there's still no relief. It seems I can't get any closer to it. I churn the pedals with wind screaming in my ears. It's as if I'm not making any progress at all. Is this a bad dream? The hazy image of the roadhouse only becomes sharper when it's right in front of me. Even then it's still blurry because sweat is pouring from my head and down my brow into my eyes.

The sheer relief is extraordinary, like nothing I have ever felt. I haven't forgotten Mundrabilla, but this has been a whole new level of pain. Rolling slowly into the shade of the servo I immediately begin to recover. And when I ask for a room,

I'm told I can get one, which is a relief, because in the lowest of my thoughts on the road, I'd concocted a dark fantasy where the plot against me had extended to being told the motel was totally booked.

⊙

The Cycling Maven and Humungous Hugh have already checked in, I soon learn, and are sharing a room, and it doesn't come to mind that they may have a third bed. Which is fine – right now, I really want to be alone. I'm happy they are here though, and pop my head into their room, which is next to mine, to say, 'G'day.'

The Maven and Humungous are both lying down and our exchange of looks tells the story: this has been one hell of a day for all of us. We don't need to say much. And we don't. We're just happy to see each other. We all just need to rest, some time to gather our thoughts, then rest some more. And then eat.

Inside my room, I draw the curtains to block out the burning sun. The darkness is instantly soothing. I prop my bike against the wall, take off my helmet, sunglasses, gloves and shoes, and empty the contents of my jersey pockets on the desk. I hobble to the bathroom for a towel, then put the towel on one of the beds, conscious of not staining bed covers with my sweaty shorts, and sit down. I drop my head into my hands. I am absolutely broken. *What am I doing here?* I ask myself. It's the first time I have really doubted being on the IndiPac. Somehow I have to find the answer. At least I'm on my own.

The welcome calm allows me to check in on my social media, emails and text messages. I can do with a lift of the spirits but am taken aback by the number of messages relating to my third flat, 50 kilometres earlier. I had recorded a live video for Facebook of the moment and now, reading the feedback and comments, I realise the extent of my meltdown over the tube sizes.

As so many messages remind me, 25 mm tubes are just as applicable to use as 28 mms . . . So I had absolutely no cause for concern. Now I do feel stupid, even more so than before. I had made a trying situation so much harder. I have never been known for being good – or even sound – with bike technology and mechanics, and now I have exposed my weakness in that domain to all and sundry on Facebook. Dumb . . .

◉

My thoughts are broken by the sound of knocking on the door. It's Tracking Jack. He's just arrived, and has heard I had booked a room. He peers behind me and sees that there are two beds.

My heart sinks. Not that Tracking Jack has done anything wrong – it's just that I really need to be alone. Jack would pay for a share of the room, as we've been doing in various permutations throughout the IndiPac, but in my current state of mind I can't think of a rational answer to dissuade his interest in rooming with me, other than to clumsily say, 'Umm . . . I'm doing something right now.'

Tracking Jack senses my reticence. 'I can see you need some time alone,' he says. 'I'll tell you what . . . I'll go and eat dinner, you do what you have to do and we can discuss it later.' I'm surprised he still wants to share a room with me in light of my badly phrased welcome. But I agree, understanding that the costs of staying in roadhouses are high and sharing rooms with more than one bed is only fair. He'd do the same for me.

Now I feel guilty. Many a time I have been told by Libby that I have a stare that sends a message of being pissed off, a look that doesn't need words – and sometimes when I don't mean it. That said, despite being generally easygoing, my moods can change quickly, and I suspect I have just given Tracking Jack the look. It's not his fault, just the timing. He arrived just as I was feeling utterly broken and enjoying the respite of solitude and I reacted in a completely unmediated way. All I knew is that I just needed some time alone. Right now I opt to simply deal with the present and take a well deserved shower.

◉

Tracking Jack's arrival also serves to trigger the routine of must-dos at the end of each day. I carry them out then put on my shorts and the undershirt I haven't ridden in today, and meet up with Tracking Jack in the dining room where he is eating. He looks up as I reach his table. I hand him the room key, saying, 'It's all yours.'

I order my usual IndiPac meal – a hamburger with the lot and a large serving of chips. After a while some other riders return to share some chat, eat, rehydrate and openly re-think their approaches for the race ahead. I think of the race leaders. They must be counting mere minutes lost, while I don't dare put my mind to the hours I'm spending just trying to regroup mentally, let alone recover physically. They really are a superior genre of athlete.

By now, Kristof Allegaert is still leading and is already well into Victoria. But even he is showing some wear and tear. He had hoped to reach Kingston South East in South Australia at the 3,130 kilometre mark the night before. When he arrived at the Salt Creek Roadhouse 84 kilometres earlier and at night, however, he was feeling fatigued. With a sense of 'being on a film set surrounded by decorative pieces' he realised he was hallucinating, so he stopped and slept on the terrace of a restaurant for a few hours until daylight emerged. A few hours later, though, in the light of day, Kirstof said 'everything seemed much nicer than in the dark'.

On this eighth day of the race, while I struggled to the Nullarbor Roadhouse, Kristof rode 400 kilometres to Portland on Victoria's Great Ocean Road. But this wasn't without its challenges. He restarted without drinking and on an empty stomach, and faced a day of extreme heat. In his IndiPac diary, he recalls the hunger and thirst he felt when he arrived later in the morning at a large service station on the outskirts of Kingston: 'I rushed inside to buy everything in duplicate . . . and then ordered the same again. The lady at the sandwich bar looked at me as if I was a bit strange, but for me it was a question of restoring my energy reserves.'

Even while refuelled, Kristof still struggled with the wind. Before the road turned inland from Kingston, he took the opportunity to stop at the beach and take a swim in the ocean: 'I scrubbed all the dirt off my body. That chance was really too good to let it pass!'

After arriving in Portland at night, with a total of 3,423 kilometres ridden, Kristof lamented not being able to see the Blue Lake in Mount Gambier. But at least he was in the lead.

By the time Kristof reaches Portland, I am still at the Nullarbor Roadhouse, 1,738 kilometres back. But at least I'm lying down. I still feel the need to be alone so I take advantage of the last hours of light, get up and walk slowly across to the old roadhouse. As I walk around it I think of the days when travellers would stop here and I wonder what state they were in when they arrived. Before 1956 this was the Nullarbor Station, which covered 1.25 million acres. It was known for sheep, horse and cattle grazing, and dingoes and wombats.

In 1956, the station manager Elwyn – or 'Scobe' as he was nicknamed – opted to sell petrol. He hand pumped it from drums into gallon tins and sold it to locals. Soon a small shop was built, and Elwyn's wife Coral started cooking and selling homemade scones, cakes and meals. She wrote a book called *Our Life at Nullarbor* and the shop's popularity grew – to the extent that by 1976, when the Eyre Highway was finished, the current Nullarbor Roadhouse was built next to the old shop.

As the sun sets my spirit dips with it. I'm still wondering what I'm doing here. It worries me that I am feeling so down. I think of Libby and if I should call her, but I dismiss the idea. *This is a solo race*, I remind myself. I can't just expect to call home and have my problems sorted out. Most importantly, I don't want to worry Libby. It's not fair on her. I try to breathe deeply and take the time to absorb the beauty of the desert. Hopefully it will reinvigorate me, but it doesn't work. Dejected and with a brewing sense of defeat, I start aimlessly throwing small stones at the ground from the handful I have gathered. I don't even have it in me to chat to the new arrivals Chris Barker, AKA 'Caveman Chris', and Mick Eyb, who met up with each other at Southern Cross and have ridden together since.

Chris approaches me with a smile. I can see he wants to chat, but I just sit there, still throwing pebbles in front me, and can barely respond, despite his attempts to cheer me up. Perhaps I gave Chris the same look I gave Tracking Jack. I feel terrible for being so rude. It is not Chris's fault. Everyone is tired, and I soon realise it's time I got a grip on things.

After several more minutes alone, I return to the roadhouse shop to check if I should buy anything more while I'm still up and about. But fatigue and the need to lie down in bed quickly take over. I waddle back to my room, still not sure what time I'll resume riding.

Jack is already in bed with an eye mask on and ear plugs in. I tiptoe in but he senses I am there. I have no choice but to tell him I have to work on my bike, and assure him I will be as quick as possible. It's awkward. As easygoing as he is, I know he can hear me tinkering, and that puts pressure on me.

'Let me help,' Jack soon offers, peering out from behind his eye mask.

'I'm fine, Jack . . . I'm fine,' I say, tersely.

It's frustrating for all of us. We've all had a torrid day. Although we're virtually strangers, we've shared experiences with each other in ways we would never have done before, even with some of our nearest friends and family. Out here on the Nullarbor Plain, we're dealing with all levels of intimacy in a bid to show empathy for each other.

To his credit, Tracking Jack takes my response well. He puts his eye mask back on, replaces his ear plugs and lies back down.

I check my bike and make sure all my gear is in place. For the first time on the IndiPac, I don't think about when I will wake up, but of the sleep I'm about to fall into. For me this is no longer a race, but a journey. And just to finish it will require everything I have in me.

11

LET GO OF MY ANGER, TAKE A DEEP BREATH

Day 9: Nullarbor Roadhouse to Nundroo

Start: 1.25 pm   Finish: 8.15 pm

Riding time: 5 hours 39 minutes

Distance: 143.6 km   Metres climbed: 601 m

Average speed: 25.4 kmh   Temperature: 21–45 C

Serenity embraces the Nullarbor Roadhouse but the building orange glow to the east heralds imminent change. The day is poised to start with headwinds and temperatures are forecast to reach the mid-40s. I'm grateful for having had some sleep, and have even gone for a short walk to take in the stunning view towards where I will later ride.

As I start walking, a slight headwind picks up, but I have heard that after peaking the winds will switch to the north-west, offering a tail wind, which will be very welcome. After the punishment of yesterday's ride, I'm super keen to milk every assistance Mother Nature offers, and cycling with a tail wind is as good as it gets. While the headwinds will pick up before any shift in direction, I'm optimistic about my plan to ride 146 kilometres to Nundroo, sheep country which was settled by graziers in the 1860s. By the 1870s the grazing land was incorporated into the larger Yalata and Fowler's Bay sheep runs that extended hundreds of kilometres east–west. By the 1880s, however, land was opened up for more extensive farming, including wheat.

I'm in no rush to leave the Nullarbor Roadhouse. Sure, there is a chance I could make good headway early should the headwinds not peak till later in the day, but the temperature will soar soon, which will leave me cycling in peak heat for longer than I need to. Riding at the back end of the day allows me to ride as temperatures are dropping.

Today will throw up a refreshing change of terrain – rolling hills on either side of Yalata, 90 kilometres down the road. Yalata had a roadhouse but is now only the site of a police station and several houses. Hopefully it will offer IndiPac riders the opportunity to find shelter from the heat if they're stuck on the road. But with the relatively short distance I plan to ride, I prefer to cycle straight through to Nundroo, especially if the headwinds winds shift to cross and then tail, and I can pick up an assisting run. I just have to decide when it's best to go. Until then I'll be best served by resting, rehydrating and fuelling up, starting with breakfast. At least having a plan, I feel in control of affairs again.

I call Libby, and tell her about my woes of the day before, and my arrival at the roadhouse, broken.

'Oh, Lib . . . this has been so hard,' I say. 'I feel much better now, but jeez, yesterday I was wishing it would end. Why weren't you a good wife and stop me from doing this?'

The latter remark was said in jest, but with a touch of honesty, as Libby suspects.

'You were the one who wanted to do this,' Libby replies laughing. 'As if I was ever going to stop you.'

We leave the chat there, bar a few domestic details. Libby can tell I'm back in a positive mindset and feel in control, and is happy I've had a good rest overnight.

But of course I remember that I felt in control of affairs when the day began yesterday, and look where it ended up. Most of the day had gone well – until I got the puncture, I felt that I had managed everything pretty well, even though I was fatigued, which I would expect to be this far into the race. And the Great Australian Bight was beautiful to see. After that I'd felt the wear and tear, but with the frustration of the puncture, and the confusion over the tube sizes, suddenly all the pain and fatigue I'd managed to contain had flooded through my body and there was no turning back.

It's fascinating looking back on yesterday's turn of events, now I've had a good amount of rest and gained some perspective. This race is teaching me how to handle moments like those – for better or worse. I came on the IndiPac to be stripped bare physically and emotionally. And I have been.

◉

I am not alone in delaying my departure from the Nullarbor Roadhouse. Tracking Jack is still there at breakfast time, as are Humungous Hugh, the Cycling Maven, Mick Eyb and Caveman Chris, who I continue to feel guilty for having been a sook with the previous day. The longer I wait the more I will be locked into an afternoon departure. And waiting in itself brings its own frustrations, such as wanting to get going after a big breakfast.

Sitting in the shade and air conditioning it is easy to forget the building heat outside. But one step out the front door is a reminder. It is a veritable furnace. Gone is the orange glow and the soft breeze of early morning. Now firmly in place for the day are the bright glare of a fiercely burning sun and strengthening headwinds that are being showcased by the flattened line of Nullarbor Roadhouse flags pointing directly from east to west.

While I wait for a window of time to leave, I keep eating. My body is burning calories at an incredible rate, even when I'm not cycling, and I have to feed the machine, literally, as well as keep up the fluid intake, which is easy to forget to do, being inside.

Then, out of the blue, I can see on the tracker that Steve Watson, AKA the Cloudrider, the guy who found my phone, is on approach to the Nullarbor Roadhouse. Riding just ahead of him is Kerwyn Ballico, who has just retired as a Navy helicopter aircrewman. Any question about whether to wait longer or get going is answered. This will be a great moment to reclaim my phone and, more importantly, thank Steve.

While I wait, I set about preparing me and my bike for departure soon after. For my bike, the only extra task is to fill the 2-litre water bladder and strap it onto my handlebars with gaffer tape. The last thing I can afford to do is run dry of water out in the desert. So far the rainy weather has made hydration easier to address, but with today's predicted rise in heat I can't risk that, despite the relatively short distance I plan to ride. I fear I won't have enough with only the three 750-millilitre bottles I have been using.

Soon Kerwyn arrives and soon after him, Steve. I allow Steve time to recalibrate as he steps into the cooling environment of the roadhouse and enquire about what rooms are available. It's clear he's also had a torrid time on the run to the roadhouse.

Yesterday, we'd all swapped stories of woe. Tracking Jack told of his saddle sores. The Cycling Maven confided he was in such a fatigued state he had to draw on the inspiration of Facebook messages read out to him on the phone by his partner Hannah– some from cancer sufferers. 'It was amazing,' the Cycling Maven says. 'They were from people who had been ill, saying they were inspired. I couldn't believe it. And it kept me going, and able to reach the roadhouse.'

Humungous Hugh was not only suffering from the heat, but also the building pain from an injured knee. We had all been stretched to our limits.

I can see that Steve needs some space before I introduce myself and ask how he found my phone. As does Kerwyn who, we learn, has slept out on the road overnight and is suffering from a serious wound to his arm after crashing 100 kilometres earlier. Kerwyn's injury is so bad that he intends to stop, but he continues on when he can't get a lift out and ends up patching up his arm and rides on later in the afternoon. He sleeps out on the road again that night before finally reaching Penong with 1,908 kilometres ridden, where he gets a lift to Port Lincoln hospital, and eventually gets home to Nowra on the New South Wales coast.

When I do approach Steve, he is pleasantly obliging. 'It's nice to meet you, Rupert. I have been chasing you for a week!' he quips with a laugh.

Steve explains how he got a Whatsapp message from his wife saying that I had lost my phone somewhere between 10 and 50 kilometres out from Norseman.

'When I got to the 50-kilometre mark, I thought, "I'll keep an eye out". It was pretty clear off to the side of the road and in a lot of grass and weeds. I was thinking, "If you're cranking along at a decent speed as I was that particular morning, this phone could have cartwheeled 5 or 10 metres off the road and I would never have seen it."'

I had thought the same thing when I went back to look for it that afteroon. Steve's better eyesight, or maybe the sharper morning light, or both, had produced a better result.

'It was there, off the side of the road and looking slightly worse for wear,' Steve says. Then he reaches into his rear pocket and hands it over. 'It's an extra 250 grams I have been carting around.'

It's in a plastic seal-strip bag, shattered beyond repair. Hopefully the data on the SIM card can be retrieved when I get home. Steve, I learn, has some experience in these matters. He has twice ridden in the Tour Divide race in the USA, and in the inaugural Race to the Rock from Adelaide to Uluru, and on each occasion had his own mobile phone disasters.

'This is a matter of some hilarity in my family,' Steve says, before explaining how he lost one phone in the first six hours of his first Tour Divide, another due to technical issues in the first two hours of his second start, and a third in the Race to the Rock due to wet weather damage in the first twenty-four hours.

When I ask how his IndiPac is going, Steve replies with a whimsical smile. 'Ah . . . slowly. I call us the seagulls at the back of the food hall.'

And how is the IndiPac compared to other races he's done?

'They're all hard,' he says. 'The long straight roads and the wind have been absolute killers. I'm really looking forward to getting into some scenic country, some hills and regular food stops where you can replenish your supplies. Strategically it's been tough getting across here. And it's difficult to knock up 250 to 300 kilometres a day given the wind, and we've had several atrocious days with the rains as well. It's been very tough.'

I ask Steve about his plan for now.

'I'm thinking I will grab a cabin . . . It's predicted it will be 44 degrees here today. I can't ride in the heat and I need to get to Ceduna hospital, to casualty.'

Steve reveals he has a pretty savage cyst in his groin that is giving him grief in the saddle. His agony reminds me how fortunate I am to have not yet suffered the same. He suspects it will need to be lanced, cut out, or at least surgically cleaned and treated with antibiotics. I tell him the nurses there have already been alerted to the possibility of more saddle sore sufferers.

I thank Steve again for his help.

'I hope I'm in front of you at the finish,' he replies with a wry grin. 'That's the main thing, Rupert.'

◉

The Nullarbor Roadhouse is busy now. There's hesitant IndiPac riders trying to decide when to ride, those like Steve Watson and Kerwyn Ballico who have just arrived, and the usual mix of truck drivers and holidaying families with their caravans. There are also two police officers from South Australian Police (SAPOL); one of them is Caucasian, and the other Aboriginal. Tracking Jack is soon chatting away with them.

But as their chat goes on, curiosity gets the better of me. I find myself drawn towards them, thinking perhaps they are providing Tracking Jack with some valuable advice. Heaven knows, advice from local police will help me, too. While the officers are completely friendly and helpful, I suspect they have more pertinent matters to attend to when they start to go back outside to their truck. Just as they're leaving the senior of the two officers says we can stop at his house in Yalata to refill our water bottles. If he's not there, we can use the hose that he'll leave by the side of the front porch. On a scorcher like today, I classify that service as falling within the category of 'trail angel'.

My urge to get going is mounting. I can tell the Cycling Maven is feeling the same way. And Tracking Jack too, I suspect, is getting itchy feet. Humungous Hugh is a little wary. And for good reason. It's now 45 degrees Celsius outside.

However, my thinking is that the heat will only last for so long, and every drop in degree as the afternoon extends will provide some relief. By leaving sooner I'll be further down the road to capitalise on the winds when they turn to tail and within reach of Nundroo before dark. Waiting much longer will now compromise those chances. I also know that despite the forecast and every positive indicator, fate can so easily and cruelly turn on me. But I can't second guess everything and have to set out sometime.

I'm confident I'm well hydrated, having drunk copious amounts of water since I woke up. I keep going to the toilet for a pee every 10 minutes, and my urine is crystal clear. And now I know that I have access to additional drinking water to what I am carrying from a hose in Yalata. And while I know it will be uncomfortable, I know I can handle the heat, having done so often in Ironman triathlons, including the Hawaii Ironman and its scorching lava fields.

At 1 pm it's time to go. Little is said. One by one, we each set off, at our own pace. The heat is as searing as I imagined it would be, but I soon put it out of my mind and slip into a rhythm and feel relatively comfortable. The landscape is changing; there are more trees and their shade by the side of the road is handy for some relief – either by riding under larger trees when possible, or standing in it when I decide to stop for a pee or a stretch. After so much desert the change provides some welcome mental stimulation.

The scorching conditions are far, far better for me than the hell of the day before. Even the hills offer solace. They require a change in gear and a pedalling position out of the saddle, which takes the weight off my sore backside. Finally, as Yalata nears, the shift in the wind arrives, first from head to cross and then at last to an assisting tail.

Arriving at Yalata at 5 pm, I'm alone.I have no idea where the others are; I assume they're not far behind. I'm feeling happier, stronger and more confident than I have since leaving Fremantle nine days earlier. I focus on finding the policeman's house, his hose and hopefully him, to say thanks and if possible have a chat about his job and his life.

◉

At first sight there's not much to Yalata. A road best suited for four-wheel drives leads to remote coastal camping sites and one of the most select fishing spots in the Great Australian Bight. The roadhouse is no longer operational. It ceased trading in February 2006 due to safety concerns. The building still stands, despite calls for its demolition and fears about exposure from asbestos, and it's been subjected to break-ins and vandalism. Seeing it tells of better times as an Aboriginal-owned enterprise providing employment and self-esteem in the community.

I stop to stretch but an attack of march flies forces me to move towards the handful of residential houses. I assume one of them is where the policeman lives. No sooner do I find the house and the hose, the front door opens and out steps the policeman. Brevet Seargent John Carroll introduces himself and offers a can of cold Coke from his fridge inside. I'm so tempted to accept, but politely decline, explaining the race rules, knowing he'll likely offer the same to the others when they come. I accept a glass of cold tap water instead of hose water and drink it outside on his porch. I know I'm in a grey area of the IndiPac laws . . . A decision that seems so simple – whether to take a glass of tap water or hose water – is actually a difficult one to make. Logic says, take the tap water – it's colder, fresher and chances are it is cleaner; but then is that deemed as outside help? Who is to say that this same offer has been made to anyone else before me, or will be after? As I wrestle with the conundrum, John introduces me to his wife Kate.

John is happy to chat. He's originally from Mount Gambier, on the IndiPac route, and a few months into a two-year stint at Yalata. In the oppressive heat that only seems worse now that I don't have the wind cooling me down, and through a constant barrage of attacks by march flies, I ask John what his duties are. He tells me his brief extends to Penong, 120 kilometres to the east, and to the Western Australia border 300 kilometres west, and to 450 kilometres north.

The Yalata Lands are occupied by the Anangu people, many of whom come from the spinifex country far to the north near Ooldea and close to where the Indian Pacific Railway runs. The Anangu were forced off their land in the early 1950s, when the Australian government used their land for the Woomera Rocket testing range and the British government for atomic testing.

The Anangu people of Yalata maintain strong ties to their traditional lands and for John working closely with the Indigenous community is vital. 'Our main focus is policing the community, keeping the people safe, making sure the alcohol doesn't come in,' he says. 'Doing our best to prevent domestic violence, and any acts of violence, and generally getting to know the community. It's quite a pleasant place to live and it's a nice community, but like any other it has its problems.'

John adds that alcohol 'is the main root' of many problems. His role is about social responsibility as much as law enforcement. He says, 'In an isolated area like this and in a small community, the main focus is getting the community on side . . . for the community to understand our role, and what we're trying to do.'

The thought of how John lives out here with the march flies comes to mind. They are everywhere, swooping in from every direction as we stand on the outside deck of his house. I am constantly swiping at them, unleashing cries as they land and bite. In one attempt to hit one, I even strike John by mistake – and then wonder if that's classified as assaulting an officer.

He reassures me with a laugh that it isn't, then swipes at one himself.

As for the IndiPac, John is impressed but has one major concern, having had a near-miss with an IndiPac rider.

'I have been really impressed with the endeavour, the commitment, the fitness, the mental strength of you guys,' he says. 'One problem I had was in the early hours of the morning, when I was driving to the east – the direction you guys are travelling in. It's not a problem in the afternoon, but in the morning, when the sun is low in the sky, it's very difficult to see any riders in front.'

John's near miss could have ended tragically. When he saw a truck on the other side of the road coming towards him, his focus was on the truck. He only noticed a cyclist ahead of him on the left at the last minute. 'It was a close call. The rider didn't come into view until they were about 20 metres in front of me,' he says. 'I made the effort to turn around and go back, firstly to apologise – not that I was at fault – but to make them aware that in those early hours, it's really difficult for drivers to see riders.'

This isn't a hazard I'll be facing now. It is 5.30 pm and my focus is on reaching the Nundroo Roadhouse before dark. John is confident I will make it, but as he speaks the Cycling Maven arrives. And several minutes later Humungous Hugh rolls in.

John's hospitality continues. Even though he said he and Kate were due to see friends soon, we chat for another 30 minutes. The sun is still out, and the winds have turned fully tail, although for how long? Once we bid John and Kate farewell, I slip back into the pace I was in before Yalata.

It's a good thing too. Before long, the winds shift again, back to cross and then cross head from the right with gusts that require me to lean into them. The heat is still intense, and I feel that I'm burning inside and out. In the desert, when the sun starts to set, it sets fast, and I find myself racing against imminent night. I just keep my pace on. *The sooner I arrive, the sooner I will get to book a room and rest*, I tell myself. As I churn the pedals I'm thinking of a shower, that simple but fabulous sensation of water cleansing the sweat, salt, grime and dirt of the day from my body. That shower is the trophy I am racing for today. It's all I want.

◉

I lose the race against sunset, but when I arrive at the Nundroo Roadhouse at 8.15 pm in the dark I can't be happier. I'm even grinning when I say hello to the young English woman serving at the counter. I ask if I can just sit down and think about what I need before ordering. 'You have fifteen minutes,' she replies. 'We close at 8.30.' Then she tells me there's no hot food, only what's on the shelves, and if I want a room, I'll need to book now.

Whoa, I think to myself. *Too many decisions needed at once.*

'There's several more riders on their way,' I say. 'Can you allow a bit more time for them?' Then I tell her that I definitely want a room, and am almost certain the others will also want beds. She is firm, though – she will close at 8.30, no matter what.

I try to do the maths. I can't count clearly how many riders are coming, so I just offer to book and pay for two rooms. Then I grab whatever food I can and times every item by three, in case the others arrive too late – much as the Cycling Maven did on the night finish at Mundrabilla. Three sandwiches, three muffins, three Kit Kats, three Cokes, three waters. And I see beer in the fridge! I grab three. No, four. I know I will drink two easily.

The woman behind the counter is mortified to see so much food in front of her so quickly. 'Can I see your ID or driver's licence?' she asks, adding that it's necessary to buy the beer. I am surprised. I even think she's joking. Why does a balding fifty-five-year-old need to prove their age? But I learn that we are in a dry zone where take-away alcohol can only be sold when there is identification to prove that you are not a local from the area, or that's my understanding. As I plan to take the beers to the rooms, they are seen as 'take away' beers.

'I don't drive, but I have my media pass with my photo on it,' I let her know. She leaves to check with her boss, who is wining and dining in the adjoining restaurant, but returns to say no. I'm astounded, then crestfallen. How sensational that first swig of beer would have been.

Then the Cycling Maven, Humungous Hugh and Tracking Jack arrive. I realise I've only bought supplies for three of us, not four; I feel terrible. They're too late to purchase anything. And it's too late for goodwill.

'It's been a long day,' implores the Cycling Maven.

'It's been a long day here,' the woman replies abruptly.

We just look at each other, bewildered.

I tell the Maven that two rooms are booked and paid for, and that the food in the cartons on the counter is for us. Few words are exchanged. We're all exhausted. I give the Maven the key to the room he'll share with Tracking Jack. Humungous Hugh and I take the other.

The bathroom light in our room doesn't work, so the bedroom door has to be left open while I shower. It doesn't matter. Feeling hot water fall on top of my head and all over is more than satisfying. Hugh, who took his shower first, is devouring some of the food I bought. I soon join him.

Then it's time to telephone Libby. The regular connection not only reassures her that my day is done, but gives me a sense of balance to what many might deem a crazy adventure. But there's no wireless connection and I'm too tired to get dressed into shorts, so in a cycling under-vest and with a towel wrapped around me I walk outside. The only access I get is at the road-house entrance and restaurant where, unbelievably, the owner is still wining and dining, and has now been joined by the shop attendant.

I sit on a block of rock and call home. As the dial tone sounds, I let go of my anger, take a deep breath and look into the star-lit sky above me. I imagine how good it would be to have a satellite photo from up there, a photo of me in a white towel and under-vest, sitting in front of the tacky neon-lights of a roadhouse in the middle of Australia. I have to laugh.

12

WE CROSSED THE BLOODY NULLARBOR

Day 10: Nundroo to Minnipa

Start: 5.14 am   Finish: 9.30 pm

Riding time: 13 hours 13 minutes

Distance: 325.9 km   Metres climbed: 1,251 m

Average speed: 24.1 kmh   Temperature: 13–31 C

It's 5 am, I'm really happy to see the back of the Nundroo Roadhouse. It's not the friendliest or most welcoming of places I have stopped in. The room was not comfortable and for breakfast I had to make do with what little I had left from my on-road stocks and the junk food I'd bought the night before.

But today marks the end of my journey across the Nullarbor Plain, which started at Norseman 1,048 kilometres back and will end at Ceduna 150 kilometres away, and for that I'm in a buoyant spirit. I quickly find my rhythm. The stiffness in my limbs abates. I don't force the early pace, just let the legs roll and wait for the body to warm. It won't be long before dawn presents its customary show. I have every reason to feel optimistic about the day ahead.

As daylight emerges, the land is no longer red desert dotted with spinifex and knee high shrubs. There are more trees and farming land divided into pastures. As simple as the sight is, it warms my soul. I have now ridden a large chunk of the 5,470 kilometres of this IndiPac – 1,829 kilometres, to be exact – and dare to imagine good times ahead.

◉

After almost three hours and 80 kilometres of steady riding, I stop in the calm to gather my thoughts. I'm on the outskirts of Penong where I plan to enjoy a much-needed meal. I'm longing for scrambled eggs, bacon, sausages, toast, fruit juice, coffee and chocolate milk.

The golden silence is broken by the chirping of a bird, then the rumbling swoosh of a road train passing by. Now comes the soft humming of bike wheels, powered by the Cycling Maven who steadily rides by me.

I'm pretty happy to have almost all of the Nullarbor behind me. It was a hard crossing, with more than a couple of 'what am I doing?' moments. But I think everybody has had those. Doubts like that were always going to be part of the package. It was interesting to see how I responded to those moments too.

They were not my finest times, but you take what life throws at you. I knew it would not be easy, but I am still excited about being part of this very first IndiPac. I decide that as I get further to Ceduna and then head towards Adelaide, I'll try to savour the local regions and people much more. At long last, I feel that I have returned to civilisation.

On the Nullarbor, each day was a leap of faith as well as a huge effort to make sure I reached water and food. The cocktail of emotions, mental fatigue and confusion almost did my head in, but I know there are many more challenges ahead. I think of the mountain passes I will need to cycle, through the Victorian Alps and Kosciuszko National Park. But right now, I'm really proud of myself, although reluctant to admit to it too much, fearing that it will make me cocky and lead me into a new crisis. But it wasn't so long ago that I'd never even imagined cycling across Western Australia and the entirety of the Nullarbor. Whatever happens now, I am pretty rapt for having achieved that.

◉

My plan at the moment is to stop at Penong for another breakfast, then cycle to Ceduna to notch up my first 150 kilometres of the day, then ride the 93 kilometres to Wirulla. I'll still allow for re-evaluation as I go, pending my mindset, physical state and the weather conditions.

Riding into Penong is heartening. Finally, a town that seems to have a real sense of community, rather than the transient atmosphere of a desert roadhouse. The town is on the western edge of South Australia's grain growing belt and surrounded by silos and windmills that pump water from the Anjutabie Basin. It's a small place, but still the most pleasant of sights. The area also produces 100,000 tonnes of salt annually, harvested from brine pools, and its gypsum deposits are the largest in the Southern Hemisphere, covering 87 square kilometres to an average depth of 4.8 metres. And 21 kilometres south is Cactus Beach, regarded as a world class surfing location.

I roll into town, ravenously hungry, but cycle straight past the service station. I've stopped at enough of those. The Penong General Store and Post Office is where I want to go. I slow to a halt and lean my bike against a nearby tree. Entering the shop, I see the Cycling Maven, who passed me while I was recording a live video, who is already looking at the breakfast menu. I just say 'Make it two' to whatever he opts for: the eggs, bacon, sausages, baked beans and toast I had longed for when I left Nundroo.

Soon we have more company: Humungous Hugh, Tracking Jack, and one of the Dutch riders, Eelco Wijmans, who bivvied overnight. After days of seeing the same faces, Eelco triggers fresh conversation. He's a friendly guy with a beaming smile and is enjoying himself, riding the IndiPac at his own pace, knowing that among the race leaders are two other Dutchmen, Matthijs Ligt and Jan-Willem Bobbink.

health inspector steps out from his shelter to politely ask if I am carrying any fruit, vegetables, or other plants or plant products; illegal luggage across the border into South Australia.

'It's been a while since I've had anything as good and tasty as that,' I reply, laughing. The inspector laughs, too, having seen a number of IndiPac riders pass through before me.

'On ya, mate . . . well done,' he says, smiling and waving me on. 'Enjoy the rest of your ride.'

I have officially crossed the Nullarbor, I say to myself, clenching a fist in private celebration. There's still such a long way to go, but I have learned to count my wins as much as I must handle my losses in this race. And crossing the Nullarbor is a pretty big win.

It's not long before I'm steering right off the highway and into the car park of the BP 'On the Run' Station for lunch and a well deserved break. It doesn't even cross my mind to ride past the Ceduna Golf Course on the left and into town to find a quiet place to eat with a picturesque view over the ocean. It's just habit now: reach a town, and find the first open servo with food, toilets and an ATM. But this servo is different to the stops I've had along the way. It's bigger for a start but more importantly the food options are aplenty. I've seen photos on Facebook of Kristof Allegaert and Mike Hall stopping here to replenish and recuperate. Kristof, still leading, rode into Ceduna late at night on day four. He'd tallied 480 kilometres for the day and stopped over for a sleep.

The BP Station is a veritable oasis of IndiPac needs and desires. Being able to go to the toilet in an air-conditioned, clean environment feels great. But while I'm standing over the toilet the yellow clip-on fluorescent arm band on my right arm suddenly flips off and falls into the bowl. Which would have been fine if I hadn't just peed into it. I don't want to lose the arm band – but I also don't like the prospect of reaching in to pull it out. Ugh. This simple little arm band could save my life. With my rear light issues, I've tried to increase my visibility by putting any reflective item I had on me and my bike.

There's nothing else for it. I plunge my hand into the toilet bowl, but to my horror the sudden movement causes a surge that sucks the band further into the S-bend. I grit my teeth and just push my hand in further, trying not to think about what may be lurking there. As soon as I feel the band, I grab it and pull it out. I feel triumphant – and safer. And now I need to wash my hands – straight away – and very, very well.

Back in the dining area, there's no sign of any of the other riders who I've passed since leaving Penong. Maybe they've ridden past into town. I order my food and sit down to reflect on how day eleven has gone so far, and take time to phone Libby. It is great to chat with her with me in such a positive spirit for a change, rather than attempting to pass the buck and asking her, 'Why did you let me do this?' I feel terrible about that.

Then the Cycling Maven arrives. I really have taken some time on him, but it's good to see him and I want to chat, even if it means I'll lose more time. I also still have to buy a new rear light.

'Mate,' he says, elated. 'It's behind us . . . No more Nullarbor. How good is that?'

'Too good to measure,' I respond. 'Think about it though . . . We crossed the bloody Nullarbor . . . On bikes!'

The Maven takes his gloves off, still smiling: 'Fantastic, mate.' Then he adds that it's something that I should be really proud of, especially after the struggles we endured on the desert. 'Rupe . . . this is a really good moment. To think we were on the brink a couple of days ago,' he says. 'It shows what we can do if we really want to. Just to finish this will be an amazing thing to do, you know; but if I do, I'll be so happy.'

The Cycling Maven's words help clear my mind – I have settled into survival mode, but can now acknowledge that if I were *really* racing, I wouldn't have spent this long in the servo at all. Allegaert, Hall, Hammond – they don't stop like this. I have heard stories firsthand about them rushing into shops with a food buying and eating plan already in place – by the time they get to the front of the queue to pay, they have already started consuming their chosen items.

Eventually I get going. And as expected, the Cycling Maven gains time on me. A few hundred metres beyond the service station, he turns left out of town on the road to Wirulla, while I ride into the centre of town to look for the sports store that I have found online to buy a new rear red light. The shop is easy to find, and I buy two lights to make sure I'm covered. I've ridden 2,000 kilometres by now, a huge feat for me, but there are still almost 2,500 kilometres to go.

◉

Riding towards the exit to the highway, I spy Humungous Hugh out of the corner of my eye. I don't stop – he's probably just arrived and no doubt wants to eat quietly by the seaside, which is only a few hundred metres away. Seeing the beach and the water on my way into town to buy my new lights is so tempting and it makes me think how good it would be to stop here for the day and enjoy the glorious sunshine. But I want to make the best of the conditions and my positive frame of mind so I ignore the thought.

On the way out of town, I laugh out loud when I see the airport – I imagine stopping there, and booking a flight to Adelaide and then Sydney. I could be back at home with a glass of wine in my hand by tonight. But Wirulla, a small grain belt town and an access point to the Gawler Ranges in the north, is my next stop, and miraculously, the next 93 kilometres fly by. I even pass the Cycling Maven.

But all the luck of this day dissipates as I arrive in town. When I turn left off the tree-lined Eyre Highway and roll slowly over the rail tracks I feel the telltale sensation of my rear tyre softening ever so slightly. Surely not. I try to think positively and continue rolling slowly into town. At the moment it's only a slow leak but I'm not sure how far it will get me before I need to change it again.

Wirulla is as quiet and empty as any outback town can be. I don't see anyone about. The Wirulla Hotel, where the Cycling Maven and I had discussed staying tonight, doesn't appear to be open, and the camping ground across the road is dead. I turn my bike and roll back out of town over the rail tracks, stopping by the corner of the highway to consider my options.

It's late afternoon. There is still plenty of light. The tailwind is still blowing. The countryside is so beautiful in the golden light. The thought of taking a room and getting a nice cold beer is quickly getting the better of me. And now I suddenly feel the fatigue of the 244 kilometres I've just covered.

Then I see the Cycling Maven. Trademark smile. Trademark enthusiasm. Trademark inquisitiveness.

'What's doing?' he asks.

We roll into town – a third time for me over those rail tracks. The Maven finds the general store, which I had missed. The owner is about to close up the kitchen, but with the friendliness we could have done with at the Nundroo Roadhouse, she says she can make us something, maybe a hamburger. We order two of her very best.

One of the biggest frustrations on the IndiPac is wasting time by stopping. But if you do stop, it should be for something beneficial, like eating and resting. After devouring our burgers, the Cycling Maven is keen to keep riding. So am I, tentatively – the accommodation options at Wirulla seem limited, but looking at my map, the next town, Poochera, is 46 kilometres away, which would make it a 290-kilometre day for me. I'm not sure I have it in me – nor am I confident that I'll reach there without tyre issues – but I decide to try, despite having heard that Poochera doesn't have a roadhouse or motel. (I later discover that is not correct.) But I figure that if I do get to Poochera, I'll be so cooked from a hard day's riding that bivvying won't be a problem – I'll sleep easily anywhere I lie down. I might as well try despite my concerns about the rear tyre.

Standing outside the shop in Wirulla, I notice that my cycling jersey and shorts are covered in stripes of white salt marks from all the sweat that's come off me today. It reminds me that over the next kilometres, I need to hydrate with plenty of water and refuel on electrolytes. The late afternoon sky is cloudless now, and it's cooler than yesterday at 28 degrees Celsius, but the sunshine has been burning with the strong winds. And now there's something else to think about – the Maven has his eye on riding a bit further on to Minnipa, an additional 34 kilometres away. He's reserved a room there and is now intent on pushing on for a guaranteed bed, shower and hot meal.

'You're more than welcome to share the room if you like,' he says.

It's a tantalising offer, though it's been such a long day already. But the thought of good accommodation, a meal, the reward of gaining some unexpected kilometres and knowing I will feel better for it once I arrive will be worth the extra effort of going all the way to Minnipa, even if it means riding into the night.

'Oh, mate . . . it'll be hard; but I'm up for it,' I reply.

◉

It's almost dark when I reach Poochera. The Cycling Maven is ahead. His rear light barely slows as he passes through the town which confirms his intent to ride on as well as his assumption that I have not changed my mind. I am nearing 300 kilometres for the day already. It astounds me that my pre-race aim was to average this distance every day, but they've been a rarity. And I feel such utmost respect for the race leaders, who are riding 400-plus kilometres every day and are now well into Victoria. Kristof Allegaert is still leading, and is now on the Great Ocean Road, hoping to reach Geelong by the end of his day.

Kristof says later in his IndiPac diary that he loved seeing the Twelve Apostles, but lamented not being able to see much of the picturesque stretch of road because he was riding in the dark. 'In any case, I now have a good reason to come back to

Australia.' In the end, he was battling strong winds and finished for the day in Torgeelo, and would hit Geelong for breakfast the next morning.

◉

My attention remains on my ride, in particular my rear tyre. It's still leaking ever so slowly beneath me and I wonder if the rail crossing in Wirulla caused it, or if there's still something else that is wrong. Either way, I know the tube is going to go down with the sun.

Over the last 50 kilometres, I stop to hand pump the tube numerous times, and each time, frustration builds. I want to get to Minnipa as fast as possible, but no sooner do I pump the tyre I feel it deflating again. I don't want to try to repair it out here in the wildnerness and the darkness, so as the evening chill kicks in, I persevere.

Then a sharp stabbing pain in my left knee strikes. I try putting more weight on my right foot and leg while pedalling, but when I ride out of the saddle to provide some temporary relief and to stretch my back, both legs have to take the weight and the pain returns.

The Cycling Maven slows down. I bemoan my lot. The tyre issue in particular is embarrassing. And I don't want the Cycling Maven to lose time. There is no real solution in the total darkness that has now enveloped us, except for him to ride on and for me to make what distance I can between re-pumps. Still, he continues to slow down and speed up again, allowing me to keep him in sight, which I really appreciate. But I do wonder how annoying it must be for him. He could just hightail it to Minnipa.

●

At 9 pm, the lights of Minnipa finally come into view. They are beautiful, not so much for their aesthetics, but because they represent the welcome end of a day that began at four this morning. My thirteen and half hours of riding have gone well for the most part, but my day is ending with a sting in the tail, which I'm now seeing typical of the IndiPac. The Cycling Maven is waiting at the turn-off from the Eyre Highway – I'd forgotten to ask him for the name of the motel and thankfully, he's realised that. We ride across railways tracks – part of the same line that I rode over in Wirulla – to where we will finally stay. It was the laying of the rail line in 1913 that turned Minnipa from two-tent town in 1878 into the township it is now.

When we arrive, the town is eerily quiet, but the Minnipa Hotel Motel is easy to see and its smiling proprietor reassures us he can still cook us dinner. By 9.30 pm, we are showered, in dry clothes and at the hotel bar. I order a beer.

'You won't need an ID for that, either,' the Cycling Maven quips with a grin.

I am happy, so happy. And to boot, we got 326 kilometres done. The beer goes down well as does a second beer with some fish, vegetables and chips.

I still need to resolve my tyre problem. I want to have a really good look inside at the tube and wheel rim. There's no bike shop in Minnipa, but there is one in Port Augusta, which is still some 270 to 300 kilometres away, not such a great solution right now. I'll have to fix the problem before I go to sleep or in the morning before I leave.

I am tempted to sleep first, especially if the Cycling Maven is keen to bunk down immediately. It is his room after all, and the last thing he'll want is trying to sleep in bright light and with the noise of me tinkering with my bike. But he encourages me to do it now, saying I'll sleep much better knowing it is fixed, rather than waking up to a problem. In the meantime he phones his partner Hannah back in Melbourne.

So for the next little while, our room is a hive of activity. As the Cycling Maven chats with Hannah, he turns the phone on loud speaker.

'Rupe is here,' he says, and beckons me with a wave of his hand to join their chat. I can tell the thrust of Hannah's conversation has been about urging the Cycling Maven to push harder and ride more kilometres.

Wow, Hannah is cracking the whip, I say to myself, amused. And once she's on loudspeaker, there is no doubt whatsoever about her feelings – and not just about the Maven's ride, mine as well!

'Hey guys, just rip the bloody bandages off and get going,' Hannah says. What she means is that the sooner we get riding again the sooner our suffering will be over.

'Hey,' I say, laughing, knowing Hannah can hear. 'We just rode 326 kilometres. Anyway, I'll look after my own motivation, thank you very much!'

I shake my head, smiling. And of course from Hannah's perspective, the sooner the ante is upped, the sooner the Maven has finished the IndiPac and is home safe – which is exactly how I suspect Libby feels about me.

As the Maven finishes his call off speaker, I concentrate on my tyre, searching for the slightest skerrick of something – anything, like the tip of a thorn to a sliver of glass or metal, or a sharp stone – that could have slipped inside and be piercing the tube. I inspect it all over, inside and out, wiping it clean, bending it every which way to make sure there's nothing there. Then I check the rim with as much forensic focus, and finally inflate the tube to look for any obvious holes, even testing it by putting it in a basin of water and watching for the tell-tale bubbles that will emerge if there's the slightest of ruptures.

I see a bubble, then correlate it with where it was sitting inside the tyre and on the rim and clean the area again. Then I put the tyre back on the rim, insert a new tube, inflate it fully and place the wheel back into place on the bike. Then I repair the punctured tube and hang it near my assortment of recharging batteries to dry.

It's almost 11 pm, and I'm exhausted. There's nothing more I can do but hope that in the morning the pressure in my rear tyre is still as firm as it is now. Meanwhile, we see that, some 2,000 kilometres ahead, Kristof Allegaert is resting 'somewhere in the woods' beyond Melbourne. His 400-kilometre day began in Torquay and since then he has battled the elements, from storm winds that limited his speed to 10 kilometres per hour to a heavy downpour of rain soon after he passed through Melbourne.

'Hannah would be impressed!' I tell the Cycling Maven, and we laugh before sleep takes over.

IT'S TIME FOR THE MAVEN TO FLY

Day 11: Minnipa to Kimba
Start: 5.38 am   Finish: 1.30 pm
Riding time: 7 hours 02 minutes
Distance: 140.7 km   Metres climbed: 754 m
Average speed: 20.0 kmh   Temperature: 7–28 C

As I ride away from Minnipa across the railway line and onto the Eyre Highway, the cold is biting right through to my bones. And this is despite my rugging up in my Rapha waterproof jacket, shoe covers – or 'booties' – and thick Sydney to Hobart Gill sailing gloves. I pull the bandana around my neck up over my mouth and nose, and breathe heavily into it to disperse a thick wave of warmth across my face. The distance to travel is the last thing on my mind as I cycle on in the blackness – I'm pedalling just to get some warmth flowing through me.

I'm well accustomed to these dark and chilly early mornings now – and it's true that the coldest part of a morning is just before the sun rises. The road appears to be continuously uphill, a good thing for now because it will require some extra effort and generate a sweat. But the most striking thing this morning is the fatigue I'm feeling. I just want to curl up and sleep forever. I haven't felt such sleepiness since leaving Border Village at midnight a few days ago.

I yawn, then a series of cavernous yawns follows. I don't understand why I'm so tired considering I've just enjoyed the luxury of a motel bed and had a good four hours' sleep. I initially attribute it to the sudden change of going from a cosy bed to the bitter cold outside – I may be awake, but my body isn't. I figure I'll be back in the groove as soon as my blood starts flowing steadily.

I tell the Cycling Maven of my fatigue as he passes me, then think that's probably not fair. I don't want to influence his state of mind. And yawning is contagious. But sunrise is coming and with it, the heat of the Australian outback. And miraculously, my rear tube and tyre appear to have no problems. The pressure feels as firm as it was when I left.

But I still can't get over the yearning to sleep. I start thinking about the next opportunity to stop and have a proper hot breakfast – maybe that will wake me up. In the meantime my wake-up feed of chocolate Kit Kats, an old muffin left over from yesterday, and yoghurt-covered muesli slices will have to suffice.

But the rate of calories I am burning up after ten days of near continuous cycling means that I must eat a substantial breakfast soon, something more nutritious than junk food.

◉

The best thing about reaching the top of a hill – apart from the end of the effort needed to get there – is the view. And just as dawn breaks, after about 35 kilometres of cycling, I reach the crest of the climb outside Wudinna, another wheat belt town. The view across the plain is simply breathtaking, and enhanced by the rising sun and the change in the sky from black to dark blue, and finally to light blue once the sun is fully up. For tourists, the real appeal is the nearby Gawler Ranges National Park, north of here and its hidden treasures like the Organ Pipes formation, the wave-like Pildappa Rock and the pristine white salt of Lake Gairdner. The Mount Wudinna Touring Route passes myriad granite outcrops like the Polda Rocks, Pygery Rocks, Little Mount Wudinna, Turtle Rock and Mount Wudinna itself, one of Australia's largest granite monoliths. But none of these are on my radar this morning.

The fresh dawn awakes other sensations. I can hear birds chirping, I can smell the remnants of bushfires on the breeze, and the feel of cool autumn air is an invigorating start to the day. I've found that the IndiPac experience is sharpening all my senses – all but one, that of taste. The more I eat, the less I can taste the difference between the foods I consume, whether it's a chocolate or a muesli bar, or a hamburger or bacon, sausage and eggs. Is it just because my body needs to treat it purely as fuel?

But just as enjoyable as the view is the descent into Wudinna where the Maven and I plan to stop for a hot breakfast. We roll into town side-by-side – not quite two gunslingers in a wild west movie, but confident and happy, though I'm still yawning.

The terrain is more rural now. There are more and taller trees by the roadside and the land is partitioned by fences and posts, the terrain purposefully kept. It's a clear marker that I'm progressing across the country. I still need convincing that the iconic Nullarbor Plain is behind me, for good. We look for somewhere to eat, but the town is yet to awake. We roll slowly to the other side where the roadhouse is open.

The Maven is feeling good – I am too, but there's an extra spring in his step. I know he's set on making Port Augusta, but I'm not sure where I will be by day's end. Yesterday was a really good ride, and while my legs feel all right I'm still really struggling to fend off the urge to sleep. One option for me is to stop 103 kilometres up the road at Kimba, which is 156 kilometres before Port Augusta. I remind myself that my overall goal is to make Sydney, not to push myself so hard every day that I run the risk of having nothing left at all. Well, that's my point of view. Obviously, for those riders at the front end it's a totally different story.

But I completely understand and respect the Cycling Maven's motivation. He can probably see his Melbourne mates, Ryan

'Rhino' Flinn and Nick Skarajew, reaching their home city well before he does and that is giving him an extra push. But I'm not chasing anyone. Now I'm riding the IndiPac to finish it, not race it, and I need to pace myself. Port Augusta would be good to get to, but if that's tomorrow, I'm fine with that.

But now my stomach is talking. It starts with a rumble, then a groan, that begs me to feed it, and quick! I'd also better order breakfast before the locals arrive to avoid finding myself in a queue. I don't do queues well anywhere. After placing our orders – yet again eggs, sausages, bacon and toast – we choose some hot items from the bain marie to appease the hunger and I scoff an egg and bacon roll, a vegetable pastie and a coffee, all of which barely touch the sides. When our food arrives, the Maven and I chat a little but appeasing the hunger takes precedence. I check on the race tracker to see how everyone is going. Humungous Hugh's dot has not moved from Ceduna. I learn that, sadly, he has left the race because of the increasing pain in his ankle. I also see a message from him to me, wishing me well. That he's taken the time to do that in the midst of his disappointment means a lot.

Getting back on the road, I'm surprised there's still a chill in the air. I am still wearing my Rapha jacket, rather than the lighter brevet, and my sailing gloves. But soon the sun finally rises high enough to bring some welcome warmth. I soon feel the first thin trickles of sweat down my brow, and then under my clothes, down my chest and back. I'm thinking about stripping down a layer when I notice the Cycling Maven has stopped by the side of the road. He is suffering from a saddle sore, not quite of the size and severity of Tracking Jack's, but it's painful enough for him to take some drastic action.

'Mate, I really need some chamois cream. Have you got any?' he asks, no longer with his characteristic grin but a look of worry that reads urgency.

I dig it out and almost immediately the Maven has his shorts down by his knees and his hand is slip-slopping away to make sure all bases are covered. Hysteria rises in me and I feel like laughing despite his obvious misery – I can't help picture the reaction of road users being welcomed by the sight of his exposed bare arse. Thankfully the moment passes and I empathise with his pain, realising it could be my agony in the turn of a pedal stroke. I stand by to alert him of any traffic that may be about to pass us.

I worry about how serious the problem is, especially with his ambition to ride long into the day to Port Augusta. But the Maven soon settles back into a nice rhythm and is soon ahead of me, tapping away well. Meanwhile, I'm still desperate to sleep; I'm still yawning. Suddenly the 100 kilometres to Kimba seems a large hurdle in itself, let alone the extra 140 kilometres to Port Augusta. Maybe digesting such a big breakfast is sapping my energy, when I had hoped for the opposite. Not that there's anything I can do about it now. The food I have eaten will serve me somehow today. I just have to push on.

After a while, the Cycling Maven slows. He turns as I approach.

'What do you want to do today, Rupe?'

I know immediately what he means: do I want to ride to Port Augusta, or not?

'I'll let you know soon, mate. I am tossing up my options,' I reply.

I appreciate that if the Cycling Maven wants to head for Port Augusta he'll want to focus on that as soon as possible, possibly to catch Nick Skarajew, who left us in the early morning at Mundrabilla, and the Rhino who bade farewell before dusk at Balladonia.

The Cycling Maven taps away again. I let distance open between us – I need to think alone, as I suspect he does too.

◉

It's not until the approach to Kimba that I let the Maven know what my call is. There's no other reason for the delay than the argument going back and forth in my mind. A part of me wants to ride on – Port Augusta would mark 2,448 kilometres ridden in IndiPac – but I can also see the sense in stopping at Kimba, allowing the Cycling Maven to ride on to do his best at his own pace and rhythm. It's clear we're both at a juncture in terms of how we want to continue and it's best to follow our own instinct.

I feel absolute relief upon arriving at Kimba, another town with a 'big' thing – in this case a 7-metre tall 'big galah' by the highway marking halfway between the east and west coasts. The town's name is derived from the local Aboriginal word for 'bushfire', and its emblem reflects a burning bush. It also has the last roadhouse before the IndiPac route turns right at Port Augusta for Adelaide and offers the last chance to get a decent feed before then. Kimba also has a proud and fascinating AFL heritage, with an incredible line up of players: Robert Schaefer played 11 games for Richmond in 1993, Shane Wakelin notched up 94 games for St Kilda from 1994 to 2000 and 158 games for Collingwood from 2001 to 2008; Darryl Wakelin appeared in 115 games for St Kilda from 1995 to 2000 and 146 games for Port Adelaide from 2001 to 2007; and Corey Enright featured in 332 games for Geelong from 2001 to 2016 and was also a six-time All Australian over 2008 to 2016, and played in the Premiership winning games in 2007, 2009 and 2011. Astonishing for a small town.

More importantly for me just now, though, is that Kimba is where I will bid farewell to the Cycling Maven. Where we might cross paths again, I have no idea. In the Victorian Alps or the Kosciuszko National Park between Melbourne and Canberra? Maybe even in the hilly and picturesque Southern Highlands of New South Wales in the final run up to Sydney and the Opera House?

I see myself as like an old diesel train, and have always wanted to get to the mountains as fresh as possible. For that

I need a bit more rest than younger riders like the Maven, who is forty-five to my fifty-five. On the vlog that I post from the Kimba Roadhouse before we part ways, the Cycling Maven is in good humour: 'It's time for the Maven to fly.'

And he confirms his plan: 'I'm going to try to make Port Augusta before 11 pm and see what happens from there. If I'm feeling good I'll push on . . . If not, I'll rest up. But I want to hit it between here and Port Augusta. It's 150 kilometres and there are no stops between, so I've got to stock up on some food now – *really* stock up.'

And stock up he does. As well as toasted sandwiches to take with him, the Maven will eat a hot curry before he goes. Meanwhile, my focus is now on the rest ahead, to regenerate and boost my chances of reaching the mountains as well as possible.

On the subject of my rest, the Maven tells viewers of my vlog with a laugh: 'So Rupe will probably pass me in four days.' Then he adds, 'It's a tactical thing. I'm going out into the heat now, so I could blow up. It's not too hot, but it's hot enough to hurt. And Rupe is going to chill. We will see what the outcome is.'

Our parting of ways becomes real and we pat each other on the back. We've spent a lot of time together, despite there being days when I would ride off and arrive at a destination hours before he did, and days when the opposite happened. But we have still forged a bond. Now, as the Cycling Maven says, laughing, 'The story will be Rupe hunting me down.'

I laugh too as I picture the prospect: he is good carrot to chase. But there are a lot of kilometres I will have to make up after I rest in Kimba.

Finally we sit down to eat together. He, with his curry; me, with just a sandwich. Having booked a room here, I'll be back for a late lunch, and then dinner and, who knows, maybe a beer.

⊙

Seated with us is a young English rider who has just arrived. He tells us the astonishing story of how he nearly abandoned during the first days. But because the line was so bad when he called home to tell his mother, he hung up, planning to tell her another day. But here he is – on day eleven, in Kimba, eating food and preparing to ride on to Port Augusta this afternoon.

It's an amazing story and I can't help but be drawn into it. But my mind is occupied. I'm still thinking about the imminent parting of ways with the Maven. I have no doubts about my decision to staying at Kimba, but I realise it will be different riding, being fully alone. And while we chat over lunch, it is not wasted time. The Maven needs to get going as soon as he can to cover as many kilometres as possible before the sun sets and night falls.

And then just like that, with his hot curry sitting pleasantly in his guts and toasted sandwiches and extra drinks packed in his jersey pockets and on his bike, the Cycling Maven is pedalling away and I am waving him off. And yes . . . I do feel alone. I turn and slowly walk with my bike to my room in the Kimba Motel Caravan Park, just behind the roadhouse.

I bypass the late lunch for some snacks in my room. I wash all my dirty gear, and hang it out in the sun to dry. I clean my bike and enjoy an hour or two watching TV before returning to the roadhouse for dinner: not a curry, but a pizza and two beers.

I feel good, almost relaxed, regenerated in mind as much as anything else. A calm and sense of self-control takes over. It is almost a sense of liberty, or independence, a feeling that now my destiny is up to what I make of it alone, rather than what I and another may make of it. I suspect the Cycling Maven feels the same. I hope so, I really do, and that he is feeling good and strong for that.

◉

As night falls I check the race tracker to see what progress the Cycling Maven is making. I also see that Tracking Jack has ridden into and out of Kimba, and is now en route to Port Augusta too. I watch the Cycling Maven's dot moving, then I see it miss the turn-off to the right from the Eyre Highway. He follows the highway directly to Port Augusta rather than take the official race route exit off the highway to the right at Caroona Road on the approach to the port city. Judging by his speed, he's unaware of his mistake until it is too late. That is, until he stops on a bridge in the town centre. Then Tracking Jack makes the same mistake.

Lying on my bed, eating post dinner snacks, I'm intrigued to see what they both do, but assume they are apart as there is some distance between them on the race tracker. The Cycling Maven is aware of his error – I have just read his social media post – but I'm surprised by how long his dot remains stationary. Having spent so much time riding with him, it feels strange to be blind to the on-road dilemma he must be facing at this late hour of 11 pm. Suddenly his dot moves – back the way it came, to where he missed the turn-off some 30 kilometres earlier. He'll be fatigued and heaven knows what else.

And Tracking Jack? His dot moves forward, onwards through Port Augusta. I'm in no position to judge him, and only feel for his suffering if he's realised his error. That horrid saddle sore will no doubt need lots of care to avoid infection, too. He has done well.

The race rules stipulate that when riders miss a turn-off they should turn around and return to the correct location. But there are also grey areas, say if the route is compromised by road works or mother nature – and it's up to riders to make a call. I'm sure Tracking Jack will figure it out.

But as I turn the lights out, I feel excited at the prospect of checking where he and the Cycling Maven are when I wake up in a few hours' time; and how much of a lead they have on me.

But hang on. I thought I'd decided I wasn't racing . . . Or had I?

I just don't know. It's intriguing how the IndiPac plays on the mind . . .

14

THE STICKY DATE
PUDDING CRISIS

Day 12: Kimba to Wirrabara

Start: 5.38 am   Finish: 6 pm

Riding time: 10 hours 08 minutes

Distance: 248.4 km   Metres climbed: 1,389 m

Average speed: 22.2 kmh   Temperature: 1–35 C

When I open my eyes I can't help but think of the American movie *Groundhog Day*, where the Pittsburgh TV weatherman Phil Connors, played by Bill Murray, wakes up to find himself in a time loop, the same day repeating itself over and over. I recall last night's dot tracking drama –the Cycling Maven's and Tracking Jack's missed exits to Port Augusta. As expected, I can't resist: I check what they did; if they returned to the missed turn-off or continued on, preferring to deal with the ramifications of their mistake, whatever those may be.

The Cycling Maven, I see, has returned to the race route exit off the Eyre Highway that he missed. It's hard not to feel for him. In a way I know what he must be thinking. I recall losing my phone on day three as I neared Norseman, then turning and riding nearly 15 kilometres back to where I thought it might be. It's as frustrating as hell to retrace kilometres already ridden. At the same time I think mischievously of the prospect of possibly catching him further down the road on the way to Sydney. 'Well, that's less of the gain he has on me.'

Tracking Jack has ridden on. Later, he explains to me that after missing the turn-off he believed he would be riding further than the official route, so he thought it was okay to continue, which makes absolute sense to me.

◉

It's 5.30 am when I leave the Kimba Roadhouse after my customary wake-up breakfast of muffins, Kits Kats and tea. And it's just me, and I do find it liberating. But by God, it's cold.

While checking on the Cycling Maven and Tracking Jack, I noticed that Steve Watson had arrived in Kimba overnight, stayed at another motel and has already resumed riding. He is now ahead of me for the first time. When he gave me back my phone at the Nullarbor Roadhouse he said that reaching Sydney ahead of me was on his mind. I knew he meant it at the time, but now I take the prospect on board even more. But wherever he is, at this hour of the morning my interests will be best served by first focusing on getting back on the road, finding rhythm in the pedal stroke and getting warm.

Not long after leaving Kimba, I see a red light in the distance, which comes in and out of sight. On a long uphill grind I realise that it is Steve. He has stopped by the side of the road by the time I catch and pass him, and he is putting on additional layers of clothing to warm up.

Steve calls and waves. It's bone chillingly cold but I am satisfied that, apart from my hands and feet, I have adequate clothing on. So I ride on steadily, trying to get some body warmth and strengthen my lead on Steve. And I soon get it, with a clarity of mind that embraces the freedom and solitude, and a spirit heartened by the new dawn. A nicely timed little tailwind helps too.

After 88 kilometres of riding and 70 kilometres out from Port Augusta, I reach the turn-off to Iron Knob, a kilometre off-route. With my body temperature back to where it should be now that the sun is fully up and some distance made, it's a good time to stop for a rest and regroup.

I think about one of the personal reasons I'm participating in the event, to promote the charity Helping Rhinos. And this morning, while checking overnight news online, I learn of more atrocities committed against rhinos by poachers. The senseless slaughter of these animals for their horns, which are sold on the black market, is awful. With such large expanses of open country all around that I think would suit rhinos, it's not hard to imagine this endangered animal running free, which I have seen on safari in Tanzania. But as the day-to-day challenges of riding the IndiPac have consumed most of my attention, I haven't been able to promote the message of Helping Rhinos as much as I had planned.

It also seems a fitting moment to think about the riders in the Tour de Kids cycling event that since 2000 has raised more than $7.5 million for the Starlight Children's Foundation. The 2017 tour, from Albury to Wollongong in New South Wales (about 850 kilometres), is the last, and I know a large number of riders who are in the peloton, which is now in the Kosciuszko National Park, near where IndiPac leaders Kristof Allegaert and Mike Hall are racing.

◉

My plan for day twelve is to first reach Port Augusta. The small city used to be a seaport but it's now an intersection for road traffic and the railway and mostly lies on the east coast of the Spencer Gulf immediately south of the gulf's head. Then, pending what time I reach and leave Port Augusta, my aim is get as far as I can towards Adelaide, the South Australian capital. I know I won't reach it today but would like to by tomorrow. I will certainly give it a crack, as I'm keen to get my bike serviced at the Treadly Bike shop there. But it's too early in the day to commit to such a target so far away.

With the tailwind still blowing, I should get going again before the cycling gods turn against me. Before getting under way though, I check where some other riders are and see there has been plenty of action up front. Yesterday, Kristof Allegaert led comfortably into the Victorian Alps. But he lost a lot of his advantage when he took a long sleep just below the top of the first major climb, the 27 kilometre long 'Back of Falls' which begins with a fabled and leg-burning 12 per cent gradient ramp that is aptly named 'WTF [What The Fuck] Corner' for the first kilometre, and then three sectors of varying gradients and lengths. After they reach the top, riders are finally greeted by the ghostly sight of a spectacularly barren plateau highlighted by dead trees that so often in the year are exposed to super cold, if not freezing, Alpine conditions. That iconic mountain climb gave second-placer Mike Hall the opportunity to close in on Kristof. While Sarah Hammond is still in third place; the race has taken a turn this morning after Kristof rode down to Falls Creek, where he stopped for supplies, knowing there would be little opportunity later.

Kristof, stopping at a shop in Fall's Creek to refuel, saw Mike ride by, turn his head and continue on. Mike, a competitor like none other, seized the opportunity to take the race lead. Later Kristof said, 'I took my time to eat my purchases knowing Mike's lead could not exceed 10 kilometres. Mike still had to stop to eat and surely to sleep.'

With almost 4,500 kilometres now ridden by the leaders, the IndiPac is getting serious.

◉

217

I am blessed. The tailwind continues to assist me all the way to Port Augusta. My one concern is that, like the Cycling Maven and Tracking Jack, I'll miss the turn-off to town from the Eyre Highway. Caroona Road passes the El Alamein Landing Ground to where the race route enters town. With the good speed I'm riding at, the wind behind me and accumulated fatigue, it's a mistake I could easily make – even in daylight.

On the approach I slow, reading the map on my Garmin Etrex 30, which I'm now using far more regularly, even though I find the map too small and a challenge to read. I reach the exit on a descent from the crest of a rise and stop to allow for a break in the morning traffic – there is a lot heading into Port Augusta on the highway. Then I look for a sign to confirm it's the correct turn-off. There is none. I double check on the Garmin and even pull out my paper map to check.

How hard it must be to see this turn-off in the middle of the night. I can understand how easily the Cycling Maven and Tracking Jack missed it. In some ways, I'm grateful they did. Their mistake has heightened my awareness to get it right.

◉

Caroona Road isn't smooth. It's a rough and tumble ride. Not only is the road pockmarked with chipped stone, but there are numerous potholes. I am so grateful I don't have any saddle sores that the slightest of bumps would painfully aggravate. But the road still takes me into some welcome solitude – far away from the noise and frenetic traffic of the highway I have just turned off. Much of the road is also a descent, with some flat stretches, and I enjoy the speed, sun and silence. My only hesitation is on entering Port Augusta. Roadworks at one intersection make me suspect I have to take another road, but I'm told by a roadworker that the gravel stretch ahead, which they are currently resealing, is definitely the road in to Port Augusta.

I enjoy the change of terrain. Riding over the soft ochre dirt beneath my wheels for about a kilometre is pleasant after the bumpy and bone-jarring ride over the last few kilometres. Finally I see the traffic lights – I have arrived in Port Augusta, the biggest city since leaving Fremantle. No sooner do I stop for a red light than a man steps out from the shadow of a tree and takes a photo of me. He is a dot tracker and has known of my imminent arrival and that of several other riders behind me, including rider Lochie Kavanagh. Lochie is closing in on me, although he has had his share of problems too. He broke his phone on day one, and in a crash suffered several broken teeth. But his courage to continue is apparently building by the day, as is his following of fans.

I'm in no rush. The day is going well, so I'm happy to chat with the dot tracker while the traffic lights change from red to green and back again over the next ten minutes.

◉

As I ride through town and over two bridges towards the eastern exit where I'll head south and then towards Adelaide, I'm actually surprised by the size and busyness of Port Augusta. I probably shouldn't be. It is a city. It is Wednesday, lunchtime. There is a lot of activity, pedestrian and traffic. Maybe it is the impact of suddenly riding into the city after riding in the wilderness for so many kilometres? But I keep going, wanting to sustain my tempo while I can, knowing that there are any number of small towns ahead where I can stop.

Out of Port Augusta, it's back to reality. The flat run on the highway towards the turn-off to Wilmington is pretty hard. A lot of traffic is heading in the same direction and a headwind is blowing to boot. The shoulder on the left side of the road is also quite narrow. There are hills to my left, and behind that range is Wilmington. I look forward to escaping the traffic and noise around me and returning to a rural landscape. The turn-off really cannot come sooner. My desire to climb is back, despite the punishment of grinding away against the wind and the noise of trucks and cars speeding by on a single lane.

Finally, I see the signpost for Horrocks Pass Road and turn left. The climb starts slowly, but soon the roadway disappearing and re-emerging in the steeper sections ahead tells me there are a number of switchbacks and the climb will be for longer than the three to four kilometres I was told it would be.

I am fine with that though and grateful to leave the noise of highway traffic below, calmly making my way up the slope

SHEER BEAUTY: Sunset on the Nullarbor is as beautiful as sunrise – nearing Ceduna where the desert ends. *Photo by Troy Bailey*

FIRST WOMAN: Jackie Bernardi was the first woman to finish the 2017 IndiPac – here between Adaminaby and Cooma. *Photo by Troy Bailey*

SAYS IT ALL: The welcome sign at the Cocklebiddy Roadhouse.

Photo by Sanne Røhe

THE EDGE: The Great Australian Bight – truly something to behold.

LOADED UP: My Curve 'Belgie Spirit' at the old Nullarbor Roadhouse in my 2018 ride.

TIME TO THINK: The loneliness of the Nullarbor Plain allows plenty of time to think, and think, and think. *Photo by Troy Bailey*

UP WE GO: Kerwyn Ballico gets stuck in on the first proper climb on the Nullarbor to Eucla in the 2018 ride.

ON THE BRINK: The ride to Mundrabilla in the 2017 IndiPac was one of the toughest cycling experiences of my life.

FOOD, FOOD, FOOD: Fuelling up at the Widgiemooltha Roadhouse during day three of my 2018 ride. *Photo by Kerwyn Ballico*

ZZZZ: Out like a light at the Wirulla Roadhouse. *Photo by Kerwyn Ballico*

AHEAD OF ME: Dot tracker Kay Haarsma rides into Adelaide with 2017 IndiPac riders (*left*) 'Cycling Maven' (Mark Ferguson) and 'Caveman Chris' (Chris Barker). *Photo from Kay Haarsma*

NICE TOUCH: The name of every starter in the 2018 ride was a great sight to see on the outskirts of Tantanoola, South Australia.

PAUSE FOR THOUGHT: The memorial for Mike Hall at the scene of his death in the 2017 IndiPac, just south of Canberra during my 2018 ride.

BENCHMARKS: Passing each of the state and territory
borders heartens a weary soul on the road.

A MOMENT TO SHARE:
Crossing the Sydney Harbour Bridge with Slovenian adventurer Bernarda Jurič in the closing kilometres of our 2018 ride. *Photo by Andy Matthews*

BIG WET II:
As befits tradition, dipping my front wheel in the waters of the Pacific Ocean – in Sydney Harbour, near the Opera House steps. *Photo by Sanne Røhe*

YES! Sydney Opera House, 11.37am, Friday 13 April, 2018 . . . After the 27 days, two hours and 15 minutes it took to cycle 5,471 kilometres in 'My Big Ride' – the 2017 IndiPac route is now completed. It's also time to turn and thank my wife Libby (*behind*). Without her support, I would not be here. *Photo by Gearoid Towey*

as it becomes steeper. I have not ridden on climbs as long as the 'Back of Falls' in the Victorian Alps or Cabramurra in the Kosciuszko National Park, two of the highlights of the last 1,000 kilometres of IndiPac, but I have trained on the 13 kilometres up Macquarie Pass near Wollongong in New South Wales with a near-full load of packs on and managed to reach the top.

Horrocks Pass steepens near the end, especially over the last few hundred metres when it ramps up, forcing me to drop into the easiest gear. I am pretty tired at the top and stop to regather my breath, which has shortened to a tight series of pants, leaving me gasping for air until I recover. Then I have a pee and finally savour the view ahead.

Behind me, Port Augusta and the traffic-laden highway near the base of the climb are shrouded by a green curtain of trees and bush. Even more pleasant is the undulating rural terrain ahead of me. I feel excited that the IndiPac route is about to change character. As I begin to descend Horrocks Pass I am treated to a vast landscape of farms and bushland.

◉

I've decided to stop in Wilmington to re-stock on food and drink for the rest of the afternoon's ride. But I spend only a few minutes at the small, pleasantly air-conditioned petrol station in the town. Soon after knocking back one more can of Coke and resting in the shade of the front awning, I'm back on the Horrocks Highway, enjoying the IndiPac as much as I ever have.

The natural beauty of the Southern Flinders Ranges is captivating. The sight of farmers toiling the land is soothing. The sound of the wind and my breathing in sync with the rhythmical hum of the bike wheels is peaceful. Not even the sight of looming rain clouds dampens my mood. When the rain falls, requiring me to put my rain jacket on, it's not a discomfort. As I ride through the quaint town of cycling-friendly Melrose and then approach Murray Town, I begin to think about which country pub to stay in. I'm tired, for sure; but tired is normal this late in the day.

After passing Murray Town, I notice Tracking Jack has stopped back at Melrose. I'm surprised to have caught and passed him, but decide to keep going. I set as my destination the former timber milling town of Wirrabara and phone the local hotel to book myself a room.

◉

With 248 kilometres ridden I arrive in Wirrabara and check in with the hotel publican Barry Hoepner. I plug my lights and Garmin in for a recharge, arrange my food supplies and refill my drink bottles, then shower and change into my regular 'evening attire' of Rapha shorts, cycling undervest and jacket.

I head to the bar and order a beer. It goes down beautifully. After another one, I remember that I'm due to take a call from SBS cycling commentator Mike Tomalaris, who is riding with the Tour de Kids group that is now near Canberra. 'Tomo' knows me well. He has followed my IndiPac progress so far and has noticed from my vlogs that I have been emotional from time to time. In a live telephone interview played on loudspeaker to the Tour de Kids group, he asks me about the circumstances that triggered those moments, about how I am faring and what my plans are for the upcoming days. It is good to chat with Tomo and it opens a few emotional valves. When Tomo asks about the emotional journey, I reflect on the highs and lows, which immediately brings any memory of them to boil and I realise my voice is quivering with feeling as I talk. 'I've experienced such a rollercoaster over the last days, I have nothing to hide now,' I tell Tomo, adding that I'm an emotional guy anyway and see no reason to be ashamed to show it.

After signing off with Tomo, I finish my beer and head to the dining room and enjoy the novelty of ordering a meal at a restaurant. It's been some time since I actually studied a dinner menu instead of buying what I see or think of first, which is usually a hamburger. As I peruse my options, I sense a presence before me. It's Tracking Jack, still in his cycling kit. He has only just arrived.

'G'day Rupe,' he says, smiling. I have some good-natured company.

Tracking Jack isn't sure what to do. 'I don't know if I'll stay here for the night and leave early, or just eat and leave,' he tells me. But he is going to eat. He sits down and we discuss his options, whether to book a room or not.

I order a chicken schnitzel, and am keen to know what his movements have been – why he stopped at Melrose, which has a reputedly good bike shop. He tells me he needed to collect a bike component that he had pre-ordered to be delivered to the shop. I'm again impressed by his intelligent forward thinking. Then Jack tells me he has finally settled on what to do – he'll sleep at the Wirrabara Hotel, too. He plans to leave at 2 am, about two hours before me.

As Jack talks, fatigue kicks in and my mind wanders to the sticky date pudding I will order once I catch the waitress's eye. I suspect I'm probably not the greatest company right now. I'm just so tired and am longing for a night alone. My heart sinks when I learn from the waitress that the kitchen is closed and her shift is over, which means I can't have my sticky date pudding. Not even the politest plea alters the situation – I'd eat it cold if I could have it straight from the fridge. Not even some plaintive begging with Barry, the publican, can sway fate my way. Barry has already paid up the staff salaries for their shift and is ready to close. I should have ordered it earlier.

I opt for a glass of wine instead and chat with Barry who tells me three or four IndiPac riders came through the hotel a week earlier.

'Steak eaters,' he says.

When I tell Barry I've just eaten a chicken schnitzel and ask if I have done the right thing, he laughs.

It's a great opportunity to learn more about the pub that is a hub for both the local Australian Rules football team and the region. Barry says he would love the six-day Tour Down Under – Australia's first World Tour professional bicycle race that has been running since 1999 – to pass through Wirrabara one day. 'We have some great roads around here that I think would suit bike racing,' he says, 'Starting at Port Pirrie, through the Port Germain Gorge, through to Wirrabara . . . perhaps over to Burra and finish up at Clare . . . a mixture of straight stretches, corners, long uphill, long downhill, all sorts of terrain. And a lot of people here would enjoy an event like the tour going through our community.' From what I have seen of the landscape so far, Barry is spot on, and I admire his passion and pride in the region.

◉

It's been a long day, and not getting my sticky date pudding irrationally irritates me. Returning to my room, I make do with a chocolate bar from one of my handlebar feed packs. There are bigger problems in the IndiPac. Then again, when you want a sticky date pudding . . .

I'm not sure what time I will try to get going but Adelaide is within reach. Finishing the Fremantle to Adelaide route that

Arthur Richardson blazed in 1896 is an achievement that I now see becoming mine. If it does, I reason, at least I can tick off one of the early 'Overlander' routes. Whatever happens after arriving in Adelaide will be a bonus.

15

ON THE CUSP OF CELEBRATION

Day 13: Wirrabara to Tanunda

Start: **4.54 am**   Finish: **8 pm**

Riding time: **9 hours 05 minutes**

Distance: **204.9 km**   Metres climbed: **1,398 m**

Average speed: **18 kmh**   Temperature: **1–24 C**

The first thing I hear today is Tracking Jack leaving his room. His steps. His bike being carefully wheeled out. The ticking of the gear block on his rear wheel turning over. He is leaving early, as he said he would. My guess is it's about 1 am, which is confirmed by a quick glance at my watch. I am still in bed. It is warm. My head drops back on to the pillow, and the next thing I hear is rain. It's about 4 am, time to get up and get going.

Getting ready is all by instinct. I barely think. Just do. And it all comes together.

◉

The rain has abated, but it's still damp outside. And it is especially cold.

As for my plan? It will be nice to reach Adelaide, really nice. But I will just let the day unravel, see what it brings and make a judgement call towards the end of it. There is always the option of stopping at Tanunda, about 80 kilometres out of Adelaide on the route. I know the town well, having been there numerous times covering the Tour Down Under World Tour.

Despite the cold, I feel relaxed. I check in on social media to see what's happening with the race, figuring yesterday's drama with Mike taking the lead must have had consequences.

Did it ever. The one-on-one engagement between Kristof and Mike was nothing short of dramatic, particularly for a race that is so long. Overnight, Kristof took back the lead from Mike after spending most of the day reasonably close to him. At one point last night they were 200 metres apart and responding to each other's accelerations of pace. Incredible.

Finally, in the thick of night, after Kristof had eaten dinner in Beechworth, he passed Mike again. Few if any words were exchanged. Action and reaction said it all really.

'Later in the evening, I had already Mike in focus,' recalled Kristof in his race diary. 'It was time to look at everything. I saw a great tiredness and I found the opportune moment to take the lead and keep up the pace. Thanks to the good sleep of the previous night, I could cross the Victorian Alps and the Kosciuszko National Park all at once. So the last mountains and slopes were suddenly behind me.'

It was clearly a defining moment: the leader, overtaken, takes back first place and then pushes on with an even more inspiring effort. I can't help but think that today Kristof will be heading to where the Tour de Kids group will be.

My departure is delayed a bit more when I read through some supportive emails and comments on social media. I don't absorb all the messages, but a quick glance is enough to draw motivation for when I am cycling alone in the dark, cold and solitude of the countryside. It's amazing how even the simplest message of goodwill can resonate on the road.

Back on the road, the cold really bites. I'd thought that with the overnight rain there might be some cloud cover which would make conditions warmer. But the sky is ablaze with stars – beautiful to see, but doing nothing to warm me. There's no wind, and I'm travelling at a pretty handy pace, but my extremities – my hands and feet – are numb with pain. I can't feel the gear and break levers, or the pedals. No matter that I am wearing wet weather yachting gloves over my mitts. At least I can cover my ears with my headband and pull my Buff up and over my mouth and nose.

After about 50 kilometres I succumb to the cold. I have to stop, if only to stretch and loosen up. I seize the chance to still appreciate how beautiful the dawn sky in the north-east behind me is. I expect the winds will pick up at some point and turn against me so anything else is a blessing. I should consider finishing the day earlier, even though I know some people are planning to greet me in Adelaide. I'll decide later.

Meanwhile, my attention is taken by the sight of the sun as it creeps up from behind a silo. The sunrise not only warms me inside and out, but reveals an expanse of pastoral land in stark contrast to the harsh desert I had become so accustomed to – a simple but stunning view.

The Nullarbor Plain seems like a lifetime away. I can see now just how challenging it was for me – far harder than I expected, or indeed understood while crossing it.

I take some time out during my stop to post a live video on Facebook about how I'm feeling and respond to a question from former Wallabies rugby union prop Ben Darwin. He asks me to describe how I have packed my bike: a question many are curious about, and one that comes with a different answer, depending on when it is asked. I have refined the packing of my Apidura packs several times since the IndiPac began, knowing now how much I'll use some things and how they need to be easy to access.

My bike isn't packed like race leader Kristof Allegaert's red Jaegher. Kristof is an absolute minimalist. But my Curve Belgie Spirit isn't as overloaded as some others are. All my sleeping gear – bivvy, mattress, plastic sheet and space blanket – is in the handlebars pack. My top bar pack includes electronic paraphernalia on one side and mechanical materials on the other. A small pack attached to the stem has my Garmin Etrex 30 inside as well as a battery pack, a small bag of mixed nuts and lollies and the as-yet unopened letter from Rod Evans 'To be Opened When Things Get Tough'. My saddle pack has my clothing in it, with the least needed gear packed firmly into the bottom, and a packet of Scotch Finger biscuits bought on the Nullarbor strapped on the top.

After all, you never know when you're going to need a Scotch Finger biscuit . . .

I also talk about my preparation for the IndiPac, explaining that I think the best thing is simply just to ride such an event and learn from the experience – the bad and good. I certainly can see where I have made mistakes. And there are plenty of things I would do differently, or better, such as more route reconnaissance, testing my electrical equipment, and boning up on bicycle maintenance. But I also admit I need to be easier on myself, not so self-critical.

◉

The next ten to eleven hours are long and punishing and a cross headwind has been blowing all day and costing me time to boot. I opt to not worry about what progress I'm making and focus more on my rhythm, which helps whittle away the time.

Arriving into Clare out of a sea of golden brown farming fields that is signature to the open countryside of the mid-north of South Australia, I have 86 kilometres accumulated in the legs for the day. It is lunchtime. Time to refuel and re-stock on food supplies with a hard afternoon of cycling to come. After cycling right through town, I turn into the service station and choose my on-road consumables automatically. I also take a salad roll from the fridge and order a hot vegetable pastie to eat on the spot. And then I'm back in the saddle.

The road out of town is long and wide, lined with trees that offer soothing shade as the afternoon heat starts to build. I stop to check my bike once more, preferring to do so now in the shade and still close to where I can find a bike shop should I need one.

A woman with a camera approaches me and asks if I'm an IndiPac rider. She introduces herself as Gabrielle, a photo-journalist from the local newspaper, *The Northern Argus*, and asks if she can take my picture and ask a few questions for a story. She has missed the race leaders, and the other riders between them and myself, many of them having shot through in the middle of the night or early morning.

I am happy to oblige, but tell her lightheartedly that as a journalist I'm sorry she hasn't landed anyone more exciting. With the photo taken and interview finished, and one last check of my bike, I finally remount. Where will the afternoon take me?

●

Over the next few hours, four dot trackers come out to see me – one on a bicycle, another on a motor bike, and two others in their cars at the halfway mark of the IndiPac outside Tanunda at sunset. They're all friendly and clearly conscious of not imposing themselves on me. Although I do learn of the distressing news regarding one rider's fate.

Somehow in the bubble that has become my world on the IndiPac I had missed the news, but am told of 36-year-old Irish rider Eoin Marshall's withdrawal three days earlier – on March 27, day 10 – due to an injury to the back of his head, grazes to the right side of his cheek and his nose and a fractured rib sustained in a collision with a car on the outskirts of Tarlee, about 100 kilometres north of Adelaide and with 2,700 kilometres ridden.

Eoin's helmet, which was split in two, took most of the impact and in all likelihood saved his life. Local police attended the scene of the accident where Eoin was initially treated before being transferred to hospital in Elizabeth Vale. A fellow rider, the 29-year-old Australian Ben Hirons witnessed the accident and travelled to hospital with Eoin, and after making sure Eoin was looked after, returned to race yesterday, day twelve. While horrified to learn all this, I'm so grateful Eoin's injuries aren't worse and also admiring of Ben's sportsmanship and humanity to stay with Eoin before rejoining the race.

I feel terrible I haven't kept abreast of what was happening outside my IndiPac world, and grateful I haven't had any major scares on the road at all. My ears soon prick up to frightening incidents experienced by others in the race. The risks are real out there on the road.

But I settle back into the pattern of the day that otherwise has been unfolding well, and it continues to, once I'm able to refocus on my ride. A sense of strength has been building in my heart and soul and I feel back on top of the IndiPac. Challenges still lurk around the corner, but the last two days have seen me turn a corner when it comes to coping with the curve balls.

By late afternoon, as the bright light of day softens, the rolling hills of the wine-making Barossa Valley are showcased in all their majesty, with row upon row of green vines still bearing their fruit, nearing the last harvest of the season. I start to weigh up my options – stay at Tanunda or go for Adelaide, knowing that if I make it to the latter, it will be in darkness.

On the outskirts of Tanunda I see a parked car. Someone waves to me. I can't see their face but wave back. The car follows me. As it passes the driver yells out that I am reaching the halfway mark of the IndiPac. Wow! I have not thought of it once since the day that I left Fremantle, let alone today as I'm closing in on it. That there is an actual marker to acknowledge such an important point in such a long race is exciting. It's still a long way from the finish line – well, 2,735 kilometres – but I don't hesitate when the driver says 'follow me'.

When I see the car stop near a giant IPWR sign halfway up a hill about 5 kilometres out from Tanunda, I really do feel like I have achieved something. I think about my other achievements: crossing the Nullarbor Plain; getting to the Western Australia–South Australia border; reaching Port Augusta. However, passing the halfway mark – painted in giant pink letters as *#Half Way! IPWR* on the road – is the biggest so far. I feel as though I'm about to lift off with exultation. But I bring myself back down to earth, saying to myself, *Geez, it's only half-way. I'm sure Kristof, Mike, Sarah and most others just sped through.*

But it's still an achievement and I know it will spur me on to Adelaide, if not tonight, which will in turn motivate me to reach Melbourne, then the Victorian and New South Wales Alps, and Canberra and Sydney. Each success feeds another.

As the sun starts to dip over Tanunda, I have no doubts about stopping to savour the moment of reaching halfway. I certainly owe it to the person who has alerted me to it, Ian Shelby-James, a local insurance broker from the Barossa Valley whose clients include some local wineries, to chat with him; but I want to as well. While not a cyclist, Ian has seen plenty of riders through Tanunda, from cyclo tourists to racers in the Tour Down Under, and now Indian Pacific Wheel Race entrants. He also has a good mate in the IndiPac, Davin Harding, who is near the pointy end and cycled by here five days ago.

When I make a quip about how far I am behind his mate, Davin, Ian replies with a laugh, 'You look in better shape though.'

Ian admits he is now a converted IndiPac dot watcher. 'I just hope everyone finishes the race, so I can go back to work,' he adds with a laugh. 'You are costing me productivity.'

As the day turns to night I ride the last 5 kilometres into Tanunda and check into the Valley Hotel. I book in and enjoy a cold beer before going back to my room, where I attend to the daily routine of recharging, refilling and organising before taking a shower.

Then I'm drawn to looking at some photos taken the night before at the Tour de Kids dinner in Canberra, which Kristof attended and was interviewed upon his arrival by Michael Tomalaris. Tomo clearly made Kristof feel comfortable and he accepted the impromptu offer to eat with them. The photo of Kristof scoffing down a giant bowl of spaghetti is something to behold – but considering just how much food is needed to get through a day on the IndiPac he could probably eat two more and not even feel it. Fleetingly, I also have a little laugh, as the image throws back to memories almost 30 years earlier when I would eat such large bowls of pasta as a lightweight rower, but then I was in the grip of bulimia and dealt with the load in the only way I knew. How different my experience of food is now – as fuel.

By 8 pm and with a medium rare steak with chips eaten and two glasses of wine helping to digest it all, I am back in my room and about to crash. I'm pretty excited about the prospect of arriving in Adelaide tomorrow. With 80 kilometres to go, it will be another early morning start. But I want to be fresh and alert, knowing I'll be riding on narrow and twisting roads. I have also been in contact with the guys at Treadly Bikes in downtown Adelaide. They have been monitoring the impending arrival of all IndiPac riders on the dot tracker and actually rang me to say they saw I had stopped at Tanunda. They offer to be open and ready to service my bike at whatever hour I want to arrive, which is really thoughtful, but I'm happy to arrive when it suits them and we settle on 9 am.

I feel such calm right now; a sense of control and readiness to tackle Part Two of the race. And with the time difference to home in Sydney now being closer – 30 minutes behind Eastern Standard Time – it's a really good time to call Libby. I want her to know how strong I'm feeling, and of course it's also good to just chat, which isn't easy when you're feeling totally drained physically and mentally after a gruelling day of cycling. Likewise for her if she's had a tough day at work, not to mention the anxiety of following my dot edge its way across Australia but not knowing the details.

Libby's delighted I'm over the halfway mark. 'But you still need to be careful tomorrow morning to get to Adelaide safely,' she says.

'I know, Lib; I will. I've had a great day. I've eaten and now I'm in bed just waiting to sleep, so I'll be rested and ready for tomorrow. I'll call you when I get to Adelaide in the morning and then let you know what I'll do. From here there are plenty of towns and places to stop and rest if needed.'

'Okay,' says Libby, 'but be careful – it doesn't mean you *have* to be there at nine o'clock. Take your time. I don't care if you leave in daylight and it's midday when you get there.'

Libby is never one to be complacent. I often call her the 'But' girl. It's not meant as a criticism, just that she will always think of all the options, especially in situations that involve risk. Having those options voiced can make a major difference, so I usually listen.

I also take some time to indulge in some dot tracking and am flabbergasted by the leaders' positions. I just can't get my head around how they do what they do. By 9 am tomorrow, Kristof Allegaert could have finished the bloody race. Barring disaster, he has already all but won it. That he is half a country ahead of me is simply amazing. The same goes for Mike Hall, who really threw it all down to Kristof in the mountains, temporarily taking the lead. Likewise for Sarah Hammond's performance, and the German Kai Edel, the fourth position holder.

Fans and followers of the IndiPac are on the cusp of celebration with the race leaders all well on their way to Sydney. The margins between the first four riders appear definitive: Kristof is 177 kilometres ahead of Mike. At 198 kilometres further back is Sarah, who in turn is 145 kilometres clear of Kai Edel. These places are in stark opposition to my halfway mark. I wonder if reaching that mark reflects achievement or indicates worse things to come.

The Melbourne crew are racing hard, too. The Cycling Maven is going great guns with his bid to chase Ryan 'Rhino' Flinn, who is leading them and well past Adelaide. And Nick Skarajew, followed by Tracking Jack, has just dropped into Adelaide. And here I am, lying on a motel bed. But good on them. I wonder how they will fare after Melbourne, and if I will come good and can reel them in. I will certainly try to make ground, in spite of my intent to engage with people and get a feel of various towns I pass through.

I am feeling okay physically, as good as can be. But now I better understand why Tour de France riders say they take one day at a time over the three-week race.

1 6

IT MUST BE MIKE HALL

Day 14: Tanunda to Adelaide
Start: 5.31 am   Finish: 9.15 am
Riding time: 3 hours 46 minutes
Distance: 79.9 km   Metres climbed: 726 m
Average speed: 21.1 kmh   Temperature: 2–17 C

This will be a special day, I tell myself. It's 4 am and it's still dark outside. In my room at the Valley Hotel, the warmth of my bed keeps me hostage. My legs are sore, seemingly too heavy to raise due to the lingering pain. My shoulders and back are stiff like boards, my right ankle is still swollen, and the balls of my feet still burn from the constant pressure on the pedals, especially my right foot. My mouth and throat are parched. The list goes on.

I felt much better when I went to bed. But a strong sense of empowerment surges through me with the thought that I'm now in the second half of the race and on my way to finishing it – which is enough to haul me out of bed and into my cycling kit.

There is still a fog in my head, like a hangover, but it clears with a few sips of fresh tea. As I arrange all for another day in the saddle, I remind myself that whatever happens after Adelaide, having made it that far means I will have completed Arthur Richardson's first 'Overlander' route. Less than a year earlier I would never have imagined attempting it, let alone trying to reach the finish line after 5,470 kilometres.

Right now the race leaders are nearing Sydney and should finish the race today. Over a few more sips of tea, another packaged muffin, a large Cherry Ripe bar and an assortment of other left-overs from the day before, it dawns on me that, as tired as I am, my body and mind are now used to the highs and lows of the IndiPac. No more overthinking, no more dwelling on fears or lamenting perceived mistakes. These I simply classify as experiences from which to learn, rather than failures. I am about getting it done, and moving on – kilometre by kilometre.

I've even managed to address my most recent problem – keeping my hands warm. This morning I've inserted my hands into small plastic bags, and then slipped them into my mitts and finally my sailing gloves which only the day before did nothing to stop my fingers from freezing to the bone. Finding solutions like this is as much about the IndiPac challenge as riding the bike for as long as you can each day is. It certainly helps serve the spirit well.

With my bicycle packed and loaded, I step out into the biting chill and haunting silence of a town yet to wake up. Once more, I double check my packs are secure and my tyres are clean of any debris or glass that could cause a puncture. I turn my light on, straddle my aching legs over the frame, clip my feet into the pedals and roll away. Another day in the saddle begins.

The route takes me along the Barossa Valley Highway to Lyndoch, then onto the Lyndoch Valley Road to Williamstown. From there the route makes its way down the sweeping bends of Gorge Road by Paracombe, the Kangaroo Creek Reservoir and then the Black Hill Conservation Park and finally to Adelaide. Being familiar with the terrain provides an added boost. I covered the Tour Down Under in this region for many years as a journalist and more recently cycled the last part of the 80 kilometres from Tanunda to Adelaide in the BUPA Challenge public ride of that race.

The spectacular scenery is made more glorious by the sunrise, which also brings warmth. It's as serene a ride as I have ever had, interrupted only by the chorus of bellbirds and my first meeting for the day with a dot tracker, who keeps pace with me on his own bike on the narrow, twisting road surrounded by bushland. He doesn't talk too much, allowing me to still keep my rhythm.

Meanwhile, Kristof Allegaert is forging ahead. He began the day with a lead of more than 150 kilometres, and now is less than 300 kilometres from the finish. The previous day, I learn, was one of lows and highs for him. He had a tough passage into Canberra, as he recalls in his diary: 'I couldn't enjoy being accompanied by other cyclists for the first time; I was locked up in my own small world. Hunger and thirst dominated my body.'

But after a brief stop at a supermarket, he embraced the national capital for what it offers cyclists: 'This city was built for real people right from the start with a good infrastructure for bicycles. I felt this whole area was a friend of the bike.' In the early evening at Bungendore, 39 kilometres after Canberra and riding in the rain, Kristof was surprised by the rapturous welcome he received at a roundabout near the entrance to town. Mike Tomalaris and the Tour de Kids crew were there; they'd arrived there earlier in the afternoon. After eating his dinner, Kristof rode on into the rainy night. As he recalls in his diary: 'The end was in sight, and that softened the pain, but after this hot meal I did not find the right rhythm to move forward.'

At Tarago, after 31 kilometres and with 5,160 kilometres ridden, Kristof saw hotel lights. 'I was unable to resist,' he says. 'The hotel was full, but fortunately two men from the same group decided to share the same room. I could take a shower and sleep in a bed. I had a comfortable lead and the last 300 km were flat, the next day could not be a problem.'

Victory for Kristof is all but assured, although he is reminded of the inherent perils when he crashes into a wombat by the roadside. 'Impossible to avoid it, so here I am,' Kristof remarked in a Facebook post along with a photograph showing a cut right thigh and knee. 'When I got up, I was not in pain anywhere and my bike was still working.' Weeks later, though, Kristof discovers he had also broken some ribs.

Near Adelaide, the traffic is building. It's about 7.30 am. My latest dot watcher and I are riding single file, him behind me. We're still surrounded by bushland, but the city is now very close. With peak hour approaching, it's inevitable there will be more traffic. Adelaide will be the first national city I've seen in two weeks after coming out of the wilderness – and that reminds me to stay alert. Libby's warning is ringing in my ears.

At that moment, out of the blue on a slightly twisting but flat stretch of the road, the flash of a white car passes me at lightning speed. It's so close I almost could touch it. Mere centimetres have separated me from potential disaster. After gathering my thoughts, I yell out to my dot tracking companion: 'That was the only near miss I've had since leaving Fremantle.' It was also the most dangerous and frightening moment I have had so far. But I try to re-focus on arriving in Adelaide.

When I am again alone and nearing Gorge Road, I start to think about what I need to do to make the best of my time in

Adelaide. I'm lucky to have many friends here but I need to balance the time I spend seeing them with being efficient and getting back on the road to climb the 13 kilometres up Greenhill Road and then ride on towards Tailem Bend as soon as possible. On the other hand, if no-one turns up to say hi, then I'll be able to continue the race at my own pace, without worry of offending anyone.

But the grand plan now is to get to the Treadly Bikes shop. Then I'll take a shower, and have a rest and a feed while my bike is being serviced – where, I don't know, but I'll figure that out when I get there. It'll be a relatively quick turn-around, I told myself, rather than the indulgent night in a five-star hotel and slap-up meal I'd envisaged.

How did this change of mindset come about? A day or two earlier I realised I no longer missed the luxuries of city life as I did during the first hard days of the race. Now I want to avoid all the comforts and instead return to the solitude of the road as soon as is reasonably possible. I have noticed already how most of my natural senses – sight, smell, touch and hearing – have been sharpened by spending so much time out in the open. My sense of taste is still on the blink, but I find more and more comfort and calm in the solitude of riding and sleeping on my own. So riding into Adelaide feels almost claustrophobic and returning to the beautiful coun-tryside is what I wish for most, away from the traffic, lights, pedestrians and noise.

As I take the long sweeping descent down Gorge Road, my train of thought is broken by the sight of a cyclist coming to me from the other direction. It is clearly another dot watcher – a woman. She stops and does a U-turn in readiness to join me for what I assume will be the final run into Adelaide.

'You must be Rupert,' she says.

Kay Haarsma then tells me about her experiences with some of the other riders ahead of me, one of them being Sarah Hammond.

By the time the IndiPac route crosses the Torrens River and joins a bike path that hugs the river, two more dot watchers have joined Kay and me. The chat is friendly, but it's difficult to keep a three-way conversation going while focusing on the narrow bike path. With fatigue starting to set in, I don't want to lose concentration and take an embarrassing deviation 'off-piste' and find myself tumbling down the embankment and into the water below. Tiredness is making hard work of some of the simpler hazards of a bike path. After riding so many kilometres alone, there are suddenly runners and walkers – some with dogs or prams – and other cyclists, most of them commuters on their way to work, to avoid bumping into.

But the sight of the CBD skyline against a blue sky on another sunny day heightens my sense of achievement. And awaiting me is the offer of a free bike service and a place to rest at Treadly Bikes. The offer is too good to refuse, especially given the issues I've had with my rear tyre and now front light, which for some reason has now started playing up. Someone more qualified that me is needed to fix them. Arriving at the bike shop, tucked away in Ebenezer Place off Rundle Street, I am welcomed by the smile of its owner Sam Neeft. He's holding a plastic bag full of homemade protein balls made for me and other IndiPac riders yet to reach Adelaide by two friends of mine, Amy de Wall and Michelle Heusse, who I met through cycling.

I immediately devour one of the balls and steer my bike to the rack for its service, explaining to Treadly mechanics Jake Thomas and Andy Rogers what I need done. Then I head next door for a coffee and yet another muffin. The eating, it never stops.

◉

At about 9.20 am I have just returned to the shop when Kay walks back in looking concerned. A few hours earlier, she says – at 6.22 am today, to be precise – an IndiPac rider was killed in a collision with a car on the Monaro Highway near Canberra. The identity of the rider is yet to be confirmed, but the ABC online report that Kay has printed out bears the key indicator.

It must be Mike Hall.

In second place and 360 kilometres from Sydney, he's the only IndiPac rider who would have been at that location at the time. And his dot has stopped there at that precise time too.

The heaviest of silences sweeps through the shop. I feel completely numb. We all just look at each other. What is only several seconds seems like an eternity. Shock is holding me up, but I have experienced tragedy before and I know it won't be long before I come tumbling down.

I walk out to the adjoining café, place my order for a coffee and take my flat white to a table. My first impulse is to telephone Libby and tell her I am okay. I imagine a national news bulletin declaring, 'A cyclist has been killed in the Indian Pacific Wheel Race in a collision with a car' – and Libby's reaction if she hears this, to say nothing of other family and friends.

I can't get through so I send her a text message. I resume thinking, or trying to absorb what has happened. It's surreal, inexplicable. Suddenly another awful incident bolts out from the cloud of memory and compounds the shock of learning about Mike's fate. I realise that today – it is 31 March – is the anniversary of the night in 2013 when Rod Allen, my good friend, died in an accident after Libby's and my shared 51st birthday party in Sydney.

That Mike's death should happen on this same date floors me. The shock of Mike's death wanes, pushed aside for the moment by the memory of Rod. I realise now that I have never really got over Rod's death, as much as I thought I had: from the sheer loss of a friend and someone who contributed so much to so many, to the circumstances of his death and the uncertainty over the final minutes of his life and what actually led to it ending. His body was found the morning after what was otherwise the most perfect of nights – and the grief of his death struck many, not only his family and friends but also the entire Sydney sporting community.

I thought that I had contained my grief. But like bubbles in a kettle as water comes to boil, it rushes uncontrollably to the surface as I also try to absorb what has happened to Mike.

My thoughts are broken by Libby's call. She is walking to a café in Sydney with a work friend, Natacha Guilbaud. Understandably, ours is an emotionally charged but short conversation and I am grateful that she has someone by her side. Her tears are of relief, but also a release of her deepest fears about me doing the IndiPac. I realise then and there that I can't ask her for any more support, let alone expect it. That would be unfair. She wouldn't be able to look at the dot tracker in the same way again. Instead of thinking I was having a rest when my dot stopped, she'd be fearing I'd had an accident.

'I'm coming home,' I tell Libby. 'I'm coming home.'

She wails in reply. 'Get off that stupid fucking race.'

I have no idea what other riders will be doing, or even the organisers. I suspect the race may be stopped. There will always be another day to ride, another opportunity.

No sooner do I return to the bike shop than I am passed the phone. It's the race organisers on the other end of the line. I am told that the IndiPac has been officially cancelled, that we are free to continue on of our own volition, but that there will be no official classification system left in place, other than the dot tracker for security and safety purposes.

I pass the phone back, then blindly make eye contact with someone in the shop I don't know. He asks if I am okay.

'It's just so sad,' are the only words I can muster before my head falls into his shoulders.

He responds with one of the most compassionate and reassuring embraces I have ever felt. I just let it all out. The tears start rolling. I glance to my right and see another pair of eyes offering support – a woman's, equally compassionate.

The guys at the shop, who have been so helpful to so many in the IndiPac, are all standing silent, as if to say, 'It's okay.'

After a tightening of the hug, a sniffle and a wipe of the nose and eyes, I smile. I am with very good people. I am so lucky.

◉

Four days later, on 4 April, I receive a message on Facebook from a Catherine Seal Yates: 'My name is Seal, we met the other day in the bike shop in Adelaide. The sad day that Mike Hall was taken from us. My husband Paul gave you a big hug that day . . . There is a story behind Paul and his hugs that you would probably like. Paul has been a paramedic for fifteen years and is now what's called an Extended Care Paramedic. He sees and treats the most horrific things you can possibly imagine. When lost for words with friends, colleagues, his patients and their family, he hugs. Not an uncomfortable man hug, a caring hug in the place of words. The day Mike passed we were so lost for words to try to console you. So Paul hugged instead. I hope you are going okay with the loss of Mike and your friend over the last two weeks. Paul is a big fan of your journalism and happy to talk with you further at any stage.'

Paul and Seal, a firefighter herself – are angels. Trail angels.

◉

Back in the bike shop, when I confirm I'm going home Jake kindly offers to pack my bike in a box while Sam arranges for me to take a shower in a bathroom shared by the small businesses in the block. Just like that, my IndiPac is coming to an end.

My next move is booking a flight back to Sydney, and then catching up with an ABC journalist friend, John Thompson-Mills, who had been waiting for me on King William Street where riders who arrived before me had been given hearty welcomes.

A large part of me wants to be alone, but it's probably best to keep busy until Mike's death becomes official. Chatting with JTM helps. He's always had a sympathetic ear. I know he'd like to interview me but his integrity shines through and we talk just as mates, and I agree to chat live on radio later on.

Returning to the bike shop, I learn that IndiPac organisers have released a statement: 'The Indian Pacific Wheel Race has been cancelled with immediate effect in light of this morning's tragic accident. Every effort is being made to personally get in contact with riders who remain on the road to inform them of the situation. The tracking devices will remain open in the interests of safety and the event is continuing to work with the relevant authorities. This is a difficult time for everyone involved, along with their families, and their wellbeing is our primary concern.'

Andy, the other mechanic, starts to demount my bike while Sam shows me the way to the shower. Standing under the warm water, I feel like I have just woken up from a nightmare. Tears roll down my face.

Then I dry off and get dressed into the only clothes I have that are no dirtier than what I was wearing: the grubby pair of Rapha shorts I have worn every day of the past fortnight between rides, my alternate pair of cycling socks, an under-shirt I have worn every second day, my gilet and my cycling shoes. *I had better get some proper clothes, clean clothes,* I think to myself, and head up Rundle Mall, looking for sales.

Kathmandu has a sale on and I head in quickly. I'm soon freshly outfitted from top to toe and walk out with my filthy gear in a clear plastic bag.

Back at Treadly Bikes, my friend Amy, who had made the protein balls, is waiting to take me for a drink and then on to the airport for my late afternoon flight. Sitting in the sunshine in Amy's courtyard soon after, the time passes in a blur. We are chatting, but my mind is still weighted heavily by thoughts of

Mike. I still can't believe what has happened. By now, I would have been past Tailem Bend and riding towards Meningie, 14 kilometres shy of the 3,000 kilometre mark – not in Adelaide sipping red wine at a friend's house in an attempt to dull the shock and grief of a fatal accident.

17

I'M HOME, LIBBY...
I'M HOME

Sitting on a plane bound for Sydney from Adelaide is not where I expected to be on the early evening of 31 March 2017. But who could have forecast the turn of events in the past twelve and a half hours?

I've spoken to Libby twice since our chat in the morning. Both short calls. Both more updates, checking in. Confirming plans. She was in tears both times.

At 5 pm, on my way to the airport, I spoke with John Thompson-Mills on ABC Radio. At that stage I didn't think Mike Hall's name had been released officially, but his mother Patricia, partner Anna and his family had then been informed of the tragedy, and it had been confirmed that it was Mike who died.

By 7.55 pm I am on the last flight to Sydney, having missed my scheduled flight. Little wonder. The hours since this morning have passed in a blur, and now I'm trying to learn more about what has unfolded. The organisers and supporters of the IndiPac have begun checking in on riders still on the course, offering support and even lifts to nearby towns or cities from where the riders could return home, or at least regroup before resuming their ride. While the race has been cancelled, a number of entrants have opted to continue.

If anything, I was lucky I had arrived in Adelaide when I did.

◉

Much appears to hinge on the response of race leader Kristof Allegaert, who was nearing Moss Vale and about 220 kilometres from Sydney when he first heard about a fatal accident. With details sketchy at the time, Kristof continued racing, awaiting further information. He was just on the other side of Moss Vale when he was met by Jesse Carlsson and told about Mike. Jesse had learned of the tragedy by telephone a few hours earlier while having breakfast with official race documentary producer Anthony Gordon at a hotel near Wollongong.

As soon as they could, Jesse and Anthony hit the road to first catch Kristof who, as race leader, was the nearest of any of the IndiPac riders. They found him at about 9 am, when he listened intently to what he was told by Jesse. The extreme shift in emotion was hard, Kristof said. One moment he was focused on imminent victory, the next he was dealing with tragedy. 'There was disbelief at first,' Kristof recalled. 'I was on the edge and my head was already in Sydney.'

The first thing Kristof did was call his wife Lien in Belgium. He decided that officially, his race would end there and he turned off his GPS tracking device. But Kristof would still ride to the Sydney Opera House. 'Had it happened in the middle of the race I would have stopped riding without thinking,' Kristof said later. 'But what is 200 kilometres, after 5,200?' But out of respect for Mike, Kristof asked that there not be any fanfare at his arrival. Kristof continued on his way to Sydney, and Jesse Carlsson left to find Sarah Hammond.

The only person with Kristof when he rode up to the Opera House in darkness at about 9.30 that night was Anthony Gordon, who in the last weeks had developed a strong relationship with him. It was a solemn moment, but finishing didn't provide Kristof with any relief. And the next day, on Saturday, he and Anthony would drive to Canberra where Kristof would identify Mike's body.

◉

As for Sarah Hammond, who had been in third place behind Mike, I learn that she stopped racing at Adaminaby on the outskirts of the Kosciuszko National Park with 4,983 kilometres ridden. I feel for Sarah, heavily so. She had been riding so strongly and had been such an inspiration for so many.

For several days she had been in third place, about 100 to 150 kilometres behind Kristof and Mike as they tried to outwit and outride each other. But her consistency was a threat, should either of them slip into a physical or mental hole. Kristof and Mike liked and respected Sarah, as much as she did them; breaking the news of Mike's death to her would have been a difficult and delicate thing to do, especially this close to the end.

Other lead riders who have stopped include Kai Edel, who was behind Sarah, Matthijs Ligt, and Juliana Buhring, who had been virtually time-trialling her way back through the field since returning to Perth for treatment after her adverse reaction to medication for a knee injury, and starting the race from Fremantle all over again.

Kai was in the Kosciuszko National Park, climbing to Cabramurra, when he learned of the tragedy. As he did, he felt as if all the energy had been sapped out from him. 'I wasn't really able to ride anymore,' he said. Just a couple of days earlier, Kai had been riding with the Belgian Kim Raeymaekers; they were chatting about how dangerous some parts of Australia's highways are to cycle on. 'We hoped everyone would make it safe to Sydney,' he says. 'Also, Mike posted about the really dangerous sections of the highways and told everyone to be extra-cautious!'

Kai defied his lost motivation and strength and pushed on to Cabramurra, where he tried to sort out what would be best for him to do. Three friends of his from Ulladulla on the New South Wales south coast offered to drive him to Sydney, but Kai figured the best way to deal with his emotions was to ride on to Adaminaby. 'Riding gives me the happiest moments in life,' Kai said, guessing that it would also help him deal with the tough, sad reality.

In Adaminaby, Kai saw Sarah Hammond, who was with Jesse Carlsson. 'After a whole day of riding, trying to deal with my emotions alone, it was good to see them and talk about the accident, side-by-side.' Kai was still wrestling with it all: from the news, how abruptly it came, and the scant detail of the accident.

The next day, Kai decided to continue, to as far as the accident site near the Williamsdale Road exit onto the Monaro Highway, just south of Canberra. There he paid respect 'to Mike and his legacy', and then his Ulladulla friends drove him to Sydney, where a tribute ride would be held for Mike the next day. 'Every racer dealt differently with the situation. Some flew straight to Sydney. Some flew home or kept riding. My IndiPac ended there, on the Monaro Highway.'

◉

Kim Raeymaekers was placed 'about fifth' when he learned about Mike's death. He decided to stop riding and head straight to Sydney. He was just coming off a solid six-and-a-half hour sleep and had hit Walwa in north-east Victoria when he heard the news. He knew wasn't going to finish on the podium, so he was just enjoying his ride through the country. 'Since Australia is on the other side of the globe for me, I didn't want to waste the scenery by riding at night.'

Kim had been feeling good physically and mentally, but he'd had some technical issues with his phone so he didn't know what was unfolding. Australian rider Adam Hunter told him about the accident and Kim was so shocked he had to be shown the report to be convinced it was Mike. 'I couldn't believe it at first,' Kim said. 'He was a guy I knew . . . a friend. One of the best in the bikepacking scene; he organised the Transcontinental Race. He was always hammering on about safety. So I thought, no, this is not happening. It's got to be someone else. But I finally had contact with Jesse Carlsson and he confirmed it for me. I cried for a few minutes. All the emotions of the last two weeks came out.'

After getting a grasp on what happened, Kim decided he needed to get to Sydney as soon as he could.

'Mike was a role model of the sport and I knew he would have wanted me to keep going. But the motivation was gone, so I quit, with 4730 kilometres done,' he said. Labouring under the weight of the grief, Kim cycled to the next town, hoping to find a bus or a train. A group of cyclists saw him and asked if he was one of the IndiPac riders, and where he was hoping to go. They offered to drive him to Canberra. 'They were so friendly and welcoming,' said Kim. One of them even bought Kim a bus ticket to Sydney, so he could take part in the tribute ride for Mike the next day. 'I barely got time to talk to him,' said Kim, 'and he paid for my ticket. All he wanted was a selfie.'

◉

The night before Mike's death, Matthijs Ligt was in about eighth place and heading towards Omeo in north-east Victoria. Apart from a saddle sore he was feeling quite good, and confident he'd hold his position or even catch some slower riders ahead of him. But on the long arduous climb up 'The Back of Falls' in the Victorian Alps the next day, any thoughts of his race were swept aside when he learned of the accident in a text message.

Alone and on the first of the two biggest mountain climbs of the IndiPac, Matthijs didn't know what to do. The shock left him in denial, so he called home for more information. 'I couldn't comprehend it,' he recalled. 'I just sat down on the road in disbelief, I was speechless. I felt tears streaming down my face.' Full of clouded thoughts and confusion, Matthijs slowly continued his lonely climb up the Back of Falls and when he reached the summit he received confirmation that Mike had died in a collision with a car. Matthijs didn't have to wait to hear the race had been cancelled. 'There was no way I would continue, because this sport is first of all about enjoying the ride, and that was no longer the case.' Then he learned of the tribute ride for Mike in Sydney in two days' time and has no second thoughts. 'I needed to be there,' he said.

◉

Juliana Buhring had stopped for a couple of hours' sleep at a service station in Ceduna the night before Mike's death. She was 1,980 kilometres into her re-started race and feeling really strong. She had made incredible progress since leaving Fremantle again. 'I'd had a great day, covering 450 kilometres, and my target was to reach Port Augusta that night. I had started passing the tail-end of riders and was intent on catching the middle group.' Juliana felt really positive she was going to make a fast time, and had come so far, quitting was the furthest thing from her mind. 'At that point, nothing could have stopped me from getting to the end,' she said.

At 10.30 the next morning, Juliana received a message, but due to fatigue and hunger she didn't fully register the news until another message confirmed Mike's death. 'Then it was like getting punched in the gut,' she said. 'All the wind got knocked out of me and I couldn't breathe on my bike. I just started big hiccuping sobs. All the determination I'd felt, all the joy of the ride and the adventure, all the energy, just left me instantly. I felt so tired and weak and devastated. I stopped at the first service station I came to, and the moment I got off my bike, I lost all the will to get back on it again.'

'My ride was finished,' she said. 'I had started racing with Mike, and it felt like this was some kind of ending. I decided to hitch a ride to Adelaide to try and get a flight out to Sydney in time to get to the tribute ride.'

◉

Meanwhile, there are still dots on the tracking system for the Cycling Maven, Nick Skarejew, Tracking Jack and Steve Watson amongst others. I'm not yet sure if this is temporary or if they're heading home, as I am. But in such a tragic scenario there's no right or wrong reaction. It's up to each person to make their own decision. And I am comfortable with mine.

Sitting in my seat on the flight back to Sydney, I'm simply numb. I feel a strong need to express some thoughts about what's happened on video for my Facebook page – not judgements, assumptions or speculations, but simply where my head is at. I have a whole row of seats to myself and edge across to the window. When the race began I pledged that my reports would be honest, raw portrayals of my experiences, so although I'm hesitant, I speak as honestly as I can.

Naturally, my thoughts are of Mike and my deepest condolences are with his mother Patricia Hall, his partner Anna Haslock and his family and friends, but I feel for everyone associated with the race – from riders to followers. I start by recounting how my day unfolded up to hearing about the tragedy. Even before Libby and I spoke and the race had officially been called off, I knew immediately that I should withdraw – for me, as well as for Libby and my family.

Mike's death on the anniversary of Rod Allen's reinforced just how fragile our existence really is. Life is so tenuous and the simplest of decisions or accidents can interrupt it brutally. Fate can swing us from one extreme to the other, and today is a reminder of that.

I don't make any comment about what may have led to Mike's death on the Monaro Highway. That is for the police to investigate and a coroner's inquiry to determine. Like many on the IndiPac, I didn't know Mike well. I knew of his prodigious reputation as an ultra-endurance rider and met him in the days before the race started in Fremantle. He was immediately charming and generous of his time and counsel, from sharing riding tips and racing knowledge to safety. I know how far and wide around the world his reach was – grief in the cycling community will be global.

My last words are for those who haven't just followed and supported me on Facebook and beyond, but everyone who has got behind the riders in the IndiPac. As the Cycling Maven said so fittingly, it has to be 'the most supported unsupported race in the world'. The dot watchers have been as much a part of the IndiPac as the racers, and their infatuation with following riders on the tracking system was infectious. Having written and reported on cycling for more than thirty years, I've never seen a cycling event in Australia with such a widespread following and so little pre-event publicity.

On my mind as I fly home is also Jesse Carlsson, the instigator of the IndiPac. His vision for the event was recognition of the pioneering Overlanders of the late 1800s and early 1900s and the race gave us all the opportunity to share in something daring; but it also gave people from widely varying lives, professions, backgrounds and countries the chance to forge potentially lifetime bonds. I'm so grateful myself for having been embraced by the close-knit but very open community of ultra-endurance riding, a community in which Mike Hall was a leader and mentor.

◉

I arrive from the airport at our apartment block in Sydney's eastern suburbs with my bike box in tow. It's 10.30 pm. By now I know that tribute rides in Mike Hall's memory are being planned for the next Sunday in Sydney, Melbourne, Canberra, Perth, Brisbane and elsewhere. This is a family I want to remain a part of; I will be there.

I fumble for the keys to the front door. Libby has heard the clatter and walks out to greet me. She's standing in the corridor. The tears are still flowing.

We just hug.

'I'm home,' I tell her. 'I'm home.'

18

THE AFTERMATH
AND FALLOUT

It's Easter Saturday, two weeks since the IndiPac has been cancelled. I'm in the middle of Centennial Park in Sydney, sitting in the shade of a tree, near the coffee van at the southern end of Busby's Lake, following a club ride. The sun is shining and it's warm, despite the imminent onset of autumn.

I'm not yet fully recovered from my thirteen days of riding in the IndiPac. I've put back on a bit of the weight I lost, and am now back up to 80.2 kilograms, compared to the 79.7 kilograms I weighed five days before the race started. I never got around to weighing myself when I got home from Adelaide, but I would have been well under my starting weight. My feet are still sore – the constant pressure on the pedals has given me burning pins and needles in the balls of my feet, especially my right. And my left hand aches from the base of my palm to the end of my little finger.

I am also finding it hard to ride a high cadence and at speed. Maintaining a 24 to 25 kilometres per hour average on a pack-free road-bike is now a challenge, when once I would have averaged 27 to 30. But I have to remember I've just ridden for close to two weeks between 12 and 20 kilometres per hour with ever-present headwinds, an 11-kilogram load of packs and of course ever-present fatigue.

There are still twenty or so entrants out on the IndiPac route who have continued riding after the cancellation. Sarah Hammond initially stopped and returned home to Melbourne, but then regretted it. This morning, which is her birthday, she has resumed her ride at Adaminaby, about 100 kilometres shy of the 5,000-kilometre mark in the race. Others still out there are the American Anders Petersen, Chris Barker AKA Caveman Chris, Lochie Kavanagh and Christie Hamilton.

Now, a growing number of IndiPac riders are in Sydney. Some have come after stopping their race, others have finished riding the route. Among them are Kim Raeymaekers, Australians Adam Hunter, Heath Ryan, Davin Harding, Jackie Bernardi, who was the first woman to finish, Michael Crutch and Michael James; German-born Briton Juliana Buhring; Englishmen Mike Sheldrake and Frank Proud; Americans Nathan Jones, an organiser of the Trans Am Bike Race and who was riding the IndiPac as part of his around the world ride, and Doug Migden; and South African Ryan Flinn – minus the toy eagle he bought on the Nullarbor Plain and strapped to his handlebars. Michael Crutch was greeted at the Opera House not only by his partner Emma and me, but also by Kristof Allegaert, who offered to make a surprise finish-line cameo before flying home to Belgium.

The past fortnight has been a restless one for me. Seeing the looks of satisfaction on those who finish the IndiPac plants the seed of my desire to have another crack at it. It's also given me some time to read about Mike Hall, the person on and off the bike, and his legacy of ultra-endurance cycling. He was the owner and director of the Transcontinental Race in Europe which, along with the Tour Divide in the United States, has been the benchmark event for solo unsupported cycle races like the IndiPac. Since his death there has been much conjecture about what the future of the IndiPac might be, although it's still too early to judge.

I want to reflect positively on the race. I got so much out of it, despite the tragedy. Sure, I didn't finish, but I don't see that as having 'given up' in the pure sense of not having been able to handle the physical challenge and the mental stress. I never once felt the need to reach into my pack and take out the private letter that Rod Evans had given me back in Bruce Rock on the first day – which was only to be opened if I was on the verge of quitting. His letter is still very much sealed, the envelope slightly shabby, but its contents as unknown to me now as it was when he gave it to me. Knowing it's there helps. I know that opening it represents a last act before I think I am about to tip over the brink. That I haven't opened it is, to me, a sign of strength that I can tap into.

No, a big catalyst for me not continuing on the IndiPac was that I didn't want to put Libby through any more anxiety, the constant worry about whether I was safe. In fact, I may well have underestimated just how punishing it was for her. But then some may regard that as a component that is part and parcel of the challenge of racing events like the IndiPac that entrants need to be ready to deal with, and that not finishing – no matter what the reason or cause – is exactly that: not finishing. Part of me laments not having finished the race. I can admit that now.

It's been an emotional time for me, too. I've realised that the death of my mate Rod Allen has been in the shallows of my mind and my memory and I have spent time thinking about him and our friendship since my return. And the accident of Mike Hall's death has told me that there was nothing I could have done to have prevented Rob's. Fate plays its cards, no matter how cruel it may seem.

◉

That the cycling community was collectively mourning Mike's death was evident very early on. Tribute rides, under the banner of #bemoremike and #Ride4Mike, were organised all over Australia within days and attended by large numbers of cyclists.

Mike's mother, Patricia Hall, acknowledged the gesture and posted her support on Facebook: 'This is such a fitting tribute to Mike. I will be thinking of you all around the world riding with my son in your heart. I have not realised the great impact my son had on this sport, how well loved he is, and want you to know I do so appreciate everything Jesse and Kristof have done. Mike will be riding up front with you all.'

The Sydney ride starts at 7.30 am and sees several hundred cyclists pedal from the Rapha store in Crown Street, Surry Hills, down Oxford Street to Whitlam Square, and through the CBD to the steps of the Opera House. Thirty-six hours earlier Kristof had arrived there as the unofficial first finisher. Riding on empty streets and with my emotions still heavy, it helps to be flanked by my fellow Eastern Suburbs Cycling Club members Lexi Ford, Mara Garanzini, Geraldine Denny and Kerry Pittman.

After Kristof leads everyone to the Opera House steps, Jesse Carlsson invites any IndiPac riders to assemble before the throng of mourners. There were twelve of us: Jesse, Kristof, Sarah Hammond, Irishman Donncha Cuttriss, Briton Frank Proud, Germans Kai Edel and Juliana Buhring, Dutchmen being Jan-Willem Bobbink, Matthijs Ligt and Eelco Wijmans, Belgian Kim Raeymaekers, Canberran Steve Watson, and myself. After a minute's silence, Kristof lays a bunch of white flowers further up the steps then addresses the gathering. He asks people to not only grieve, but also to remember Mike as the 'fucking hard racer' he was. His words are brief but powerful.

The final ride back to Surry Hills is quiet, with most cycling in small groups or alone. And by the time the smell of freshly brewed coffee welcomes us at the Rapha store, spirits and smiles have begun to return. We feel we have all been part of something very special. Afterwards, there is a barbecue for the IndiPac riders there, international and Australian, which gives them a chance to chat and reflect further. 'It was like a safe bubble with really special people who have been going through some rough days together,' said Kai Edel. Kim Raeymaekers also felt the gathering afterwards was important because it allowed them all to catch up on their memories of Mike more privately, and share their own stories. 'I lost one friend on 31 March 2017,' Kim said. 'But after that tragic day I gained a lot of new friends. I think that sums up the race.'

For Juliana Buhring, who'd arrived on a flight from Adelaide the night before, the tribute ride failed to help her gain any closure. She felt as though Mike was still out there where he died, 'So I decided to ride to the finish for him.' The next Tuesday, Juliana got a lift from photographer Troy Bailey to the site of the crash, and then cycled the rest of the route to the Opera House. 'It was an emotional last ride for all of us,' she said.

◉

At a time of a tragedy and grief, it's easy to forget the good things. Three days after Rod's death, I addressed our squad cycling training group – many of whom were at the ill-fated birthday party. 'Some of you met him, others did not, but please don't forget him. He was a fabulous guy. But likewise, please don't forget the great night we had – don't be shy talking about it. He wouldn't want that.'

Likewise, with the IndiPac, as tough as many moments in the isolation and wilderness were for me, it was truly a powerful experience up until Mike's death. To not recognise that would be such a waste. I learned so many things in the IndiPac that I would like to put into practice. For example, on day eight on the Nullarbor Plain, struggling with a third puncture, standing in the heat and wind, and being ravaged by march flies, former Wallaby prop Ben Darwin's message to me, 'Work the solution', wasn't only timely but inspirational. It made me realise how you can get so bogged down with a problem that you can't look ahead and find a solution. It applies whether you're on a bike or stuck with a work or personal problem – when the smallest of issues grows to Herculean size and becomes a threat. Just for Ben's advice alone and putting it into practice in the rest of my life, the IndiPac was worth it.

◉

In the days following the tribute ride, the course was finished by Sarah Hammond and Christie Hamilton, both real highlights for me. While Sarah resumed riding on Easter Saturday to finish what she'd started, Christie was the very last finisher after an amazing six weeks that had everyone following in awe for her sheer determination to grind it out.

It was terrific to see Sarah dipping her front wheel into the Pacific Ocean at North Bondi. Jesse Carlsson was there too, having ridden the last stretch of the route for Mike from where he was killed. It seemed fitting. Three months later, Sarah did a video interview for Curve bikes. 'It was an incredible race,' she said, saying it was *the* race to do, with the perfect line-up with the perfect course, despite its terrible ending. For Sarah, it had been a chance to put a year's worth of riding to the test. When the race was cancelled she'd decided not to continue riding, but as soon as she arrived home she knew she had to go back to Adaminaby and finish. It was closure for her, and crossing the Harbour Bridge on the approach from Homebush was a difficult moment for her emotionally.

Christie Hamilton arrived at the Opera House on a glorious Friday evening with the Mango Rider, Michael Crutch and Lochie Kavanagh, who had all finished earlier but returned and rode with her over the final days to Sydney. Her smile was as bright as the gleaming white sails of the Opera House itself. Christie called the 5,470 kilometre route 'punishing', but a fun adventure too, noting you can't be happy all the time, because then you don't get the highs. She'd had seven flats and two broken spokes since Bright, and admits there was one day she was fantasising about hitch-hiking off the race. 'I'd thought through quitting before I started, and the strategy was, if I wanted to quit I had to go to a town and eat and sleep for twenty-four hours before I was allowed to tell anyone.' And she'd made it, with her trademark spirit and humour.

◉

In the weeks and months ahead, the measure of Mike Hall's reputation in ultra-endurance cycling becomes clearer. Newspapers around the world report on his death, and international magazines publish tribute features on him and his achievements, which include winning the 29,000-kilometre World Cycle Race in 2012, the 4400-kilometre Tour Divide from Canada to Mexico across the Rocky Mountains in 2013 and 2016, and the 2014 Trans Am Bike Race across the USA. A 'Just Giving' page is put together by James Hayden to help Mike's mother Patricia Hall, his partner Anna Haslock and other family to cover the costs from his death. In the first forty-eight hours, £65,170 (over $100,000 Australian dollars) are raised.

At the accident site, near the corner of Williamsdale Road and the Monaro Highway just south of Canberra, there's a memorial for Mike. A bicycle painted white, dubbed the 'ghost bike', has been erected on a paddock fence and cycling mementos and other offerings like beer, water, food, tubes, a cycling jersey – even a fold-away stool – have been left in tribute. Meanwhile, as the investigation into Mike's death continues and Australian

Capital Territory police submit a report to the coroner's office, arrangements begin for formally farewelling Mike.

Aside from a family funeral, two memorial services have been organised in which people were invited to come by bicycle and in cycling kit. The first memorial is held on 2 May at Pavilions of Harrogate in Yorkshire where Mike came from. The second memorial is over a weekend in early June, starting in the Welsh village of Abbeycwmhir where Mike lived. Locals have allowed attendees to camp in the Abbey grounds before a 20-mile (40-kilometre) ride through some of Mike's favourite riding areas – from Abbeycwmhir along the local lanes to Rhayader, over the Elan Valley to Cwmystwyth, to Ty Mawr farm in Ysbyty Cynfyn, where a party is held for what would have been his 36th birthday weekend. As Anna recalls later, 'It was a beautiful day for a ride and we carried Mike over some big climbs and great views in the part of Wales he loved best . . . The party at the end was just right – outside a big fire, we cooked two whole sheep in a big pit and drank good beer, and kids and dogs were running around and playing. There was a slack-line, and tents and campervans dotted around. He would have loved it. It was such a lovely way to remember him and so sad not to share it with him.'

Anna also opens up about how she feels about losing Mike: 'One of the things I most admired about Mike was his independence and self-reliance. To me he was indestructible. He was vulnerable in some ways as we all are, but out on the road I felt he was in his element. He knew exactly what he was doing, what the job was he needed to do and how to achieve it . . . In the short time I knew Mike, only just over three years, he became the centre of my world. He was so many things to me. My best friend and my love, my messy housemate and my adventure playmate, my business partner and my boss, my most demanding critic and my biggest fan . . . Even while he was away racing I would be glued to his dot, feeling almost as if I was there with him. His loss was the biggest trauma I have ever had to face.'

◉

Where the IndiPac might go to from here no one knows. Everyone has opinions and I have mine. But work commitments soon require me to turn my focus elsewhere. I'm covering the Giro d'Italia in May 2017 and the Tour de France in July where, at both races, I will get to catch up with the Cycling Maven as he will be there, too, filming videos, with his partner Hannah. We will no doubt reminisce about our IndiPac experience. Working on these races limits my time to cycle regularly enough to make it worthwhile. So I run instead, and when in Italy and France as much as possible in the mountains where the wilderness beckons. The IndiPac has given me a strong desire to escape into the outdoors, and I find myself compelled to run very early in the mornings – even in the dark – and through the most isolated settings I can find.

MY BIG RIDE

'YES!'

This one simple word comes out of my mouth with a charge of sheer elation.

I'm standing at the foot of the Sydney Opera House steps, under dazzling golden sunshine and a bright blue sky, holding a 26-kilogram titanium bike in the air. I feel like a weightlifter who has just produced a winning clean and jerk.

It's 11.35 am, Friday, 13 April 2018. Behind me are 5,470 kilometres, which I have just finished cycling from Fremantle to Sydney. It's taken me 27 days, 2 hours and 15 minutes, but my time isn't important; neither is my position – there are still a handful of the 50 or so individual entrants behind me. That I finished is all that matters.

The lifting of my bike is more than a full stop to a journey that began a tad under four weeks ago. It's an exclamation mark to a mission that has taken 18 months to complete – that's if

I'm not counting the years of struggling to find closure to the insecurities that have manifested themselves in various ways in my life.

I'm not sure how I've managed to lift my bike. Last night I'd given it a go in my room at Boyles Hotel at Sutherland, just south of Sydney. It was too heavy, and I dismissed the idea as a way of signing off on my cross-Australia ride.

But here I am, lifting my bike into the air – and and so is fellow rider Bernarda Jurič, an adventurer from Pjuc in Slovenia who is on her fifth visit to Australia, her first with a bicycle. We're sharing the same cocktail of joy, elation, satisfaction and relief for finishing our rides, and are now pretty drunk on the experience.

It's such a special moment, one we've been anticipating since we left Sutherland. We'd stopped on the Harbour Bridge for some photos, then resumed riding arm in arm, all the way down Macquarie Street.

'Bernarda . . . it's here, the finish,' I said as we rode the last metres towards the Opera House and the crowds outside. 'Can you believe it? We've done it!'

Bernarda's smile lit up her face as she waved in joy to all and sundry. 'I know, I'm so glad I have finished with you,' she replies.

Somehow we navigated our way through the masses to the steps, and there, waiting for me are Libby, my mother-in-law Elva and sister-in-law Genelle and other friends, while for Bernarda is her best friend who has flown from Brisbane, a throng of Sydney-based Slovenians and even representatives from one of her Slovenian sponsors. Our bond is tight; even though we met only by crossing paths during the ride, and have only spent the last night and days together.

The emotions are swirling through my mind too rapidly to contain. I feel more stunned than anything – my brain is like a hard drive overloaded with data. I'm shocked by the numbers of people who have come – friends, but strangers, too, many from the fabled legion of dot watchers who have come out to support the cyclists in this ride. I can't stop grinning, hugging, shaking hands.

And I cry. I shed them on Libby's shoulders as I embrace her on the Opera House steps. She cries too, and then says with a smile, 'You're not doing this bloody race again.'

I laugh and enjoy the moment. As we're reminded all too often, life hinges on a thin thread of fate and we can't take it for granted. So I don't – and appreciate the joy of these precious minutes. Right here, right now, I feel as assured and confident as I have ever been in my 56 years.

The route across Australia I have just finished riding is brutal – on the mind and the body – but so beautiful, too, and so rewarding. From Fremantle, across the fabled desert of the Nullarbor Plain to the city of Port Augusta, and through the hilly vineyards of the Clare and Barossa Valleys to Adelaide, where my first ride ended. And then on, as I rode through on this second ride, to Murray Bridge and Tailem Bend to the picturesque Coorong National Park and the Great Ocean Road, the climbs of the Great

Otway National Park, then back to the coast for the run to Bells Beach and then Torquay, Geelong and Melbourne before crossing the Dandenong Ranges and from Bairnsdale, up through the Victorian Alps and Kosciuszko National Park before Canberra, through the Southern Highlands of New South Wales ... and to the Sydney Opera House where I stand right now.

If it's a mouthful to describe, the route is one of the hardest to ride across Australia. But it has it all, from deserts to vineyards, wind exposed rural plains and farmlands to ocean roads, mountains and mind-numbing bicycle inner city paths. And in conditions from hot to freezing, it not only exposed me to my vulnerabilities but helped me to discover my strengths.

Looking back at my second ride, there were moments of mental and physical duress, moments when I longed for the agony of any given day to end. There were certainly very tough days on the Nullarbor. A year before, on day five, cycling from Balladonia to Caiguna, I'd given myself little hope of returning. Standing on the desert roadside to record a live video for Facebook, I said, 'This is probably the only time in my life I'll ride this road. I got to enjoy it for that reason alone.' I coped much better on my return, taking five and half days to cross it this time against a week in 2017 – but I didn't finish without being pushed to the brink once again. On the second ride, and on the second of back-to-back scorchers, from Mundrabilla to the Nullarbor Roadhouse, I almost ran out of water in 45 degree temperatures – as did a number of other riders. At the time I couldn't help but think, 'What a clichéd way to go – dying of thirst in a desert.' But luckily for me, some concerned drivers who stopped to ask if I was okay gave me some of theirs.

In 2017 I rejected such offers, citing IndiPac race rules, but this time there were no rules – the circumstances of this ride being very different. In all reality, I would have made it to the Nullarbor Roadhouse, but I wasn't going to refuse the offer when there was no reason to. However, it made me pause to think of Jerome Murif, one of the original Overlanders, and the description of his own thirst crossing a hot windy desert. On his 1897 ride from Adelaide to Port Darwin, wearing pyjamas for added comfort and high length boots to stop the sand from getting in, he wrote: 'If I had one good long drink of water, hot or lukewarm, I could die joyfully.' I know how he felt.

There were also brutal mountainous days in the last 1,000 kilometres between Melbourne and Sydney that forced me to draw on every ounce of physical and mental strength. Climbing the 'Back of Falls' in the Victorian Alps on day 21 was tough, especially the first five of the mountain's 27 kilometres, which begin with the brutal wall of the aptly dubbed 'WTF corner' – after four and a half kilometres I was forced to dismount and walk for about a kilometre. Another highlight was the remote 92 kilometre stretch from Tallangatta to Walwa that largely hugs the mighty and majestic Murray River, but most challenging – but rewarding – was the 177 kilometres I rode through the Kosciuszko National Park from Kanhcoban to Cooma on day 24 which saw me labour through 3,465 metres of climbing. It was the perfect challenge and strengthened me for the next day, the ride into Canberra, where'd I'd meet up with Libby and catch up with some friends for a barbecue that night.

That day was set to be my most emotional after the 31 March anniversary of Mike Hall's death, which fell on day 15 of my second ride. At 6.22 am, when Mike's tracker stopped, I got off my bike 15 kilometres out from Robe to pay my respects by standing alone in the dark in silence for a minute. The ride to Canberra, though, was the day I passed the site of Mike's death on the outskirts of Canberra.

I had been readying myself for the moment ever since committing to the ride. I wasn't even sure what I would do when I reached the white 'Ghost Bike'. The memorial was set up by Todd Bonney, a local rider who looks after it and brings fresh flowers every month. I saw Todd in his van on my approach to the site – I pulled over and we chatted for half an hour. After parting ways, I was still thinking about Mike, about his impact and all that has unfolded since. Suddenly, my stomach was gripped in a knot, and my eyes started to well. Thoughts of Mike, his death and the senselessness of it all overcame me and I wept.

Kilometres passed and my tears dried, and then I saw it on my left – the 'the Ghost Bike'. I was filled with calm, a sense of

finality about the reality of what happened, and an acknowledgement that I would keep riding, lovingly, and to the end.
I wrote a message on a card to leave there, and looked at the
other memorabilia, taking a photo to mark the occasion. Fittingly,
after sitting there for about half an hour, the sun broke through
the overcast sky. I stood up, slowly walked with my bike to the
road and remounted.

'See ya, Mike,' I said, then I pushed on, looking forward to a
happy reunion with Libby in Canberra.

Soon after reaching the national capital and Parliament
House, I set off to find the hotel where I was meeting Libby, with
Michael James's help, who came out to greet me after finishing
his ride several days earlier.

I was excited to see Libby after everything that had happened,
and opening the door of our room at the hotel, there she was. I
walked in and we hugged.

'You stink,' said Libby with a laugh.

She was right. No sooner had I brought all my gear in than
I was doing what I had been doing for the last weeks: plugging
in electronics, refilling water bottles and finally showering. But
the one big fantastic difference was that I was with her, and able
to escape from the tunnel vision of my ride for a few hours and
enjoy an evening with friends.

The next day I would be on my way to the Southern Highlands
of New South Wales, and then the final run in to Sydney. I had
arranged to stay with Richard Vollebregt and his wife Pamela,

a local cyclist who'd set a new Guinness World Record in 2006 for the fastest assisted direct cycle across Australia. Richard would ride the last kilometres into Moss Vale with me. And it would be at the Moss Vale Hotel, owned by an old school mate Tom Porter, where Bernarda and I would unite for our final run in to Sydney – she arrived into town while we were eating dinner and Richard offered her a room to sleep that night, too.

The time I spent thinking on my way from Canberra into the highlands was invaluable, and some of the most memorable for me – my last hours alone in this great adventure were from Bungendore to Bundanoon where I met Richard, and I accompanied my thoughts with the soundtrack of my 'IndiPac Playlist' one last time.

Music had done wonders for me in this ride across Australia, especially in the Nullarbor. My selected songs – the music, lyrics, and rhythms – motivated me to ride at levels I would normally shy away from over extended distances. I hadn't felt the need to take any music in the first race – it had crossed my mind, but I thought it might be a distraction and put me at risk of road trains, caravans and cars, and animals, if I couldn't hear them coming. But used wisely, when the roads are relatively quiet like in the calm of a mid-week afternoon in the Southern Highlands, the music was a revelation – it pulled me further into myself and provided a gateway for my deepest thoughts on the ride.

As I thought about all that had happened to this point, pure emotion broke through like sets of waves at the beach – joy at all but having completed my ride, regret that this incredible experience was coming to an inevitable end, and gratitude that I had my health and the love of life, and family and friends to support me.

◉

I began the 2018 ride with a number of objectives, and of course these were all part of my broader goal to finish in Sydney – and safely. I also wanted to show it was possible to ride a course like this and still have fun and maintain good overall general health – all objectives that I achieved. My plan was to stop each day at sunset and resume in the early morning in the dark, rather than ride into the night when I and so many on the roads were tired. I also aimed to chat with nearly every dot tracker who came to see or ride with me, and took time to engage with anyone I would see at night, at motel or pub – and I nearly always enjoyed a couple of beers each night with dinner!

But perhaps the first of all my goals was to put into practice what I learned from the 2017 race. Apart from being physically stronger, and being more efficient with the practicalities and planning of the ride because of the experience, my biggest development was in my composure – not allowing problems to overcome me, like the flat tyre on the Nullarbor did in my first ride, and making the best of the opportunities that arise, such as those magnificent tailwinds that push you along on the road.

Deep down I knew I would finish, barring accident. I knew I would not need to open the letter Rod Evans had given me for the 2017 IndiPac for 'when things get tough', but had still brought it with me on this ride as a sort of talisman. I knew getting beyond Adelaide would be a test and a symbolic moment. And I came through with flying colours – I may have ridden into the unknown, but the confidence I had in myself to respond to conditions and problems as they arose made up for any lack of experience of the route or the terrain, even though the mountain passes were some of the most challenging rides of my life.

◉

Considering all the gains of my second race – 'My Big Ride' – it's remarkable it ever got underway, considering its wavering prospects in the tragic aftermath of the inaugural IndiPac. After months of speculation, the event organisers, Dragon Face Pty Ltd, announced in late 2017 that a second race would be held in 2018, on 17 March and at 6.22 am, the time that Mike's dot stopped.

The new race would have a stricter qualifying system and new safety and security measures that included riders being required to have two front and two rear lights, a rear reflector, reflective ankle straps and reflective tape on their bike's crank arms and seat stays. Riders would also have to wear a reflective vest and have their lights on between 4 pm and 8 am and when visibility was poor.

The field would also be limited to 70 entrants plus 10 invitational starters, and this time it would include four-rider relay teams with each member riding one of four main legs – Fremantle to Adelaide, Adelaide to Melbourne, Melbourne to Canberra and Canberra to Sydney. This time around, all entrants had to undergo a three-tiered application process, which included supplying proof they had ridden at least 800 kilometres in a ride, and explaining how they would manage their sleep, as well as signing a waiver accepting they were their own organiser, and their next of kin signing a letter confirming they supported them racing in the IndiPac.

It didn't take long for the 2018 IndiPac field to fill. After the first entry deadline, entrants waited anxiously to learn if they had passed phase one of the process. That included me, even though Libby was reluctant – she had signed the next of kin support letter, but on the proviso we continue to discuss me actually starting. All this was enough for me to start planning and plotting – and training. I was confident of being able to reassure Libby with the new safety measures in place, and agreed to discuss any concern she had and find the best solution, as well as taking any extra measures to help ease her anguish during the race.

Getting back into the groove of training wasn't so hard. The 2017 IndiPac had given me a good base to start from, as well as the running I continued with after last year's race. This time around I decided to style my own training program – thankfully I had limited my weight gain in the meantime.

I continued training with the cycling squad on Tuesdays and Thursdays in Sydney's Centennial Park, and added extras, and kept twice-weekly gym sessions with my trainer, Nicola Vrachnas working more on strength and skills which helped develop my level of mental alertness under stress. In the 2017 race, my most vulnerable decision-making moments came when I was most fatigued.

I also decided to enter the inaugural Revolve 24 event, which would be held over the 13th and 14th of January, at the new brand new motor racing circuit called The Bend at Tailem Bend, about an hour's drive east from Adelaide. Revolve 24 is held on a closed circuit and the challenge of racing twenty-four hours straight is big, but it would also help me re-adapt to riding at night and give me a good lead-in experience to focus on.

My plan unfolded well over the next weeks in the gym. My lost muscle returned, and my weight, BMI and body fat levels started to drop. That is, until I came down with a left inguinal hernia. I opted to have surgery as soon as possible, even though it meant postponing a long-promised holiday to Hawaii with Libby. But with 22 November the first date I could have the surgery, the window for recovery and rehabilitation was narrow at best. Within days of going under the knife, though, I was powerwalking for up to three hours, and within a week I was back on the spin bike. After two weeks I was riding easily with the cycling squad and making good progress in the gym.

By week three, I was pushing myself in training. If anything, I felt fresher for the enforced short break.

By week six, in January 2018 – the weekend of Revolve 24 – I was racing better than I could ever have imagined. With the terrific backing of my 'all Greek' support crew of my trainer Nicola and Adelaide bicycle mechanic Bill Dragos, I placed ninth from thirty-four soloists, with a tally of 586.5 kilometres ridden in the twenty-four hour window. I didn't sleep, but took a total of two hours in breaks for food and drink. My IndiPac 2018 project could not be going better.

But on Tuesday 6 February, an email at 8.43 pm reminded me how the best plans can go awry. From Dragon Face Pty Ltd, the missive announced that the 2018 IndiPac had been called off. At a meeting that day of parties involved in the ACT coroner's inquiry into Mike Hall's death, which would be held later in the year, it was agreed the 2018 IndiPac would be cancelled.

Everyone responded differently, but my initial desire is still to ride the route. It may not be the IndiPac, but it could still be 'My Long Ride'. There was no shortage of motivation – from honouring Mike and all he stood for, to promoting the freedom to safely cycle where and when we want, to finishing unresolved business, and tapping back into the purity of cycling on your own.

I knew not everyone would be happy about me wanting to still ride the route, including Libby – and I didn't waste any time testing the waters of her position on it.

One night I asked her, 'Are you relieved the race has been called off?'

'Yes,' she said simply, walking away down the corridor of our apartment.

'But it doesn't mean the ride has been cancelled,' I called out. 'I can still ride the route.'

There was silence. Libby had stopped in her tracks. I heard her coming back, and her face said enough: she was dead set against it. 'You still want to ride it? I don't think so,' she said.

I didn't push the issue. I had already lobbed one hand grenade too many for the night.

The ensuing weeks passed by quickly. I continued my training and preparation calmly, but at home, discussion about the IndiPac – from its cancellation to talk of me still riding – became limited. While Libby knew of my intent to still ride, I didn't want to push the subject unless she raised it, but I also didn't want to dismiss her concerns by not talking about it. It became the elephant in the room.

But gradually the subject emerged more often between us, and when it did I tried to focus on addressing any of the issues she raised. My preparations mounted, and my program culminated with a three-day gravel tour with three friends in the Kosciuszko National Park on the weekend before Libby and I flew to Hawaii. We would be on holiday there for a week and a half, and then I would fly to Perth for the start of the race.

In Hawaii, I still tried to temper my open enthusiasm open for the ride but freely answer any questions Libby raised, and I continued to train, running and cycling on an indoor spin bike, and hiking with Libby. She still had understandable anxiety about it all – and that kind of angst can't be underestimated; I understood. But there's also considerable selfishness in taking part in something like this ride, and I was rightly reminded of that, one night at dinner.

'So when are you flying to Perth?' Libby asked.

'Next Wednesday,' I replied with wine glass in hand. 'Look, I know it's a pretty selfish thing to do—

'Selfish?' Libby interjects. 'It's bloody selfish.'

I have no answer . . . She's right, I thought.

Silence swept over our table for a while. Then Libby asked, 'If I asked you not to go for me, what would you do?'

My delay in answering condemns me. What were several long seconds felt like minutes.

But Libby's question is so pertinent. We leave the restaurant in silence and she goes for a walk in the hotel resort. I head to our room, thinking. There are only two ways this can go. I choose not to go, because she doesn't want me to, and I will resent that, and her. Or I choose to go, and she will resent that, and me.

Stalemate – or just the recognition of the intricacies of a long-term loving marriage, where there is push and pull on both sides? I totally understood where Libby was coming from, but this far down the track, I knew I would still go, and Libby knew I would too.

Accepting all of these things, we didn't talk about it again. And the next day our holiday resumed on its happy way to the end. I was committed to the ride, but I was just as committed to doing all I could to allay Libby's fears along the way.

And to her eternal credit and with my eternal gratitude, Libby committed just as strongly to supporting me to ride it.

◉

In the end, 54 cyclists registered of the MAProgress tracker to start the ride despite the official event being cancelled – at least 50 riding as individuals or as members of relay teams plus several riders who had not registered on the tracker but were committed to riding. With no official organiser behind it, there were no rules or restrictions about how anyone should ride. And there were also no restrictions on what kind of support the public – dot watchers and road angels alike – could offer to riders on the way.

And the public took it to heart, nurturing the 2018 ride from its start to its end, with riders being offered all sorts of resources for a safe, enjoyable and rewarding passage across Australia. Key to the success of the unofficial ride was the creation of a public Facebook page, 'Indian Pacific Wheel Ride (Dot Watchers)'. The site stated clearly that it wasn't in any way officially connected or affiliated with the Indian Pacific Wheel Race or its organisers, but would become a hub of information and communication for anyone taking part in or interested in the ride, and attracted 4,000-plus followers.

From those who lined up at the South Mole Lighthouse in Fremantle on 17 March 2018, a number were there to race – and race hard; some were there to race but with an open mind; some, like me, were there to ride the route but with concerted effort to not waste time; and finally there were some who would take their time and stop for several days to take in the sights and the people before finishing.

There were only six in the field who also started in the 2017 race. This doesn't include Heath Ryan, a publisher from Melbourne who finished the IndiPac in 2017 – for the 2018 ride, he opted to follow the Fremantle to Sydney route ridden by Sir Hubert Opperman in 1937 instead of the IndiPac course. He wanted to pay tribute to Mike Hall, but also to honour 'Oppy', a superstar in his time, who on top of his intrepid rides and point to point races, also placed respectably in the 1928 and 1931 Tours de France.

Of the six who rode the IndiPac route a second time, three claimed back-to-back finishes – Ryan 'Rhino' Flinn, Chris 'The Caveman' Barker, and Michael James, who all bettered their 2017 times – the Rhino in 18 days against the 25 days he took to finish the 2017 race; Chris in 22 days – 10 days better than the year before; and Michael, who took 23 days in 2017 and finished with Chris. Claire Stevens, a surgeon from Melbourne, reached Sydney on day 23, and I manage to finish too on day 28. And I'm sure Kerwyn Ballico – a retired Navy search and rescue helicopter crewman who I met in the 2017 race and who I rode and shared a room with for several days and nights while crossing the Nullarbor in the 2018 ride – would have finished if he hadn't developed a saddle sore, which ended his ride at Port Augusta. Kerwyn had to stop in 2017 due to infection of a cut in his arm after crashing on the Nullarbor Plain.

And of course there were many new faces, with some exceptional individual performances. Take Abdullah Zeinab, one of a growing number of vegans in cycling. Melbourne-based Abdullah is a videographer who has his own YouTube channel 'The Glucose Factory', and filmed a documentary of the 2017 IndiPac in which he shot some captivating moments between Kristof Allegaert and Mike Hall. Abdullah returned in 2018 to race and lead from the start – after averaging 450 kilometres a day, he became first finisher in 14 days, 28 minutes and 10 seconds. In second place was the experienced French ultra-endurance rider Stéphane Mehdi Ouaja, who finished on day 16. Australian Matt Sully held third place later on day 17, followed by Australian Mark Croonen, AKA 'Grumpybug' on day 18 in fourth, followed on the same day by the Perth-based New Zealander Callum Henderson in fifth, and then Ryan 'Rhino' Flinn in sixth, Rowan McMurray in seventh and former Fremantle Dockers AFL footballer Brad Bootsma in eighth place, in an effort that saw him raise $7,050 for the Chemo Club to honour his friend Mark Rimell, who died in 2013 from oesophageal cancer.

We were also treated to the impressive performances of Pawel 'Pico' Pulawski from Poland and Joseph Kendrick from England, who both cycled on fixed-wheel bikes and finished on days 20 and 21 respectively. Kendrick even continued on after reaching Sydney, riding to Cairns, which he reached on the evening of 5 May for a journey that totalled 8,500 kilometres.

Another incredible performance was by Melbourne bike courier Elizabeth Long, who I rode with and chatted to for most of day one to Bruce Rock. Liz rode off into the night towards Merredin and went on to finish eleventh and become the first woman to finish the ride on day 20.

Purdie Long, a Victorian Police detective who races bikes in road events for the Total Rush team, finished on day 22; as did Newcastle fitness trainer Su Pretto, a dot watcher in 2017 who was told by her son, 'Stop talking about the Indi, Mum, and just bloody do it', and Sydney-based Briton Rob Leslie, AKA 'Boyracer'.

Danish rider Sanne Røhe, a former airline pilot and now psychologist, passed me when I was in Canberra and reached Sydney on day 27; Vikram Singh, an Australian Army Reservist from Western Australia, who started 14 hours late due to shooting range duties but swept through the field to finish on day 21; and Naresh Kumar, riding to continue his worldwide campaign to raise awareness and funds in the fight against sex trafficking, rode into Sydney on day 25. When Naresh heard of the IndiPac in 2017 he was already on 'Freedom Seat', another fundraising expedition to stop sex trafficking, this time riding 3,330 kilometres from north to south in New Zealand on a tandem bike, picking up strangers who donated funds. After 35 days he had raised $60,000.

There were so many other exceptional people who I met and rode with. But in my mind, no one threw themselves into the 2018 ride more than Jaye Fatchen, who raised more than $10,000 through her fund raising efforts to help a severely disabled little girl named Paige and her family. I first met Jaye in Fremantle on the eve of the ride at Bathers Bay where we dipped our rear wheels, then she was seemingly everywhere . . . first riding in a relay team named 'Stranger than Fiction' as their Nullarbor crossing member and then, after she finished her leg, offering support to all and sundry with offers of food and accommodation at her family's Café Milche at Falls Creek in the Victorian Alps. She also helped riders on the climb up Tawonga Gap, where she and her friend, Roz Bradley, laid picnics for riders at the top of the climb, and also cycled with a number of riders, supporting them through the Victorian Alps and Kosciuszko National Park. And all this before riding on to Sydney where she arrived on day 35, several hours after Melburnian Heny Yates.

In the days following my own race, being there to welcome those I could as they hit the Opera House was almost as enjoyable as finishing myself, and included Dale Tan, a remote nurse from Cooktown in Far North Queensland, Western Australian Brad Ewings AKA 'Mrcycology', Perth's Justin McLean, who at 17 was the youngest rider, and the last rider on the tracker, Briton Josh 'Burty' Burt.

⊙

And just like that, it all came to an end: an adventure that for me began when I read that first advertisement asking: 'Is the Overlander in you?' – one that became so much more than I had ever bargained for.

I still don't know if I have what it takes to be an Overlander, not in the true hardened sense like those who forged the way back in the late 1890s, and even those who are forging ahead today with what has become a resuscitation of their heritage. But I am certainly proud and extremely happy to have finished a ride of the scale of the IndiPac on the second attempt.

And no question: I'm so grateful that I got to have a second crack at it, and am so appreciative of the support of everyone who got me through it – from Libby, of course, to family, friends and a public whose enthusiasm for every rider in both attempts was so humbling.

But while finishing such an epic ride was so satisfying and certainly went a good way to helping me deal with some of my issues – my self-confidence, self-esteem and trickier spin-off issues such as my bulimia – I'd be lying if I said it had eradicated them. They are all still a part of me, components of my make-up, but now they're components I can now openly recognise and manage, rather than try to hide them or bury them.

Far more experienced ultra-endurance riders have told me they are always learning; that every race teaches them something. I used to think they were referring to their ride or performance, but now I see they mean far more than that. Certainly I can see areas of my performance that I can still improve on, particularly if I want to 'race' rather than 'ride' an ultra-endurance event again.

Perhaps the best thing I've learned is not to be afraid of failure, or of exposing myself for my vulnerabilities by daring to try something I have not taken on before. For that reason, I can say the IndiPac – both official and unofficial – is complete for me. I have learned so much about myself as a person – my strengths and skills, but more importantly my weaknesses and flaws and that I have no reason to be ashamed of them. After all, I'm just a human being. But hopefully now I'm better equipped to not only accept who I am, but embrace it.

NOTES

Page xiv: from Harris, Bret, *Tour de Oz – The Extraordinary Story of the First Bicycle Race Around Australia*, HarperCollins Publishers, 2018, p 3.

Page 34: from Murif, Jerome, *From Ocean to Ocean: Across a Continent on a Bicycle – An Account of a Solitary Ride from Adelaide to Port Darwin*, George Robertson & Co, 1897, p 12.

Page 155: from Murif, Jerome, *From Ocean to Ocean: Across a Continent on a Bicycle – An Account of a Solitary Ride from Adelaide to Port Darwin*, George Robertson & Co, 1897, p 47.

Page 283: from Murif, Jerome, *From Ocean to Ocean: Across a Continent on a Bicycle – An Account of a Solitary Ride from Adelaide to Port Darwin*, George Robertson & Co, 1897, p 47.

BIBLIOGRAPHY

Books

Burston, G.W., *Round About the World on Bicycles – The Pleasure Tour of G.W. Burston and H.R. Stokes*, George Robertson and Company, 1890.

Fitzpatrick, Jim, *Wheeling Matilda – The Story of Australian Cycling*, Star Hill Studio Pty Ltd, 2013.

Guinness, Rupert, *Power of the Pedal – The Story of Australian Cycling*, National Library of Australia, 2018.

Harris, Bret, *Tour de Oz – The Extraordinary Story of the First Bicycle Race Around Australia*, HarperCollins Publishers, 2018.

Murif, Jerome, *From Ocean to Ocean: Across a Continent on a Bicycle – An Account of a Solitary Ride from Adelaide to Port Darwin*, George Robertson & Co, 1897.

Richardson, Arthur C.J., *The Story of a Remarkable Ride*, The Dunlop Tyre Co. of Australia, 1900.

Websites

Boles, Mike, *A Free Guide to Cycling Across Australia's Nullarbor*, Travelling Two, www.travellingtwo.com/13620

Brown, Meaghen, *The Longer the Race, the Stronger We Get*, Outside Online, May 2017, www.outsideonline.com/2169856/longer-race-stronger-we-get

Buhring, Juliana, *In Memory of Mike Hall, the Man Who Inspired a World of Cyclists*, Outside Online, April 2017, www.outside online.com/2173576/mike-hall-man-who-inspired-world-cyclists

Gallivanting Oz, Perth to Adelaide (Nullarbor) Travel Route, www.gallivantingoz.com.au/travel-routes/perth-adelaide

ACKNOWLEDGEMENTS

When reflecting on an event like the 2017 Indian Pacific Wheel Race and the unofficial version of it in 2018, as powerful as the good, bad and most significant memories may be is the impact of those who have supported me in my attempts to finish the 5470 kilometre route and the writing of this book. But foremost, I must look to those whose love for Mike Hall saw them pay the heaviest of prices with his tragic death – Mike's mother Patricia Hall and his partner Anna Haslock. Both are still passionately involved with the bikepacking fraternity, Patricia through her open engagement with members of the community, and Anna through her continued direction of the Transcontinental Race that Mike created and ran with her. May every strength, success and happiness come to both of you.

As for me and my experience that led to this book being commissioned before the 2017 IndiPac and now published, I owe thanks to so many that naming everyone is a challenge.

My gratitude starts with the dot trackers and people who have followed my Facebook, to those like Jesse Carlsson, Adam Lana and Ryan 'Rhino' Flinn who backed me with moral support and technical backing from Curve bicycles, Andy Pike and Adam Taylor-Campbell at Rapha Apparel, Chris Peacock and his replacement George Huxford at Apidura bike packs, Paul Molyneux from Métier cycling attire, Kerry Staite from K-Lite lighting, Mark Fenner at FTP training, Nicola Vrachnas, my personal trainer from Longevity Training run by Jarrat Wood at Russell Cox's Regenesis gym, Frank Conceicao from Albion Cycles and his staff, my fellow Eastern Suburbs Cycling Club clubmates and other riders who have supported me (special tilt of the lid to ESCC president Colin Iremonger, Stu MacDougall, Jen Benson, Peter 'Cipo' O'Connor, Phil and Jude Mathewson), Sydney University Cycling Club patron and good mate, Mike Tomalaris of SBS fame and Andy Matthews, especially for their support during my 2018 ride, and my Revolve 24 mechanic Bill Dragos.

I owe a big shout out to Anthony Gordon who I first talked to about riding the IndiPac and from which he produced a fabulous documentary that was seen on many a Qantas flight with his equally as helpful driver Troy Grice. Anthony has since been a huge support and mate. Also big thanks to photographer and cyclist Troy Bailey, who shot some beautiful work of the 2017 race and has supplied some great photographs for this book; and Arran Pearson for his advice on preparation and packing.

Then there are the riders I got to know through the 2017 IndiPac and 2018 ride, some I saw over and over in both, to those I met back in Sydney, and later through social media. On social media, many noted the 'bromance' between myself and The Cycling Maven – Mark Ferguson – in the 2017 IndiPac. I got to know the Maven well after our first meeting the year before at the 2016 Tour de France, and we spent some excellent time together until we parted at Kimba on day eleven – whether that was chatting in the saddle or at roadhouses while consuming far too many hamburgers, chocolate milks, chocolate bars, chips, muffins, jelly beans . . .

There are still many others who booked a place in my soul in both of my 2017 and 2018 rides across Australia. From the 2017 IndiPac, I think of Jesse Carlsson, Sarah Hammond, Ryan 'Rhino' Flinn, Nick Skarajew, Sam O'Dea, the Mango Rider (Ben Cadby), Americans Anders Petersen and Doug Migden, Humungous Hugh (Hugh Moore), Tracking Jack (Jack Heyward), Dutchman Eelco Wijmans, Michael Crutch, Michael James, Sam Jeffries and James Raison and all who I stood with at the Opera House at the tribute ride for Mike in Sydney. Add to that Australian endurance legend Rod Evans, who gave such great insights to us all before the 2017 race, then gave me a personal letter in an envelope titled 'For When Things Get Tough' which still remains unopened with my 2018 ride finished. I'll also forever be grateful for the warmth and support I received in Adelaide after learning of Mike Hall's death – the crew at Treadly Bikes, owner Sam Neeft, and mechanics Jake Thomas and Andy Rogers;

Catherine Seal Yates and Paul Black for their compassion in Adelaide when I was on the brink; and Amy de Wall for nursing me to my return flight back to Sydney.

There are also those who I got to know better following the tragic end to the 2017 race through time spent together in Sydney soon after it and especially when I sought information about their race: the first finisher, Belgian Kristof Allegaert, who has kindly written the foreword for this book; fellow Belgian Kim Raeymaekers, Dutchmen Jan-Willem Bobbink and Matthijs Ligt and Germans Kai Edel and Juliana Buhring.

Then to the 2018 unofficial ride, or 'My Big Ride'. I am indebted to having ridden at varying times with Elizabeth 'Liz' Long, Claire Stephens, Purdie Long and again Michael James, and of course Kerwyn Ballico, Shane Beaumont and Haydn Bevan and finally, after several cross-paths along the way, the tremendous Bernarda Jurič. A tilt of the lid again to Michael Crutch for his support via Facebook; also to Rowan McMurray for backing up from his own ride to welcome me, as did Michael James on my entry to Canberra with a swag of goodies; likewise to 'Caveman' Chris Barker for offering some photos and helpful insights on his 2017 race and 2018 ride. I also want to pay tribute to the Indian duo, Naresh Kumar and Vikram Singh, Finnish Sanne Røhe, Australians Tan Dale and Brad Ewings, the Thai Korpong Engtrakul ('Bombwhiskey'), Australians Justin Marshall, Henry Yates, Jaye Fatchen, former AFL player Brad Bootsma, whose personal insights near the end of writing this book helped provide me with some clarity of thought, Damian van Loon for his assistance with some facts and figures, and the ever-positive 'lanterne route' Josh 'Burty' Burt from Great Britain.

Of course, this book would not have been possible were it not for the support of my agent and friend Jeanne Ryckmans, and the superb team at Simon & Schuster Australia, especially my publisher Roberta Ivers whose sheer enthusiasm is matched by her patience; Janet Hutchinson for her sharp edit of the manuscript and suggestions, cover designer Christa Moffitt, and PR and marketing campaign manager Kirsty Noffke, and Director of Publicity Anna O'Grady, and the whole Simon & Schuster sales team there who have done such a great job getting this book into bookshops around the country. Similarly, I am indebted to Crossing the Line for their support and encouragement and allowing me time to go on my 2018 ride – to founder Gearoid Towey and Communications Manager Lorna Hankin, thanks so much.

Last but definitely not least, I owe so much to my long suffering but supportive wife Libby, who I have really put through the mill with my pursuits. Despite her angst and fears she has been ironclad in her support through the good and, most importantly, bad, sad and challenging times. The day after I finished my 2018 ride, I left Libby some flowers in the kitchen with a card to express my thanks and love for her, but I also said 'I am sorry' for putting her through hell. If anyone showed strength through all of this, it was certainly Libby.

LIST OF GEAR TAKEN ON THE ROAD

MY BIKE

Frame: Curve 'Belgie Spirit' Titanium Disc

Forks: Curve full carbon tapered CCRD FM12mm

Handlebars: ZIPP Service Course

Aaero bars: Clip on TI+ Profile Design

Headset: Curve sealed bearing

Stem: ZIPP Service Course

Brake levers: SRAM Force 22

Brakes: SRAM Force 22 disc

Front derailleur: SRAM X7 2×10 HDM

Rear derailleur: SRAM X7 Type 2 10 Speed

Cranks: SRAM Force 172.5mm

Gears: SRAM Force 22 compact 50/34T 11 speed

Bottom bracket: SRAM GXP

Chain: SRAM PC1051 10 Speed

Pedals: Crank Brothers Candy 1 mountain bike (green)

Saddle: Curve Velo saddle

Seatpost: Curve Titanium

Wheels: Curve G4 35mm × 25mm Road Disc

Front hub: LED-Scheinwerfer Edelux SONdelux dynamo

Rear hub: White Industries USA

Tires: Bontrager 700 × 28

Bottle cage: 2 × Bontrager RL (lime green)

ON THE ROAD IN THE 2017 INDIPAC
Cycling kit

1 × 'Helping Rhinos' Velotex cycling jersey

1 × Rapha short sleeved brevet jersey

1 × Rapha 'Pro Team' blue short sleeved base layer

1 × Rapha 'Pro team' pink short sleeved base layer

1 × Rapha jacket

1 × Rapha Brevet insulated gilet

1 × Rapha bib 'n' brace shorts

1 × Easts Cycling Champion System gilet

1 × Easts Cycling Champion System bib 'n' brace shorts

1 × Gill wet weather sailing gloves

1 × Easts Cycling Champion System cold weather gloves

1 × Easts Cycling Champion System hand mitts

1 × Kask cycling helmet – green
and black

1 × Easts Cycling Champion
System cap

1 × Rapha sunglasses

1 × Helly Hansen thermal beanie

1 × Montbell ear warmer/headband

1 × neck Buff

1 × Rapha black merino cotton arm
warmers

1 × Crane Performance white arm
warmers

1 × Rapha black merino cotton
knee warmers

1 × Rapha mountain bike shoes –
black

1 × Unbranded winter booties

2 × pairs socks (1 × Rapha cotton,
1 × Easts Cycling Champion
System)

Mechanical
4 × oxygen 'bombs' with valve
connection

4 × Bontrager spare tubes

1 × Bontrager AIRsupport hand
pump

1 × Bontrager multi tool kit

1 × Swiss Army knife

1 × Thumbs Up puncture repair kit

1 × 120ml bottle Squirt dry chain
lubricant

1 × set tyre levers

1 × small roll of gaffa tape

1 × small roll packaging tape

1 × roll electrical tape

1 × tube Super Glue

1 × half-dozen spare spokes

1 × set of spare plastic ties

Computers/lights/electrics
1 × Garmin Edge 520

1 × Garmin heart rate monitor

1 × Spot Gen3 device

1 × Garmin Etrex 30

1 × iPhone and earphones

1 × smartphone as back-up

1 × K Lite dynamo front light
system, 1300 Lumens

1 × Sinewave Revolution USB
system

1 × ZMI 5000mAh powerbank, 120g

1 × Fuse recharging adaptor for
3 items

1 × pack 12 XX alkaline batteries

1 × Moon Mask 5 LED rechargeable
front light, 70 Lumens

1 × Moon 360 helmet light,
360 Lumens

1 × Zefal Spy rear view mirror

3 × Azur rechargeable rear lights,
100 Lumens

3 × ankle/arm reflectors

5 × re-charger cords

Personal hygiene and care
1 × toothbrush

1 × tube toothpaste

1 × jar of McEwen chamois cream

2 × Rapha chamois cream sachets

1 × 100 Water purifying pills

1 × pack bandages and medical kit

1 × massage ball

1 × pack of Voltaren

1 × pack of Nurofen

1 × jar multivitamin pills

1 × tube sunblock cream

2 × Shotz electrolyte drink tablets

2 × Gel energy sachets

Extras
1 × bike lock

1 × small plastic bottle

1 × whistle

1 × spare cord/rope

1 × Quad Lock to hold iPhone on headstem

1 × chamois sports towel

1 × hair net

1 × Hawaiian shirt

1 × pair Rapha 'Randonée' shorts

1 × wallet: cash, 2 credit cards, bank card, Medicare card, BUPA card, Cycling Australia card, professional identity card

2 × Platy Bottle 2 litre water bladders

2 × Ocky straps

3 × Kathmandu dry sacks (three sizes)

3 × 750ml drink bottles

3 × Kathmandu seal bags

6 × Apidura packs (1 rear saddle, 1 under top tube, 1 on top tube, 1 under handlebars, 2 pouches for drink and/food)

Sleeping items

1 × Kathmandu Bivy XT bag 600 grams

1 × Mountain Designs silk sleeping bag sock, 100 g

1 × Exped air pillow 4 grams

1 × Seat to Summit Ultra Light air mattress, 345 g

1 × Seat to Summit Pump Sack, 48 g

1 × Kathmandu Emergency v3 blanket, 60 g

1 × plastic sheet

ON THE ROAD IN THE 2018 'MY BIG RIDE'
Cycling kit

1 × Easts Cycling Champion System jersey

1 × Rapha 'Pro Team' blue short sleeved base layer

1 × Rapha 'Pro Tour' pink short sleeved base layer

1 × Rapha jacket

1 × Rapha bib 'n' brace shorts

1 × Métier Beacon gilet

1 × Easts Champion System gilet

1 × Easts Cycling Champion System bib 'n' brace shorts

1 × Gill wet weather sailing gloves

1 × Torpeako thermal gloves

1 × Bellwether cold weather gloves

1 × Circuit Glove yellow hi-viz hand mitts

1 × Kask cycling helmet – green and black

1 × Easts Cycling Champion System cap

1 × Bollé sunglasses

1 × Helly Hansen thermal beanie

1 × Montbell ear warmer/headband

1 × neck Buff

1 × Easts Cycling Champion System arm warmers

1 × Crane Performance white arm warmers

1 × Easts Cycling Champion System knee warmers

1 × Rapha mountain bike shoes – black

1 × pair ASSOS winter booties

2 × pairs socks (1 × Rapha light blue cotton, 1 × Nike Dri Fit)

Mechanical

4 × oxygen 'bombs' with valve connection

4 × Bontrager spare tubes

1 × Lezyne Pressure Drive hand pump

1 × Bontrager Multi tool kit

1 × Swiss Army knife

1 × Thumbs Up puncture repair kit

1 × 120ml bottle Squirt dry chain lubricant

1 × set tyre levers
1 × small roll packaging tape
1 × small roll of gaffa tape
1 × roll green electric tape
1 × tube Super Glue
1 × half-dozen spare spokes
1 × set of spare plastic ties

Computers/lights/electrics

1 × Garmin Edge 520
1 × Spot Gen3 device
1 × Garmin Etrex 30
1 × iPhone and earphones
2 × smartphones as back-up
1 × K Lite dynamo front light
system, 1300 Lumens
1 × Sinewave Revolution USB
system
1 × Kathmandu 5200 mAh power
bank, 125 g
1 × ZMI 5000 mAh power bank,
120 g
1 × Fuse recharging adaptor for
3 items
1 × pack of 6 AAA lithium
batteries
1 × pack 6 XX alkaline batteries
1 × Cygolite Dash rechargeable
front light, 460 Lumens
1 × Moon 360 rechargeable helmet
light, 360 Lumens
1 × Azur rear light, 100 Lumens
1 × Axiom FastFlash DHL mirror
2 × Cycgolite Hotshot Micro
rechargeable rear lights,
30 Lumens
3 × ankle/arm reflectors
5 × re-charger cords

Personal hygiene and care

1 × toothbrush
1 × tube toothpaste

1 × jar of McEwen chamois cream
1 × 50 water purifying pills
1 × pack of Bandaids
1 × pack of Voltaren
1 × pack of Nurofen
1 × tube sunblock cream
1 × lip balm
1 × 'Cool pop' used as ice pack
when frozen
2 × PowerBar5 electrolyte drink
tablets
2 × Gel energy sachets
2 × Kathmandu pocket hand
warmer pads

Extras

1 × Topeak handlebar iPhone
holder
1 × pair Rapha 'Randonée' shorts
1 × pair $1 flip flops, 280 g
1 × wallet: cash, 2 credit cards,
bank card, Medicare card,
BUPA card, Cycling Australia
card, professional identity card
2 × Ocky straps
3 × Kathmandu dry sacks (three
sizes)
3 × 750ml drink bottles
6 × Apidura packs (1 rear saddle,
1 under top tube, 1 on top tube,
1 under handlebars, 2 pouches
for drink and/food)
6 × Plastic ziplock bags for foods

Sleeping items

1 × Sol Escape Bivvy bag, 241 g
1 × Kathmandu v3 Emergency
blanket, 60 g
1 × Exped air pillow, 4 g
1 × Seat to Summit Ultra Light air
mattress, 345 g
1 × Sea to Summit pump sack, 48 g

ABOUT THE AUTHOR

Rupert Guinness is a veteran sports journalist for major news outlets in Australia and around the world, and the bestselling author of 15 books. He has written about many sports, especially cycling, rugby, sailing and rowing. Guinness received a Walkley Award commendation for his inside story for *The Australian* on the 1999/2000 Sydney to Hobart yacht race, during which he crewed on board the line honours-winning maxi yacht Nicorette. A former triathlete, club cyclist and elite lightweight rower, Guinness still rides, runs in marathons and is always open to new adventures. He lives in Sydney.